LOW SODIUM DIET COOKBOOK FOR BEGINNERS

1000 Days of Flavorful Low-Salt Recipes to Live a Healthy Lifestyle.| with

28-Day Meal Plan to Kick start

MICHELE D. BUTLER

Table of Contents

Introduction

M any people love sprinkling salt on top of their salads, fruits, and even on cooked food. Salt can add delightful flavor to the food but a lack of salt can make food taste bland. However, it is highly recommended to follow a low-sodium diet to manage certain medical conditions.

This book shows you easy and quick ways how to live a low-sodium life by cooking healthier. A great book for people of all ages!

Though changing eating habits can be a little challenging, an easy guide and easy-to-prepare low-sodium recipes in this cookbook make the low-sodium diet journey more satisfying and fulfilled. This book provides nutritious and delicious heart-healthful low-sodium recipes without compromising flavor.

Those who are thinking of switching to a low-sodium diet should go through this cookbook containing numerous recipes and a 4-week meal plan. It will help in improving your health by handling various diseases, such as kidney problems, diabetes, high cholesterol, and heart problems. Learn how to eat, choose the right and healthy ingredients, and cook your meals by reducing fat and sodium intake.

But, before moving further, it is good to know more about Low-Sodium Diet and other useful information that will help you to learn how to enjoy your new meal plan while limiting your sodium intake.

The average American consumes around 5 or more teaspoons of salt every day. But, do you know this amount is nearly 20 times more than what your body needs? The human body needs only one-fourth teaspoon of salt a day. In fact, several foods that do not taste salty may contain a high amount of sodium. These can be canned, processed, and convenience foods, as well as foods that are served at fast food restaurants.

Though sodium is an important mineral that helps in performing various functions in the body, excessive sodium consumption can trigger certain medical conditions. Consuming too much sodium can lead to high blood pressure and cause fluid retention. Limiting sodium in your diet means eating less than 2,000 milligrams of sodium a day.

Chapter 1
Basics of Sodium

Comforting Prospects of Sodium

First, let's talk about the positive sides of sodium. Just like other minerals and vitamins, the body gains sodium through what we eat. So, it is recommended to consume it enough, but not too much. Sodium in your body helps in:

Health Benefits of Sodium

Regulates fluid

Balances ions

Prevents loss of water

Prevents cramps

Removes excess CO2

Develops the brain

Sufficient sodium

Improves teeth

Improves the skin

Prevents dryness

BALANCING FLUID

In addition to other minerals, sodium too can be called "electrolytes", which is important for keeping the fluid balance amid the inside and outer of the cells. Consuming too much sodium can lead to fluid retention and swelling in the legs and arms.

CONTRACTING MUSCLE

Electrolytes produce nerve impulses and are quite necessary for muscles to contract. If you ever experience muscle cramps while doing exercise, this happens due to electrolyte imbalance. No doubt you drink water to rehydrate yourself, but it does not replace electrolytes that have been lost in sweat.

INCREASING BLOOD

Taking enough sodium can improve the amount of blood in your body. But too much sodium increases the amount of blood, which in turn causes high blood pressure. On the other hand, low sodium decreases blood volume and makes it difficult for your heart to pump blood to your body organs.

An inadequate amount of sodium in your body can cause headaches, nausea, and muscle cramps, and it can even lead the patient to coma in severe cases.

What Happens when you Consume a Diet High in Sodium?

Many people move to a low-sodium diet because of their recent medical conditions or health diagnosis. Excessive salt can upsurge blood pressure and can put your body at risk of cardiovascular disease. As per several types of research, it is found that limiting sodium can help significantly in controlling or improving certain medical conditions. A diet high in sodium can impact your health adversely. Some of the possible results of high sodium in food include the following:

HIGH BLOOD PRESSURE

Consuming a high amount of sodium results in the buildup of this mineral in the body. This forces your body to hold on to extra fluid to weaken the excessive sodium. This in turn forces your heart to work harder to pump the blood and causes hypertension. Chronic hypertension can lead to damage to the blood vessels and increases the risk of severe heart and kidney diseases. The common signs or symptoms of high blood pressure are headaches, shortness of breath, nose bleeding, etc. When you eat a diet low in sodium, it allows your body to control fluid retention and blood pressure.

HEART DISEASE

Consuming too much salt causes the accumulation of excess fluid in people with heart failure and can be a life-threatening situation for them. People dealing with high blood pressure are more prone to experience stroke and

other heart diseases. Therefore, health experts recommend the low-sodium diet to people with heart conditions, especially heart failure. People even with mild heart failure are advised to reduce their sodium intake i.e., 2,000 – 3,000 milligrams a day. On the other side, people with moderate to severe heart failure are recommended not to consume sodium more than 2,000 milligrams a day.

KIDNEY DISEASE

Your kidneys' health is also at risk if you have a high sodium intake daily. Consuming too much sodium can make your kidneys unable to excrete the excess in your blood and find it hard to excrete enough fluid to balance. You may feel swelling in your hands and feet due to fluid retention. If your kidneys are not able to function optimally, it causes the buildup of waste products in the blood. People with chronic kidney disease should strictly adhere to a low-sodium diet. This is important to support your kidney function and prevent any further damage. Additionally, chronic hypertension and various other factors can be responsible for kidney diseases.

MENIERE'S DISEASE

This disease is caused by the accumulation of fluid in the inner ear and the patient experiences dizziness, hearing loss as well as ringing in the ear. The exact cause of Meniere's disease is not determined yet. But the doctors recommend patients limit salt intake because salt can cause fluid buildup in the inner ear. Following a low-sodium diet can help ease the symptoms of Meniere's disease for many patients. Though this disease has no cure, limiting salt and avoiding caffeine, smoking, and alcohol can help deal with it and reduce attacks.

OSTEOPOROSIS

Osteoporosis, a skeletal disorder, occurs due to the higher calcium excretion and increases the risk of bone weakening. The consumption of sodium plays a great role in influencing the amount of calcium excreted from the body through urination. High sodium intake leads to a great loss of calcium and is one of the main risk factors for osteoporosis. Multiple studies show that a high-sodium diet significantly affects bone health, especially in older women.

What is a Low-Sodium Diet?

Low-Sodium diet means limiting the consumption of high-sodium foods and beverages. Whole foods such as vegetables, fruits, and poultry have a lower amount of sodium. Also, plant-based foods have less sodium as compared to animal-based foods.

Processed and packaged foods such as chips, frozen foods, and fast foods have a higher amount of sodium. During the processing of these foods, salt is added to improve flavor. Another contribution to sodium intake is when you add salt to food while preparing it or as a seasoning before you eat food.

Healthcare experts recommend avoiding or limiting the consumption of these foods to treat health problems, such as high blood pressure or heart disease. They recommend keeping sodium intake less than 2,000 – 3,000 milligrams a day.

Following a low-sodium diet is something that makes many health-conscious people eager to incorporate it into their daily life. Sodium consumption at an appropriate level helps greatly in making people live healthier lives.

The Dietary Guidelines for Americans acclaim that an adult should keep sodium intake less than 2,300 milligrams a day, which is far less than 3,400 milligrams, the average sodium consumption by Americans daily.

Changing your normal meals to a low-sodium diet can be challenging at first. But nothing can stop you from gaining your health goals if you are determined. Learning what foods to eat, what foods to avoid, and what ingredients to add for preparing low-sodium recipes can help a lot.

Chapter 2
Start your Low- Sodium Diet Journey

Benefits of a Low-Sodium Diet

Incorporating a low-sodium diet means making important changes in the way you eat. Though sodium is found naturally in some foods, adding sodium to several foods can make reducing its intake a challenging task.

REDUCES BLOOD PRESSURE

As stated earlier, high sodium intake increases the risk of high blood pressure. On the other hand, a low-sodium diet is highly effective in decreasing blood pressure. Several studies have concluded that shifting to a low-sodium diet can result in significant changes in blood pressure. This change is highly helpful for people with elevated blood pressure levels. It has been also proved that even a moderate reduction in salt intake for a few weeks can lead to a decrease in blood pressure in patients dealing with high and normal levels.

DECREASES CANCER RISK

A high-sodium diet is associated with certain types of cancers. A higher intake of high-sodium processed foods increases the risk of stomach cancer. As per the research, a high-sodium diet can damage the mucosal lining of the stomach. This also increases inflammation and bacteria that may raise the risk of stomach cancer. On the other side, a low-sodium diet with fruits and vegetables helps in lowering the risk of stomach cancer.

IMPROVES DIET QUALITY

Several foods are very high in sodium, which means if you over consumption these foods very often you may experience negative effects on your health. Junk foods, processed foods, frozen meals, and even various packaged foods not only contain a high amount of sodium but are also high in unhealthy fats and calories. The consumption of these foods leads to obesity, diabetes, heart disease, and other health conditions. The low-sodium diet works greatly in improving your overall diet quality and preventing and managing certain medical conditions.

IMPROVES KIDNEY FUNCTION

Studies also conclude that patients with kidney problems can benefit from lowering the intake of sodium in their daily diet. The research determines that excessive sodium consumption interferes the kidney function. The transition to a low-sodium diet can help in treating various health conditions, including chronic kidney disease.

It is extremely challenging for people following a cardiac diet or those dealing with high blood pressure. Because experts recommend these people to consume less than 1,500 milligrams of sodium a day. Similarly, patients with heart failure can benefit from a low-sodium diet because the high amount of salt can lead to water retention, fluid buildup, and deteriorating symptoms of hypertension.

Recommended Foods on a Low-Sodium Diet

One of the easiest ways to reduce your sodium intake is to add certain foods to your daily meals. The experts suggest selecting the following foods to keep your diet low in sodium.

- Fresh fruits and vegetables
- Canned vegetables or beans stating 'low in sodium' or 'no added salt' on a label.
- Frozen foods without added salt or sauce
- Low-Sodium salad dressings
- Low-Sodium bread and grains
- Fat-free or low-fat dairy products
- Salt-free herbs and spices

People need to be very careful while buying food items from the grocery store. Make sure to check the label on each food product before buying to help you opt for brands with low sodium. It is a good idea to buy foods with 5% DV (daily value - the recommended amount) or less sodium. If you see 'salt', 'sodium', or 'soda' words on the label, the food has sodium in it.

Certain foods that are high in sodium should be avoided when on a low-sodium diet. These include – fast foods, salty snack foods, frozen meat dishes, frozen pizza, processed meats, salted canned foods, salty packaged soups, cheese, high-sodium baked products, baking mixes, packaged meals, pickled vegetables, salty seasonings, sauces, and condiments.

Recommended Daily Sodium Intake

Health professionals say that the human body needs at least 500 milligrams of sodium a day to function properly. But, when you consume a high amount of sodium daily, it leads to various kinds of health problems, such as high blood pressure, heart disease, kidney disease, and stroke.

As per the United States Department of Agriculture (USDA), the adult should consume up to 2,300 milligrams of sodium a day, while the American Heart Association (AHA) recommends a maximum of 1,500 milligrams of sodium intake a day. But the research shows that the average American adult consumes nearly 3,400 milligrams of sodium a day. 9 out of 10 American adults consume high sodium (100%) from packaged processed foods (65%), restaurants (25%), and home-cooked food (10%).

You would be surprised at the amount of food that doesn't taste salty but contains a high level of sodium. Such food items are bread, canned foods, cookies, cereals, and much more. Therefore, the best way to decrease sodium intake is to prepare your own meals. Learn about low-sodium recipes and try cooking them at home using the right ingredients in this book!

You will enjoy healthy changes to your diet, along with putting flavor at the forefront.

Week 1

Are you ready to experience a healthy body and healthy mind through a dietary change? Well, this 28-Day meal plan helps you get started on this journey today only.

Meal Plan	Breakfast	Lunch	Dinner	Motivational Quotes
Day-1	Avocado and Egg Toast	Chicken and Vegetable Stir-Fry	Salmon Shrimp Burgers	Keep it simple, especially when you are starting out.
Day-2	Peaches and Greens Smoothie	Hot and Sour Soup	Shrimp & Corn Chowder	Don't let a mishap in the road put an end to your journey.
Day-3	Slow-Cooker French Toast	Turkey Meatballs	Spiced Pumpkin Soup	Don't dig your own grave with your own knife and fork.
Day-4	Slow-Cooker French Toast	Salmon Shrimp Burgers	Curried Cod	It's much easier to stick to your goals if you're not constantly fighting temptation.
Day-5	Strawberry Yogurt Smoothie	Shrimp & Corn Chowder	Hot and Sour Soup	Don't let a stumble in the road be the end of your journey.
Day-6	Slow-Cooker Quinoa and Oats	Quick & Easy Pork Wraps	Chicken Legs with Rice and Peas	When you want to give up, remember why you started.
Day-7	Slow-Cooker Quinoa and Oats	Quick & Easy Pork Wraps	Chicken Legs with Rice and Peas	When, if not now?

Week 2

This meal plan not only helps you replace high-sodium foods with healthier and tasty low-sodium substitutes but also makes you learn to keep track of your sodium intake and choose ingredients wisely. Just allow your taste buds to incorporate a healthy diet into your daily meals by reducing sodium week by week.

Meal Plan	Breakfast	Lunch	Dinner	Motivational Quotes
Day-1	Steel-Cut Oats with Blueberries and Almonds	Oatmeal-Crusted Chicken Tenders	Oatmeal-Crusted Chicken Tenders	Fall seven times, rise eight times.
Day-2	Steel-Cut Oats with Blueberries and Almonds	Herb-Encrusted Lamb Chops	Halibut with Greens and Ginger	Every step, no matter how small, is a step in the right direction.
Day-3	Peaches and Greens Smoothie	Slow Cooker Pineapple Chicken	Two-Pea Jollof Rice	With the new day comes new strength and new thoughts.
Day-4	Make-Ahead Fruit and Yogurt Parfait	Mint Spiced Lamb Skewers	Lentil Sloppy Joes	The past cannot be changed, the future is yet in your power.
Day-5	Blueberry-Oatmeal Muffin in a Mug	Pasta-less Beef Lasagna	Baked Flounder Packets with Summer Squash	With each new day comes new strength and new ideas.
Day-6	Cantaloupe Smoothie	Shrimp and Mushroom Fried Rice	Bean Pasta with Arugula Avocado Walnut Pesto	Stop slacking and start making things happen.
Day-7	Creamy Blueberry-Banana Smoothie	Slow Cooker Pineapple Chicken	Pasta-less Beef Lasagna	The past is unchangeable, but the future is still within your grasp.

Week 3

From Chorizo Sweet Potato Hash to Apricot Chicken, Asparagus Soup, Salmon Veggie Kebabs, and Lentil-Walnut Mushroom Tacos, you will find plenty of delicious options for low sodium meals for any time of the day. This meal plan too represents the author's mission of helping people solve a variety of health problems with the right eating habits.

Meal Plan	Breakfast	Lunch	Dinner	Motivational Quotes
Day-1	Avocado Toast with Basil Pesto	Coconut Chicken Curry	Salmon Veggie Kebabs	You will never win if you never begin.
Day-2	Honey-Lime Quinoa Fruit Salad	Beefy Whole-Wheat Pasta	Lentil-Walnut Mushroom Tacos	You can never win if you never start.
Day-3	Chorizo Sweet Potato Hash	Apricot Chicken	Tomato Peach Soup	You are your only constraint.
Day-4	Orange-Almond Muffins	Easy Scallop Quinoa Paella	Fajita Chicken Wraps	Success is not an accident: it is the result of hard work and perseverance.
Day-5	Orange-Almond Muffins	Beefy Whole-Wheat Pasta	The Best Black Bean and Beet Burger	You will reap the benefits of what you plant now.
Day-6	Orange-Almond Muffins	Asparagus Soup	Coconut Chicken Curry	It does not matter how slowly you go, as long as you don't stop.
Day-7	Orange-Almond Muffins	Turkey Chili	Turkey Chili	Never let your fears dictate your destiny.

Week 4

This is the final stage of our 4 week's low-sodium diet meal plan. This week's plan will surely help you in enjoying the last step toward a healthier lifestyle. This is something that will make you understand the unsurpassed combination of taste and low-sodium content.

Meal Plan	Breakfast	Lunch	Dinner	Motivational Quotes
Day-1	Overnight Oatmeal with Banana and Chocolate	Spinach-Stuffed Turkey Burgers	Creamy Cauliflower Butternut Squash Mac and Cheese	It is never too late to make amends.
Day-2	Cheesy Pasta Bake	Chicken Salad with Creamy Tarragon Dressing	Cabbage and Salsa Soup	The net will appear if you leap.
Day-3	Cheesy Pasta Bake	Oregano Baked Beef & Beans	Ground Turkey–Brussels Sprouts Skillet	You are your only limit.
Day-4	Peanut Butter and Banana Smoothie	Crustless Vegan Mushroom and Sweet Potato Mini Quiches	Old-Fashioned Saucy Bean Salad	You get what you concentrate on, so concentrate on what you want.
Day-5	Banana Cream Pie	Caffeinated Beef Roast	Crispy Fish Sandwiches with Creamy Coleslaw	Yes, I believe I can.
Day-6	Chocolate-Mint Truffles	Roasted Cajun Blackened Salmon with Asparagus	Spinach-Stuffed Turkey Burgers	Don't give up until you're satisfied.
Day-7	Chocolate-Mint Truffles	Roasted Pork Loin and Potatoes	Avocado Egg Salad	A small amount of progress each day adds up to big results.

Chapter 4
Kitchen Staples, Condiments, and Sauces

Perfectly Poached Eggs

Prep time: 15 minutes | Cook time: 5 minutes | Serves 4

- 2 teaspoons white vinegar
- 8 large eggs

1. Pour about a gallon of water into a stockpot and bring to a gentle simmer (160 to 180°F). Stir in the vinegar. Place a few pieces of paper towel on a plate next to you.
2. Stir the water a bit to create a whirlpool. Crack one egg into a small bowl, then slowly slide it into the simmering vinegar water. Repeat this process with the other 7 eggs. Cook for 3 to 5 minutes, until the egg whites are set.
3. Remove the eggs with a slotted spoon and place them on the paper towel–covered plate.
4. For leftovers, place the eggs into a microwaveable airtight container. To reheat, microwave on high for 30 to 60 seconds, until heated through.

PER SERVING

Total Calories: 142; Total Fat: 10g; Saturated Fat: 4g; Cholesterol: 422mg; Sodium: 140mg; Potassium: 0mg; Total Carbohydrate: 0g; Fiber: 0g; Sugars: 0g; Protein: 12g

Simple Tomato Salsa

Prep time: 15 minutes | Makes 3 cups

- 3 ripe tomatoes, cored and quartered
- ½ red onion, peeled and quartered
- ½ jalapeño pepper, seeded
- ½ cup fresh cilantro
- Zest and juice of 2 limes
- ¼ teaspoon kosher or sea salt
- ½ teaspoon ground black pepper
- ½ teaspoon granulated sugar

1. Place all the ingredients in a food processor and pulse until the desired consistency is reached. Taste and adjust the seasoning, if necessary.

PER CUP

Total Calories: 51; Total Fat: 0g; Saturated Fat: 0g; Cholesterol: 0mg; Sodium: 206mg; Potassium: 360mg; Total Carbohydrate: 9g; Fiber: 3g; Sugars: 2g; Protein: 2g

Basil Pesto

Prep time: 15 minutes | Cook time: 5 minutes | Makes 3½ cups

- 1 cup fresh basil leaves
- 1 cup fresh baby spinach leaves
- ½ cup freshly grated Parmesan cheese
- ½ cup olive oil
- ¼ cup pine nuts
- 4 garlic cloves, peeled
- ¼ teaspoon kosher or sea salt
- ¼ teaspoon ground black pepper

1. Place all the ingredients in the bowl of a food processor and process until a paste forms, scraping down the sides of the bowl with a spatula as needed. Taste and adjust the seasoning, if necessary.
2. Place leftovers in airtight containers and refrigerate for up to 5 days, or freeze pesto in an airtight container for up to 2 months and thaw as needed. Or divide pesto into cube trays, seal in a plastic bag, and freeze for up to 2 months. Pop pesto cubes out of the ice cube tray as needed.

PER ½ CUP

Total Calories: 209; Total Fat: 20g; Saturated Fat: 2g; Cholesterol: 0mg; Sodium: 231mg; Potassium: 65mg; Total Carbohydrate: 2g; Fiber: 1g; Sugars: 0g; Protein: 4g

Chili Lime Marinade

Prep time: 10 minutes | Serves 2

- ¼ cup canola oil
- Zest and juice of 1 lime
- 2 tablespoons apple cider vinegar
- 1 tablespoon chili powder
- 1 teaspoon garlic powder
- 1 teaspoon onion powder
- ¼ teaspoon kosher or sea salt
- ¼ teaspoon ground black pepper

1. Whisk all the ingredients together, and store in an airtight container in the refrigerator for up to 5 days or freeze it for up to 2 months.

PER SERVING

Calories: 266; Total Fat: 27g; Saturated Fat: 4g; Cholesterol: 0mg; Sodium: 291mg; Potassium: 157mg; Total Carbohydrates: 4g; Fiber: 1g; Sugars: 1g; Protein: 1g.

Chili Garlic Rub
Prep time: 5 minutes | Makes ½ cup

- 3 tablespoons chili powder
- 1½ tablespoons garlic powder
- 1 tablespoon smoked paprika
- 1 tablespoon onion powder
- 2 teaspoons ground black pepper
- 1 teaspoon Mexican oregano or dried oregano leaves
- ¼ teaspoon ground cayenne pepper (optional)

1. Place ingredients in an airtight container or sealed plastic bag and shake to combine. Store for up to 2 months in a dry, dark pantry.

PER SERVING

Total Calories: 100; Total Fat: 1g; Saturated Fat: 0g; Cholesterol: 0mg; Sodium: 11mg; Potassium: 440mg; Total Carbohydrate: 22g; Fiber: 6g; Sugars: 1g; Protein: 4g

Garam Masala
Prep time: 5 minutes | Makes ½ cup

- 3 tablespoons ground coriander
- 2 tablespoons ground cardamom
- 2 tablespoons ground cumin
- 1 tablespoon ground black pepper
- 2 teaspoons ground cinnamon
- 1 teaspoon ground nutmeg

1. Place the ingredients in an airtight container or sealed plastic bag and shake to combine. Store for up to 2 months in a dry, dark pantry.

PER SERVING

Total Calories: 156; Total Fat: 5g; Saturated Fat: 1g; Cholesterol: 0mg; Sodium: 30mg; Potassium: 579mg; Total Carbohydrate: 31g; Fiber: 13g; Sugars: 0g; Protein: 6g

Taco Seasoning
Prep time: 5 minutes | Makes ½ cup

- 2 tablespoons chili powder
- 1 tablespoon ground cumin
- 1 teaspoon smoked paprika
- 1 teaspoon onion powder
- 1 teaspoon garlic powder
- 1 teaspoon Mexican oregano (optional)
- ½ teaspoon ground black pepper
- ¼ teaspoon ground cayenne pepper

1. Combine all the ingredients in a small jar or airtight container and shake to combine. Store in an airtight container for up to 5 days.

PER SERVING

Total Calories: 71; Total Fat: 3g; Saturated Fat: 0g; Cholesterol: 0mg; Sodium: 154mg; Potassium: 394mg; Total Carbohydrate: 13g; Fiber: 6g; Sugars: 1g; Protein: 3g

Homemade Chicken Stock
Prep time: 25 minutes | Cook time: 3 to 5 hours | Makes 6 cups

- 4 pounds whole chicken or chicken bones
- 2 onions, quartered
- 4 carrots, chopped
- 4 celery stalks, chopped
- ½ cup fresh parsley stems
- 4 bay leaves
- 4 sprigs thyme
- 2 tablespoons whole peppercorns

1. Pack the chicken or chicken bones, onions, carrots, celery, and parsley stems into a large Dutch oven or stockpot. Cover with cold water and place bay leaves, thyme, and peppercorns on top or in a tied sachet bag. Bring the pot to a low simmer, place the lid on top, and cook for 3 to 5 hours. Discard the bones, chicken fat, vegetables, and parsley stems. Using tongs or a slotted spoon, transfer the chicken meat to a container for future use.
2. Let the stock slightly cool, then strain. Transfer to airtight containers and refrigerate for up to 5 days or freeze for up to 6 months. Before use, skim the fat off the top.

PER SERVING

Total Calories: 56; Total Fat: 4g; Saturated Fat: 1g; Cholesterol: 22mg; Sodium: 20mg; Potassium: 54mg; Total Carbohydrate: 0g; Fiber: 0g; Sugars: 0g; Protein: 5g

Homemade Hummus
Prep time: 15 minutes | Serves 8

- 1 (15-ounce) can chickpeas, rinsed and drained
- ¼ cup tahini (sesame seed paste)
- 4 garlic cloves, peeled
- Zest and juice of 2 lemons
- ¼ teaspoon kosher or sea salt
- ¼ teaspoon ground black pepper
- ¼ to ½ cup olive oil

1. Place all the ingredients in the bowl of a food processor and process until a smooth paste forms, scraping the sides of the bowl with a spatula as needed. Taste and adjust the seasoning, if necessary.
2. Place leftovers in airtight containers and refrigerate for up to 5 days.

PER SERVING

Total Calories: 160; Total Fat: 12g; Saturated Fat: 2g; Cholesterol: 0mg; Sodium: 84mg; Potassium: 141mg; Total Carbohydrate: 11g; Fiber: 3g; Sugars: 2g; Protein: 4g

Carolina Barbecue Sauce

Prep time:10 minutes | Cook time: 10 minutes | Makes about 1 cup

- ½ cup apple cider vinegar
- ¼ cup lower-sodium ketchup
- 2 tablespoons brown sugar
- 1 tablespoon honey
- 1 tablespoon yellow mustard
- ½ tablespoon onion powder
- ½ tablespoon garlic powder
- 1 teaspoon chili powder
- ½ teaspoon ground black pepper
- ¼ teaspoon Worcestershire sauce

1. Add all the ingredients to a saucepan and bring to a simmer. Whisk occasionally until the sauce has thickened, 8 to 10 minutes.
2. Let cool, then transfer to an airtight container and refrigerate for up to 10 days.

PER ½ CUP

Calories: 136; Total Fat: 0g; Saturated Fat: 0g; Cholesterol: 0mg; Sodium: 120mg; Potassium: 487mg; Total Carbohydrate: 36g; Fiber: 1g; Sugars: 26g; Protein: 1g

Enchilada Sauce

Prep time:10 minutes | Cook time: 10 minutes | Makes 6 cups

- 2 tablespoons canola oil
- ½ yellow onion, peeled and sliced
- 5 garlic cloves, peeled and sliced
- 1½ cups Homemade Chicken Stock or store-bought unsalted chicken or vegetable stock
- 1 (32-ounce) can no-salt-added crushed tomatoes
- 2 tablespoons chili powder or dried crushed chiles
- 1 tablespoon ground cumin
- ¼ teaspoon kosher or sea salt
- ½ teaspoon ground black pepper

1. Heat the canola oil in a saucepan over medium heat. Add the onion and sauté for 3 to 4 minutes, until soft. Stir in the garlic and sauté for 30 to 60 seconds, until fragrant.
2. Transfer the onion mixture to a blender. Add the stock, crushed tomatoes, chili powder or dried chiles, cumin, salt, and black pepper and purée until smooth.
3. Use the enchilada sauce right away or divide into airtight containers or airtight plastic bags and refrigerate for up to 5 days or freeze for up to 2 months.

PER SERVING

Total Calories: 96; Total Fat: 5g; Saturated Fat: 0g; Cholesterol: 0mg; Sodium: 118mg; Potassium: 135mg; Total Carbohydrate: 11g; Fiber: 4g; Sugars: 6g; Protein: 3g

Honey Chipotle Sauce

Prep time: 10 minutes| Cook time: 15 | Makes about ½ cup

- 1 tablespoon chopped chipotle chiles in adobo sauce
- 3 tablespoons honey
- 3 tablespoons no-salt-added tomato paste
- 3 tablespoons unsalted vegetable or chicken stock
- 2½ tablespoons white wine vinegar

1. Pour all the ingredients into a small saucepan and bring to a simmer for about 15 minutes, until slightly thickened.
2. Store in an airtight container in the refrigerator for up to 7 days.

PER ¼ CUP

Calories: 136; Total Fat: 0g; Saturated Fat: 0g; Cholesterol: 0mg; Sodium: 124mg; Potassium: 348mg; Total Carbohydrate: 32g; Fiber: 2g; Sugars: 30g; Protein: 1g

Spicy Bean Chili

Prep Time: 10 minutes| Cook time: 20 minutes|Serves: 2

- 1 teaspoon of grapeseed oil
- ½ medium size red onion
- ½ Jalapeno pepper
- 1 garlic clove
- 15 ounces of low sodium red kidney beans
- ¾ cups of vegetable broth (low sodium)
- 3 fresh medium tomatoes (chopped)
- ¾ teaspoons chili powder
- ¼ teaspoon of sea salt
- ⅛ teaspoon of ground cinnamon

1. Warm oil in a saucepan with medium-high heat.
2. Add the onion and Jalapeño, after which you sauté for 5 minutes till the onion is caramelized.
3. Put the garlic and sauté until fragrant for about 30 seconds.
4. Add the rest of the ingredients and stir. Allow them to a boil 1 minute warmly.
5. Cover with the lid and simmer in medium heat for 10 minutes until well combined.
6. Enjoy.

PER SERVING

Calories 270 ;Fat 2g | Sodium 790mg;Carbs 45g ;Fiber 17g ;Sugar 5g ;Protein 17g

Fluffy Brown Rice

Prep time:5 minutes | Cook time: 50 minutes | Serves 4

- 1 cup brown rice
- 2½ cups vegetable stock or water
- ⅛ teaspoon kosher or sea salt

1. Add rice and vegetable stock or water to a saucepan and bring to a simmer. Place the lid on top and let simmer for 50 minutes, until the water has been absorbed and the rice is tender.
2. Season with the salt and fluff with a fork.
3. Place in airtight containers and refrigerate for up to 3 days.

PER SERVING

Total Calories: 172; Total Fat: 1g; Saturated Fat: 0g; Cholesterol: 0mg; Sodium: 199mg; Potassium: 100mg; Total Carbohydrate: 36g; Fiber: 2g; Sugars: 1g; Protein: 5g

Honey Whole-Wheat Bread

Prep time:40 minutes, plus 2 hours rest time | Cook Time: 30 minutes | Makes 2 loaves

- 1 cup warm water
- 2 tablespoons honey
- 4½ teaspoons (2 packets) instant yeast
- 5¾ cups whole-wheat flour or whole-wheat pastry flour, divided
- ½ tablespoon kosher or sea salt
- 1¼ cups warm low-fat milk
- 2 tablespoons olive oil

1. In the bowl of a stand mixer, whisk together 1 cup of warm water, the honey, and the instant yeast. Let sit for 5 to 10 minutes, until the mixture is frothy.
2. Add half of the flour to the mixture and whisk to combine. Let sit for 30 to 40 minutes, until foamy.
3. Place the dough hook on the stand mixer. While running on low, slowly add the remaining flour and the salt, milk, and olive oil, then let it run for about 5 minutes, until the dough sticks to the hook.
4. Separate the dough into two balls and transfer to 2 greased loaf pans. Place damp rags over the top of the dough and let it sit for about an hour, until the dough has doubled in size.
5. Preheat the oven to 350°F. Bake for 30 minutes. Let cool, then remove from the loaf pans. Once completely cooled, slice or store whole. Store in sealed plastic bags in the refrigerator for up to 2 weeks or the freezer for up to 3 to 4 months.

PER SLICE

Total Calories: 94; Total Fat: 1g; Saturated Fat: 0g; Cholesterol: 0mg; Sodium: 114mg; Potassium: 1mg; Total Carbohydrate: 18g; Fiber: 46g; Sugars: 3g; Protein: 2g

Fajita Chili

Prep Time: 15 minutes | Cook Time: 5 hours|Serves: 8

- 2 pounds boneless chicken breast, cut into 1-inch chunks
- 1 tablespoon chili powder
- 1 teaspoon fajita seasoning
- ½ teaspoon ground cumin
- 2 garlic cloves, minced
- Non-stick cooking spray
- 2 x 14½-ounce cans diced tomatoes
- ½ green bell pepper, julienned
- ½ red bell pepper, julienned
- ½ yellow bell pepper, julienned
- ½ onion, sliced
- 1 x 15-ounce can white kidney beans, rinsed and drained
- 3 tablespoons sour cream
- 3 tablespoons reduced-fat cheddar cheese, shredded
- 3 tablespoons guacamole

1. Mix the chicken with the cumin, garlic, fajita seasoning, and chili powder in a bowl.
2. Heat a skillet greased with cooking spray on medium heat.
3. Add the chicken and sauté until golden brown.
4. Transfer the chicken to a slow cooker.
5. Add the vegetables, undrained tomatoes, and cannellini beans to the slow cooker.
6. Cover and cook on a low setting for 5 hours.
7. Garnish with sour cream, guacamole, and shredded cheese.
8. Serve.

PER SERVING

Calories 225 ;Fat 16g ;Sodium 55mg;Carbs 21g ;Fiber 1.2g ;Sugar 5g ;Protein 21g

Stir-Fry Sauce

Prep time:20 minutes | Makes about 1 cup

- ¼ cup unsalted vegetable, chicken, or beef stock
- 3 tablespoons low-sodium soy sauce
- 1 tablespoon honey or brown sugar
- 2 teaspoons sesame oil
- 1 teaspoon sriracha (optional)
- 4 garlic cloves, peeled and minced
- 1-inch piece fresh ginger, peeled and minced
- 1 tablespoon corn starch

1. In a bowl, whisk the ingredients together until combined. Store in an airtight container in the refrigerator for up to 5 days.

PER ¼ CUP

Total Calories: 57; Total Fat: 2g; Saturated Fat: 0g; Cholesterol: 0mg; Sodium: 447mg; Potassium: 17mg; Total Carbohydrate: 8g; Fiber: 0g; Sugars: 4g; Protein: 1g

Barley Tomato Risotto

Prep Time: 10 minutes | Cook Time: 1 hour and 20 minutes | Serves: 4

- 10 large plum tomatoes, peeled and chopped
- 2 tablespoons olive oil
- ½ teaspoon black pepper
- 4 cups vegetable stock
- 3 cups water
- 2 cups pearl barley
- 2 shallots, chopped
- ¼ cup dry white wine
- 3 tablespoons fresh basil, chopped
- 3 tablespoons fresh parsley, chopped
- 1½ tablespoons fresh thyme, chopped
- ½ cup parmesan cheese, grated

1. Preheat the oven to 450˚F.
2. Spread the tomatoes on a baking sheet and toss them with the salt, pepper, and oil.
3. Roast them in the oven for 30 minutes and keep 16 wedges for garnishing.
4. Mix the stock with the water and boil on high heat.
5. Reduce the heat to a simmer.
6. Add 1 tablespoon of oil to a saucepan and heat it.
7. Stir in the shallots and sauté for 3 minutes, then add the white wine.
8. Cook for 3 minutes, then add the barley.
9. Stir cook for 1 minute and add ½ cup stock mixture.
10. Cook until the liquid is completely absorbed.
11. Continue adding the stock mixture while cooking the barley for 50 minutes in total.
12. Turn off the stove and stir in the tomatoes, basil, thyme, cheese, parsley, basil, and tomatoes.
13. Serve.

PER SERVING

Calories 240 ;Fat 7.4g ;Sodium 120mg;Carbs 45g ;Fiber 0.2g ;Sugar 1g ;Protein 6.2g

Arugula Quinoa Risotto

Prep Time: 15 minutes|Cook Time: 20 minutes|Serves: 6

- 1 tablespoon olive oil
- ½ cup yellow onion, chopped
- 1 garlic clove, minced
- 1 cup quinoa, rinsed
- 2¼ cups low-sodium vegetable stock
- 2 cups arugula, chopped and stemmed
- 1 small carrot, peeled and shredded
- ½ cup shiitake mushrooms, sliced
- ¼ cup parmesan cheese, grated
- ¼ teaspoon salt
- ¼ teaspoon ground black pepper

1. Add the oil to a saucepan, then heat it.
2. Stir in the onion and sauté for 4 minutes until soft.
3. Add the quinoa and garlic. Cook for 1 minute.
4. Stir in the stock and bring it to a boil, then reduce the heat to a simmer.
5. Cook for 12 minutes until the quinoa is al dente.
6. Add the carrot, mushrooms, and arugula.
7. Cook for another two minutes.
8. Add salt, pepper, and cheese.
9. Serve warm.

PER SERVING

Calories 288 ;Fat 5.1g ;Sodium 64mg;Carbs 28g ;Fiber 3.9g ;Sugar 1.4g ;Protein 6g

Lime Braised Cauliflower

Prep Time: 10 minutes| Cook time: 20 minutes|Serves: 4

- 1 medium head cauliflower, cored and chopped into 1½-inch florets
- ⅓ cup chicken broth
- 2 tablespoons minced fresh parsley
- Juice from 1 large lime
- 3 tablespoons olive oil
- ⅛ teaspoon red pepper, sliced
- 3 garlic cloves, minced
- Salt and pepper, to taste

1. Mix 1 teaspoon oil, garlic and pepper in a small bowl.
2. Heat remaining three tablespoons oil in a large skillet over medium-high heat until glistening and shimmering.
3. Whisk in cauliflower and ¼ teaspoon salt and cook, stirring from time to time, until florets become golden brown, 7 to 9 minutes.
4. Move cauliflower to sides of skillet. Pour garlic mixture to center and continue to cook, crushing mixture into skillet, until garlic begins to sizzle about 30 seconds.
5. Combine garlic mixture into cauliflower and mix well with a wire whisk.
6. Pour in broth and lime juice and bring to simmer. Reduce heat to medium-low, cover and cook until cauliflower is crisp-tender, 4 to 6 minutes.
7. Remove from the heat, and sprinkle with salt and pepper to season.
8. Serve.

PER SERVING

Calories 72 ;Fat 4.9g | Sodium 166mg;Carbs 4.2g ;Fiber 1.4g ;Sugar 1.52g ;Protein 3.19g

Chapter 5
Breakfasts & Smoothies

Microwave Quiche In A Mug
Prep time: 5 minutes | Cook time: 5 minutes| Serves 1

- ½ cup chopped frozen spinach, thawed and drained (or ½ cup packed fresh spinach)
- 1 large egg
- ⅓ cup low-fat milk
- 1 teaspoon olive oil
- Freshly ground black pepper
- ½ slice whole-grain bread, torn into small pieces

1. If using fresh spinach, place it in a mug with 2 tablespoons of water. Cover with a paper towel and microwave for 1 minute. Remove from microwave and drain the water from the spinach before adding it back to the mug. If using frozen spinach, make sure it is completely thawed and drained.
2. Crack the egg into the mug with the spinach and add the milk, olive oil, and pepper. Whisk until thoroughly mixed.
3. Add bread and stir in gently, but do not whisk.
4. Place mug in the microwave and cook on high for 1 minute until egg is cooked, and quiche is slightly puffed.
5. Enjoy immediately.

PER SERVING

Total Calories: 216; Total Fat 11g; Saturated Fat: 3g; Cholesterol: 191mg; Sodium: 268mg; Potassium: 352mg; Total Carbohydrate: 18g; Fiber: 4g; Sugars: 5g; Protein: 14g

Avocado and Egg Toast
Prep time: 5 minutes | Cook time: 5 minutes| Serves 1

- 2 eggs
- 2 slices whole-grain bread
- 1 small avocado
- 1 teaspoon freshly squeezed lime juice
- Freshly ground black pepper

1. Toast bread and cook eggs to personal preference.
2. Peel and mash avocado with the lime juice and pepper.
3. Spread avocado evenly on each slice of toast, then top each with a fried egg.
4. Serve immediately.

PER SERVING

Total Calories: 612; Total Fat: 38g; Saturated Fat: 7g; Cholesterol: 372mg; Sodium: 535mg; Potassium: 1,015mg; Total Carbohydrate: 50g; Fiber: 18g; Sugars: 7g; Protein: 24g

Overnight Oats with Bananas and Walnuts
Prep time: 5 minutes | Cook time: 5 minutes| Serves 1

- ½ cup rolled oats
- ½ cup nonfat or low-fat milk
- 1 ripe banana, mashed
- 2 tablespoons chopped walnuts
- ¼ teaspoon ground cinnamon

1. To a Mason jar or container of choice, add the oats, mashed banana, walnuts, and cinnamon. Pour in the milk and gently stir until combined.
2. Place in the refrigerator overnight or for at least 8 hours.
3. When ready to serve, top with additional milk if desired.

PER SERVING

Total Calories: 405; Total Fat: 15g; Saturated Fat: 2g; Cholesterol: 8mg; Sodium: 62mg; Potassium: 492mg; Total Carbohydrate: 62g; Fiber: 8g; Sugars: 21g; Protein: 13g

Steel-Cut Oats with Blueberries and Almonds
Prep time: 15 minutes | Cook time: 18 minutes| Serves 4

- 1 cup nonfat or low-fat milk
- 1 cup water
- 1 teaspoon ground cinnamon
- 1 cup steel-cut oats
- 1 cup blueberries
- ½ cup sliced almonds

1. In a medium saucepan over medium heat, whisk together milk, water, and cinnamon.
2. When the mixture starts to come to a boil, add steel-cut oats and bring to a boil.
3. Reduce heat to low and simmer for 15 minutes.
4. About 2 minutes before the end of cooking time, add in blueberries and almonds and stir well.
5. Serve immediately.

PER SERVING

Total Calories: 268; Total Fat: 10g; Saturated Fat: 1g; Cholesterol: 1mg; Sodium: 28mg; Potassium: 241mg; Total Carbohydrate: 39g; Fiber: 7g; Sugars: 7g; Protein: 11g

Peaches and Greens Smoothie

Prep time: 5 minutes | Cook time: 5 minutes | Serves 1

- 2 cups fresh spinach (or ⅓ cup frozen)
- 1 cup frozen peaches (or fresh, pitted)
- 1 cup ice
- ½ cup nonfat or low-fat milk
- ½ cup plain nonfat or low-fat Greek yogurt
- ½ teaspoon vanilla extract

1. Add all of the ingredients to a blender and process until smooth.
2. Enjoy immediately.

PER SERVING

Total Calories: 191; Total Fat: 0g; Saturated Fat: 0g; Cholesterol: 7mg; Sodium: 157mg; Potassium: 984mg; Total Carbohydrate: 30g; Fiber: 3g; Sugars: 23g; Protein: 18g

Strawberry Yogurt Smoothie

Prep time: 5 minutes | Cook time: 5 minutes | Serves 1

- 1 cup plain nonfat or low-fat Greek yogurt
- 1 cup frozen strawberries
- 1 cup ice
- ½ cup nonfat or low-fat milk
- ½ orange, peeled
- ½ frozen banana

1. Add all of the ingredients to a blender and process until smooth.
2. Enjoy immediately.

PER SERVING

Total Calories:82;Fat: 1g; Saturated Fat: 0g; Cholesterol: 13mg; Sodium: 170mg; Potassium: 1,284mg; Total Carbohydrate: 52g; Fiber: 6g; Sugars: 37g; Protein: 29g

Peanut Butter and Banana Smoothie

Prep time: 5 minutes | Cook time: 5 minutes | Serves 1

- 1 cup nonfat or low-fat milk
- 1 cup ice
- ¼ cup plain nonfat or low-fat Greek yogurt
- 1 frozen banana, sliced
- 1 tablespoon peanut butter

1. Add all of the ingredients to a blender and process until smooth.
2. Enjoy immediately.

PER SERVING

Total Calories: 313; Total Fat: 9g; Saturated Fat: 2g; Cholesterol: 8mg; Sodium: 136mg; Potassium: 1,037mg; Total Carbohydrate: 45g; Fiber: 5g; Sugars: 30g; Protein: 19g

Make-Ahead Fruit and Yogurt Parfait

Prep time: 5 minutes | Cook time: 5 minutes | Serves 1

- ¾ cup plain nonfat or low-fat Greek yogurt
- ⅓ cup rolled oats
- 2 tablespoons nonfat or low-fat milk
- 1 apple, skin left on, washed, cored, and diced
- 2 tablespoons chopped walnuts

1. In a bowl, combine yogurt, oats, and milk. Stir to combine.
2. Layer half of the yogurt mixture in a wide-mouth Mason jar or container. Add half of the apple and 1 tablespoon of the walnuts, then layer in remaining yogurt mixture and top with remaining apple and nuts.
3. Cover and refrigerate overnight and up to 5 days.

PER SERVING

Total Calories: 355; Total Fat: 12g; Saturated Fat: 1g; Cholesterol: 8mg; Sodium: 99mg; Potassium: 614mg; Total Carbohydrate: 43g; Fiber: 6g; Sugars: 21g; Protein: 24g

Blueberry-Oatmeal Muffin in a Mug

Prep time: 5 minutes | Cook time: 5 minutes | Serves 1

- ½ cup rolled oats
- 1 egg
- 2 tablespoons nonfat or low-fat milk
- ⅓ cup blueberries
- Cooking spray

1. Spray a large mug or small ramekin with cooking spray.
2. Add the oats, egg, and milk, and stir to combine. Gently fold in the blueberries.
3. Place in the microwave and cook on high for 1 minute, being careful to watch as it could overflow. If the muffin does not look firm, place back in for 30 seconds at a time.
4. Once ready, flip mug upside down onto a plate, slice, and enjoy.

PER SERVING

Total Calories: 259; Total Fat: 8g; Saturated Fat: 2g; Cholesterol: 187mg; Sodium: 87mg; Potassium: 159mg; Total Carbohydrate: 36g; Fiber: 5g; Sugars: 8g; Protein: 13g

Cantaloupe Smoothie

Prep time: 5 minutes | Cook time: 5 minutes| Serves 1

- ½ cup nonfat or low-fat milk
- 1 frozen banana, sliced
- 1 (5.3-ounce) carton vanilla nonfat Greek yogurt
- ½ cup ice
- 1 teaspoon honey
- 2½ cups (1-inch) cubed and peeled frozen cantaloupe

1. Place the milk, banana, yogurt, ice, and honey in a blender—process until smooth.
2. Add the cantaloupe pieces and process until smooth.
3. Serve immediately.

PER SERVING

Total Calories: 214; Total Fat: 1g; Saturated Fat: 0g; Cholesterol: 4mg; Sodium: 67mg; Potassium: 994mg; Total Carbohydrate: 46g; Fiber: 3g; Sugars: 38g; Protein: 11g

Slow-Cooker French Toast

Prep time: 15 minutes |Cook time: 2 to 2 hours and 30 minutes on high, 7 hours on low| Serves 6

FOR THE FILLING

- 2 tablespoons honey
- ½ cup low-fat ricotta cheese
- ⅓ cup sliced almonds
- ½ teaspoon cinnamon
- 3 cups finely diced apples pieces

FOR THE FRENCH TOAST

- Cooking spray
- 2 eggs
- 2 egg whites
- 1½ cups nonfat milk (or almond or soy milk)
- 1 tablespoon honey
- 1 teaspoon vanilla extract
- ½ teaspoon cinnamon
- 12 slices light whole-grain bread, lightly toasted

TO MAKE THE FILLING

- To make the filling, in a large bowl mix together the honey, ricotta cheese, almonds, and cinnamon until uniform. Add the apples and stir to coat.

TO MAKE THE FRENCH TOAST

1. Spray the inside of a slow cooker with nonstick cooking spray.
2. In a medium bowl, whisk together the eggs, egg whites, milk, honey, vanilla, and cinnamon.
3. Tear the toasted bread into 1-inch squares. Place ⅓ of the bread in the bottom of the slow cooker. Top with ⅓ of the filling mixture. Repeat twice with the remaining bread and apple mixture.
4. Pour the egg mixture over the contents of the slow cooker. Cook on high for 2 to 2½ hours, or on low for 7 hours, until set.

PER SERVING

Calories: 228; Total Fat 5g; Saturated Fat: 2g; Cholesterol: 63mg; Sodium: 238mg; Potassium: 261mg; Total Carbohydrate: 36g; Fiber: 6g; Protein: 12g

Slow-Cooker Quinoa and Oats

Prep time: 5 minutes | Cook time: 2 hours on high, 6 to 7 hours on low| Serves 6

- 1 cup gluten-free steel-cut oats
- ½ cup quinoa, rinsed
- 4½ cups unsweetened vanilla almond milk (or water), plus more for serving
- 4 Medjool dates, chopped
- 1 apple peeled and diced
- 2 teaspoons cinnamon
- ¼ teaspoon nutmeg
- 1 teaspoon vanilla extract
- ¼ cup crushed walnuts (optional)

1. Spray the inside of a slow cooker with nonstick spray.
2. Combine the steel-cut oats, quinoa, almond milk, dates, apple, cinnamon, nutmeg, and vanilla in the slow cooker.
3. Cook on high for 2 hours, or on low for 6 to 7 hours.
4. Stir well before serving. Top each serving with walnuts (if using) and a splash of almond milk.

PER SERVING

Calories: 230; Total Fat 5g; Saturated Fat: 0g; Cholesterol: 0mg; Sodium: 119mg; Potassium: 212mg; Total Carbohydrate: 44g; Fiber: 6g; Protein: 7g

Slow-Cooker Vegetable Frittata

Prep time: 10 minutes | Cook time: 1 to 1½ hours on low | Serves 6

- 1 tablespoon extra-virgin olive oil
- ½ cup sliced green onion
- 1 medium red bell pepper, chopped
- 2 garlic cloves, minced
- 1 cup shredded part skim mozzarella cheese, divided
- 3 eggs
- 3 egg whites
- 2 tablespoons milk (nonfat, almond, or soy)
- 1 packed cup chopped baby kale, stems removed
- 1 Roma tomato, diced
- ¼ teaspoon freshly ground black pepper
- ¼ cup chopped fresh parsley, for garnish

1. In a small skillet, heat the oil over medium heat.
2. Sauté the onion, bell pepper, and garlic until tender and fragrant, about 5 minutes.
3. In a large bowl, whisk together the sautéed vegetables and ¾ cup of the mozzarella cheese, the eggs, egg whites, milk, kale, and tomato. Transfer the mixture to the slow cooker.
4. Sprinkle the remaining ¼ cup cheese over the egg mixture, cover, and cook on low for 1 to 1½ hours, or until the eggs are set and a knife inserted in the center comes out clean. Serve. Season with black pepper and garnish with parsley.

PER SERVING

Calories: 139; Total Fat 8g; Saturated Fat: 3g; Cholesterol: 103mg; Sodium: 185mg; Potassium: 150mg; Total Carbohydrate: 6g; Fiber: 1g; Protein: 11g

Creamy Blueberry-Banana Smoothie

Prep time: 5 minutes | Serves 2

- 1½ cups water (or dairy or plant-based milk of choice)
- ½ cup gluten-free rolled oats
- 1 banana, sliced and frozen
- 2 cups baby spinach, packed
- 1 cup frozen blueberries
- ¼ cup mashed avocado
- 1 cup plain nonfat Greek yogurt
- ½ teaspoon vanilla extract
- 1 tablespoon unsalted almond butter
- 1 cup ice

1. Add the water and oats to the base of a high-speed blender and allow the oats to soak for 2 to 3 minutes.
2. Add the banana, spinach, blueberries, avocado, yogurt, vanilla, almond butter, and ice and blend until smooth, adding more ice or water|milk until desired consistency is reached.
3. Pour into serving glasses and serve immediately.

PER SERVING

Calories: 342; Total Fat 11g; Saturated Fat: 1g; Cholesterol: 0mg; Sodium: 82mg; Potassium: 461mg; Total Carbohydrate: 47g; Fiber: 9g; Protein: 18g

Overnight Spiced Oatmeal with Cranberries

Prep time: 10 minutes | Chill time: 8 hours (overnight) | Serves 2

- 1 cup unsweetened vanilla almond milk
- 1 cup gluten-free rolled oats
- ¼ cup unsweetened cranberries
- 2 tablespoons chia seeds (optional)
- ¼ teaspoon cardamom
- ¼ teaspoon ground cinnamon
- ¼ teaspoon ground ginger
- ¼ teaspoon ground nutmeg
- ¼ teaspoon vanilla extract
- Optional toppings: sliced almonds, additional cranberries

1. In a medium bowl, combine the almond milk, oats, cranberries, chia seeds (if using), cardamom, cinnamon, ginger, nutmeg, and vanilla extract. Cover the bowl with plastic wrap and refrigerate for 8 hours and up to overnight.
2. Before serving, stir thoroughly, portion into serving bowls, and top with sliced almonds and more cranberries if desired.

PER SERVING

Calories: 220; Total Fat 4g; Saturated Fat: 0g; Cholesterol: 0mg; Sodium: 75mg; Potassium: 89mg; Total Carbohydrate: 40g; Fiber: 5g; Protein: 6g

Overnight Oatmeal with Banana and Chocolate

Prep time: 5 minutes | Chill Time: 8 hours (overnight) | Serves 1

- ½ cup gluten-free rolled oats
- ½ tablespoon cocoa powder
- 1 teaspoon milk chocolate morsels
- ⅛ teaspoon cinnamon
- ¼ teaspoon pure vanilla extract
- ½ cup unsweetened coconut milk, plus more as needed
- ½ banana peeled and chopped
- 1 to 2 teaspoons pure maple syrup

1. In a pint-size mason jar, combine the rolled oats, cocoa powder, chocolate morsels, and cinnamon.
2. Stir in the vanilla extract, coconut milk, banana, and maple syrup.
3. Cover and refrigerate 8 hours, or up to overnight.
4. Before serving, stir thoroughly. Add a little more coconut milk if needed, to loosen it up and to get the consistency you want.

PER SERVING

Calories: 297; Total Fat 7g; Saturated Fat: 3g; Cholesterol: 1mg; Sodium: 4mg; Potassium: 306mg; Total Carbohydrate: 56g; Fiber: 7g; Protein: 6g

Cheesy Pasta Bake
Prep Time: 10 minutes| Cook time: 35 minutes|Serves: 8

- 1 ¼ cups whole-grain pasta
- 1 head Romanesco cauliflower, cut into florets
- 2 tablespoons olive oil
- 1 tablespoon corn flour
- 2 cups low fat milk
- 1 teaspoon hot English mustard
- Olive oil cooking spray
- 1 cup grated homemade Gouda cheese
- 1 cup grated Emmental cheese
- Black pepper to taste
- ¼ cup coarsely ground almonds
- ½ teaspoon ground paprika

1. Bring a pot of water to a boil and cook the pasta for about 7 minutes.
2. At the same time, bring a smaller pot of water to a boil, and cook the cauliflower florets for about 5 minutes.
3. Drain both the pasta and cauliflower and set aside.
4. Preheat the oven to 350° F. Next, make the sauce. Heat the oil in a medium pot, then whisk in the corn flour, being sure to remove any lumps that form.
5. Gradually add in the milk, whisking all the time to prevent lumps from forming. Lastly, mix in the mustard and let the sauce come to a boil.
6. Then add the grated Gouda and Emmental, whisk until they melt, and remove from the heat. Add the pasta and cauliflower into the saucepot and stir well.
7. Add black pepper to taste. Pour the pasta mixture into an oiled casserole dish, and top with the ground almonds.
8. Sprinkle over some paprika and bake in the oven for about 20 minutes until the sauce starts to bubble on the sides.
9. Rest the dish for 5 minutes, then serve hot.

PER SERVING
Calories 234 ;Fat 10g | Sodium 88mg;Carbs 23g ;Fiber 2g ;Sugar 5g ;Protein 13g

Honey-Lime Quinoa Fruit Salad
Prep time: 5 minutes | Cook time: 15 minutes| Serves 4

FOR THE FRUIT SALAD
- 1 cup uncooked quinoa
- 1 cup sliced blackberries
- 1 cup sliced strawberries
- 1 cup sliced blueberries
- 1 mango, diced
- 1 kiwi, sliced
- 1 tablespoon chopped fresh mint, for garnish
- FOR THE GLAZE
- ¼ cup honey
- 2 tablespoons freshly squeezed lime juice
- 1 tablespoon chia seeds (optional)
- 2 to 3 tablespoons water

TO MAKE THE FRUIT SALAD
1. Rinse and prepare the quinoa according to package directions. Cool the quinoa to room temperature.
2. In a large bowl, combine the quinoa, blackberries, blueberries, strawberries, mango, and kiwi.

TO MAKE THE GLAZE
3. In a small bowl combine the honey, lime juice, chia seeds (if using), and water. Drizzle the glaze over the fruit salad and toss to coat. Garnish with the fresh mint.

PER SERVING
Calories: 321; Total Fat 3g; Saturated Fat: 0g; Cholesterol: 0mg; Sodium: 15mg; Potassium: 321mg; Total Carbohydrate: 71g; Fiber: 8g; Protein: 7g

Red Beans and Rice
Prep Time: 10 minutes| Cook time: 45 minutes|Serves: 2

- ½ cup dry brown rice
- 1 cup water, plus ¼ cup
- 1 (15 ounces) can of red beans, drained and rinsed
- 1 tablespoon ground cumin
- Juice of 1 lime
- 4 handfuls of fresh spinach
- Optional toppings: avocado, chopped tomatoes, Greek yogurt, onions

1. Combine rice and water in a pot and bring to a boil. Cover and reduce heat to a low simmer.
2. Cook for 30 to 40 minutes or according to package directions.
3. Meanwhile, add the beans, ¼ cup of water, cumin and lime juice to a medium skillet. Bring to a boil. Reduce to a simmer and let cook until most of the liquid is absorbed 5 to 7 minutes.
4. Once the liquid is mostly gone, remove it from the heat and add spinach.
5. Cover and let spinach wilt slightly, 2 to 3 minutes. Mix in with the beans.

PER SERVING
Calories 232 ;Fat 2g | Sodium 210mg;Carbs 41g ;Fiber 12g ;Sugar 1g ;Protein 13g

Roasted Salmon with Smoky Chickpeas and Greens

Prep Time: 40 minutes|Cook Time: 40 minutes|Serves: 4

- 2 tbsp. extra-virgin olive oil, divided
- 1 tbsp. smoked paprika
- ½ tsp. salt, divided, plus a pinch
- 1 (15 oz.) can no-salt-added chickpeas, rinsed
- ⅓ cup buttermilk
- ¼ cup mayonnaise
- ¼ cup chopped fresh chives and/or dill, plus more for garnish
- ½ tsp. ground pepper, divided
- ¼ tsp. garlic powder
- 10 cups chopped kale
- ¼ cup water
- 1¼ lbs. wild salmon, cut into 4 portions

1. Position racks in the upper third and middle of the oven. Preheat to 425°F.
2. Combine 1 tbsp. of the oil, the paprika, and ¼ tsp. of salt in a medium bowl.
3. Very thoroughly pat the chickpeas dry, then toss with the paprika mixture.
4. Spread the chickpea mixture on a rimmed baking sheet. Bake the chickpeas on the upper rack, stirring twice, for 30 minutes.
5. Meanwhile, puree the buttermilk, mayonnaise, herbs, ¼ tsp. of pepper, and garlic powder in a blender until smooth. Set aside.
6. Heat the remaining 1 tbsp. of oil in a large skillet over medium heat. Add the kale and cook, stirring occasionally, for 2 minutes.
7. Add the water and continue cooking until the kale is tender, about 5 minutes more. Remove from the heat and stir in a pinch of salt.
8. Remove the chickpeas from the oven and push them to one side of the pan. Place the salmon on the other side and season with the remaining ¼ tsp. each of salt and pepper. Bake until the salmon is just cooked through, 5 to 8 minutes.

PER SERVING

Calories 447 ;Protein 37g ; Carbohydrates 23.4g ; Dietary fiber 6.4g ;Sugars 2.2g ;Fat 21.8g ;Sodium 556.7mg

Orange-Almond Muffins

Prep time: 15 minutes | Cook time: 20 to 22 minutes| Makes 6 muffins

- 1 large egg, separated
- 1 teaspoon extra-virgin olive oil
- 2 tablespoons nonfat Greek yogurt
- 2 teaspoons almond extract
- 1½ cups gluten-free oat flour
- 2 tablespoons wheat germ
- 1 teaspoon baking powder
- ½ teaspoon baking soda
- 1 teaspoon orange zest
- ½ cup slivered blanched almonds, divided
- ¼ cup low-fat buttermilk
- ⅓ cup orange juice
- 2 teaspoons light brown sugar

1. Preheat the oven to 375°F.
2. In a medium bowl, beat the egg yolk with a whisk until frothy. Add the olive oil and whisk some more. Add the Greek yogurt and almond extract while whisking.
3. In another medium bowl, mix together the oat flour, wheat germ, baking powder, baking soda, orange zest, and ¼ cup of the almonds.
4. Gently fold the egg yolk mixture into the flour mixture.
5. In another medium bowl, whisk the egg whites until frothy and white. Fold it into the muffin batter.
6. Slowly add the buttermilk and orange juice, gently mixing after each addition until smooth.
7. Line a standard-size muffin tin with 6 paper liners and fill each liner with an equal amount of the batter. Sprinkle the top with the brown sugar and the remaining ¼ cup almonds.
8. Bake for 20 to 22 minutes or until a toothpick inserted in the center comes out clean.

PER SERVING(1 MUFFIN)

Calories: 208; Total Fat 7g; Saturated Fat: 1g; Cholesterol: 32mg; Sodium: 211mg; Potassium: 142mg; Total Carbohydrate: 30g; Fiber: 6g; Protein: 7g

Avocado Toast with Basil Pesto

Prep time: 10 minutes | Serves 2

FOR THE PESTO

- ⅓ cup fresh basil leaves, loosely packed
- ¼ cup walnuts
- Juice of 1 lemon
- ⅛ teaspoon freshly ground black pepper
- ⅛ teaspoon garlic powder
- 1 tablespoon extra-virgin olive oil
- 1 tablespoon hot water

FOR THE TOAST

- 3 slices crusty whole-grain bread
- 1 avocado, sliced
- Microgreens, for garnish
- Freshly ground black pepper
- Extra-virgin olive oil (optional)
- Lemon wedges (optional)

TO MAKE THE PESTO

- Add the basil, walnuts, lemon juice, black pepper, garlic powder, olive oil, and water to a blender or food processor. Blend until smooth, with some nut pieces remaining for texture.

TO MAKE THE TOAST

1. Toast the bread.
2. Divide the avocado slices equally among the toast slices.
3. Spread 2 tablespoons of the pesto over the avocado. Add the microgreens to garnish and season with black pepper.
4. Drizzle with additional olive oil and lemon juice (if using), and serve immediately.

PER SERVING

Calories: 396; Total Fat 32g; Saturated Fat: 4g; Cholesterol:0 mg; Sodium: 201mg; Potassium: 538mg; Total Carbohydrate: 27g; Fiber: 10g; Protein: 10g

Chorizo Sweet Potato Hash

Prep time: 15 minutes | Cook time: 35 to 45 minutes | Serves 8

FOR THE SAUSAGE

- 1 tablespoon ground cumin
- 1 tablespoon sodium-free garlic powder
- 1 tablespoon sodium-free onion powder
- 1 tablespoon pimentón (Spanish paprika)
- 1 teaspoon freshly ground black pepper
- 1 teaspoon sodium-free chili pepper
- 1 teaspoon ground cloves
- 1 teaspoon ground coriander
- 1 teaspoon dried thyme
- ½ teaspoon cayenne pepper
- 1 pound low-sodium ground pork
- 2 tablespoons cider vinegar
- Zest of 1 lime

FOR THE HASH

- 1 (1-pound) container fresh baby or mature Brussels sprouts (or 1 package frozen)
- 2 Granny Smith apples, cored and cubed
- 2 large sweet potatoes, peeled and cubed
- 1 medium zucchini, peeled, seeded, and cubed.
- 1 medium yellow onion, diced
- 2 tablespoons extra-virgin olive oil

FOR THE GLAZE

- ¼ cup pure maple syrup
- 2 tablespoons extra-virgin olive oil
- 2 tablespoons balsamic vinegar
- 1 tablespoon chipotle pepper
- Freshly ground black pepper

TO MAKE THE SAUSAGE

1. In a mortar and pestle or a grinder (I use a coffee bean grinder), grind together the cumin, garlic powder, onion powder, pimentón, black pepper, chili pepper, cloves, coriander, thyme, and cayenne.
2. In large bowl, mix together the ground spices, pork, vinegar, and lime zest.
3. Let the sausage sit in the refrigerator for 10 to 20 minutes before cooking to let the spices meld. If desired, divide it into 8 small balls and form patties.

TO MAKE THE HASH

1. Meanwhile, prepare the hash. Preheat the oven (or a grill) to 400°F. Line a large baking sheet or roasting pan with foil and generously grease with olive oil.
2. If using mature Brussels sprouts, remove any tough outer leaves cut them in half. Leave frozen or baby Brussels sprouts whole. Transfer to a large bowl.
3. Add the apples, sweet potatoes, zucchini, and onions, and drizzle with olive oil.

TO MAKE THE GLAZE

1. Mix together the maple syrup, olive oil, vinegar, chipotle pepper, and season with black pepper.
2. Toss the glaze with the vegetables and spread them out in one layer on the prepared baking sheet. Bake until sweet potatoes are tender and Brussels sprouts are lightly browned, 25 to 30 minutes.
3. Mix in the chorizo and return to the oven to bake another 10 to 15 minutes. Once the vegetables are cooked through, toss and serve.

PER SERVING

Calories: 341; Total Fat 20g; Saturated Fat: 6g; Cholesterol:41 mg; Sodium: 58mg; Potassium: 660mg; Total Carbohydrate: 31g; Fiber: 6g; Protein: 13g

Chapter 6
Poultry

White Bean, Chicken & Green Chili
Prep Time: 20 minutes|Cook Time: 25 minutes| Serves 6

- 2 pounds tomatillos, peeled and quartered
- 1 jalapeño, halved and seeded
- ½ red onion, peeled
- 2 tablespoons canola oil, divided
- 1½ cups unsalted chicken stock
- 3 (15-ounce) cans great northern beans, rinsed and drained, divided
- 1 tablespoon ground cumin
- ½ teaspoon coarse salt
- ½ teaspoon ground black pepper
- 1 pound boneless skinless chicken breast, cubed
- 2 (4-ounce) cans green chiles with juice
- ½ cup fresh cilantro leaves, chopped
- Zest and juice of 1 lime
- Pinch granulated sugar (optional)
- ¼ cup plain nonfat Greek yogurt

1. Preheat the oven to 425°F.
2. Place the tomatillos, jalapeño, and red onion on a baking sheet and toss with 1 tablespoon of the canola oil. Roast for 20 minutes, until the vegetables are caramelized on the edges.
3. Transfer the caramelized vegetables to a blender or food processor. Add the chicken stock, 1 (15-ounce) can of beans, cumin, salt, and black pepper to the blender or food processor. Purée until smooth.
4. In a Dutch oven or stockpot, heat the remaining 1 tablespoon canola oil over medium heat. Add the cubed chicken breast and sauté for 4 to 5 minutes, until fully cooked. Add the remaining two cans of beans, green chiles, chopped cilantro, lime zest and juice, and puréed mixture to the pot and simmer for about 10 minutes. Taste the soup, and if tart, add the pinch of granulated sugar.
5. Evenly divide the soup into bowls and garnish with the Greek yogurt.
6. Divide leftovers evenly into microwaveable airtight containers and store In the refrigerator for up to 5 days. Reheat in the microwave on high for 2 to 3 minutes, until heated through, stirring as needed.

PER SERVING
Calories: 356; Total Fat: 8g; Saturated Fat: 1g; Cholesterol: 47mg; Sodium: 566mg; Potassium: 460mg; Total Carbohydrate: 42g; Fiber: 12g; Sugars: 9g; Protein: 29g

Chipotle Chicken & Caramelized Onion Panini
Prep Time: 20 minutes|Cook Time: 25 minutes| Serves 8

- 2 tablespoons canola oil, divided
- 2 yellow onions, thinly sliced
- ½ pound boneless skinless chicken breasts, thinly sliced
- 2 tablespoons Honey Chipotle Sauce
- 8 slices store-bought whole-wheat bread or Honey Whole-Wheat Bread
- 4 slices low-sodium provolone cheese
- 1 tablespoon olive oil

1. In a large skillet, heat 2 tablespoons canola oil over medium-low heat. Add the onions and cook for 20 minutes, stirring occasionally, until they are soft and caramel colored on the edges. Place them in a bowl and set aside.
2. In the same skillet, add another tablespoon of canola oil over medium heat. Place the chicken in the skillet and cook for 3 to 4 minutes per side, until the chicken reaches 165°F. Transfer the cooked chicken to the bowl with the caramelized onions and stir in the honey chipotle sauce until combined.
3. Wipe out the skillet and put back on the range. Prepare the sandwiches by placing 4 slices of bread on a cutting board. Evenly distribute the chicken/onion mixture onto each slice and top with a slice of provolone cheese. Top with another slice of bread. Brush the top slices of bread with olive oil. Place the sandwiches olive oil–side down in the hot skillet. Cook for 2 to 3 minutes, until browned. Brush the other slices of bread with olive oil, then flip and cook for another 2 to 3 minutes, until the bottom is browned and the cheese is melted. Place a lid over the skillet, if necessary, to assist with melting the cheese.
4. Slice each sandwich in half and serve.

PER SERVING
Calories: 260; Total Fat: 11g; Saturated Fat. 3g; Cholesterol: 26mg; Sodium: 308mg; Potassium: 67mg; Total Carbohydrate: 25g; Fiber: 3.5g; Sugars: 7g; Protein: 20g

Chicken and Vegetable Stir-Fry

Prep time: 15 minutes | Cook time: 20 minutes| Serves 4

- 2 tablespoons sesame oil
- 1 pound boneless, skinless chicken breasts, cubed
- 3 cloves garlic, minced
- ½ of an 8-ounce package sugar snap peas
- 4 scallions, chopped
- 1 (16-ounce) bag frozen stir-fry vegetables, thawed
- 8 ounces water chestnuts, drained and rinsed
- 2 teaspoons Chinese five-spice powder
- 2 teaspoons reduced-sodium soy sauce
- 2 tablespoons balsamic vinegar
- 2 teaspoons hot sauce

1. In a wok or large sauté pan, heat ½ tablespoon of the sesame oil over medium heat. Add the chicken and cook until lightly browned, 5 to 7 minutes. Transfer the chicken to a bowl, cover, and set aside.
2. Add the remaining 1½ tablespoons sesame oil to the pan along with the garlic and snap peas. Cook until the peas begin to soften and the garlic begins to brown, 3 to 4 minutes. Add the scallions, stir-fry vegetables, and water chestnuts and cook, stirring constantly, for 2 minutes.
3. Add the five-spice powder, soy sauce, balsamic vinegar, and hot sauce. Return the cooked chicken to the pan and stir, cooking for 2 additional minutes, until the chicken is warmed through and the ingredients are combined.

PER SERVING

Calories: 255; Total fat: 9 g; Saturated fat: 1 g; Cholesterol: 55 mg; Sodium: 331 mg; Potassium: 279 mg; Total carbohydrates: 16 g; Fiber: 6 g; Sugars: 6 g; Protein: 26 g

Crispy Walnut Chicken with Steamed Broccoli

Prep time: 15 minutes | Cook time: 30 minutes| Serves 4

- ½ cup chopped walnuts
- ½ cup flaxseed meal
- 1 teaspoon sweet paprika
- ½ teaspoon freshly ground black pepper
- ⅛ teaspoon salt
- 4 boneless, skinless chicken breasts (4 ounces each)
- 4 cups broccoli florets
- 1 lemon, quartered

1. Preheat the oven to 350°F. Lightly coat a baking dish with cooking spray.
2. In a food processor or blender, process the walnuts into a meal.
3. In a resealable plastic bag, combine the walnut meal, flaxseed meal, paprika, black pepper, and salt. One at a time, place a chicken breast in the bag, seal the bag, and shake until evenly coated. Transfer the coated chicken breast to

the prepared baking dish and sprinkle with any remaining walnut/flaxseed meal. (Do not keep the walnut/flaxseed mixture for another purpose as it has touched the raw chicken and you want to avoid cross-contamination.)

4. Transfer the chicken to the oven and bake until no longer pink in the center, the juices run clear, and an instant-read thermometer inserted in the center reads 165°F, 25 to 30 minutes.
5. Meanwhile, about 5 minutes before the chicken is done, place the broccoli in a microwave-safe dish and pour about 4 tablespoons water over the top. Cover with a microwave lid or paper towel and cook on high for 3 minutes. Remove the lid carefully and check to see if the broccoli is tender. If not, microwave in additional 1-minute increments. Carefully remove the broccoli from the microwave and drain.
6. Serve the chicken with the broccoli, with lemon quarters for squeezing. If desired, season the dish with a dash of salt, pepper, and paprika.

PER SERVING

Calories: 310; Total fat: 18 g; Saturated fat: 1 g; Cholesterol: 55 mg; Sodium: 308 mg; Potassium: 407 mg; Total carbohydrates: 14 g; Fiber: 8 g; Sugars: 2 g; Protein: 31 g

Fajita Chicken Wraps

Prep Time: 10 minutes | Cook Time: 6 minutes | Serves: 2

- 12 ounces skinless chicken breast strips
- ½ teaspoon chili powder
- ¼ teaspoon garlic powder
- Non-stick cooking spray
- 1 red or green sweet pepper, seeded and cut into strips
- 2 tablespoons bottled ranch salad dressing
- 2 x 10-inch whole-wheat tortillas
- ½ cup salsa
- ⅓ cup reduced-fat cheddar cheese, shredded

1. Mix the chicken strips with the garlic powder and chili powder.
2. Heat a skillet greased with cooking spray on medium heat.
3. Add the chicken and sweet peppers. Cook for 6 minutes.
4. Toss in the ranch salad dressing.
5. Divide the mixture into warmed tortillas.
6. Top each tortilla with cheese and salsa.
7. Roll each tortilla and cut them in half.
8. Serve.

PER SERVING

Calories 245 ;Fat 17g ;Sodium 42mg;Carbs 8.7g ;Fiber 0g ;Sugar 1g ;Protein 38.5g

Pistachio-Crusted Honey-Mustard Turkey Cutlets

Prep time: 15 minutes | Cook time: 20 minutes| Serves 4

- 1 cup unsalted pistachios
- ½ teaspoon freshly ground black pepper
- ⅛ teaspoon salt
- ½ teaspoon sweet paprika
- ¼ cup honey
- ¼ cup Dijon mustard
- 1 teaspoon fresh lime juice
- 2 tablespoons extra-virgin olive oil
- 1 large egg
- 4 turkey breast cutlets (4 ounces each), such as Honeysuckle White
- 1 cup thinly sliced radicchio
- 1 cup broccoli slaw
- 2 medium carrots, cut into ribbons with a vegetable peeler

1. Preheat the oven to 400°F. Line a large baking sheet with parchment paper.
2. In a high-powered blender or food processor, combine the pistachios, black pepper, salt, and paprika and pulse a few times until the mixture is crumbly but before it forms a paste, 20 to 30 seconds. Transfer the mixture to a large shallow dish.
3. In a small bowl, combine the honey, mustard, lime juice, and olive oil and whisk to combine. Reserve half of the mixture for dressing the radicchio slaw and pour the remaining half into a separate shallow bowl and whisk in the egg until well combined.
4. Working with one cutlet at a time, coat with a thin layer of the egg/mustard mixture, gently shaking off the excess, then coat on both sides with the pistachio mixture, gently shaking off excess. Place the cutlets on the lined baking sheet.
5. Transfer to the oven and bake for 8 minutes, then carefully flip and continue baking until the cutlets are slightly browned and crispy, for an additional 8 to 10 minutes.
6. Meanwhile, in a medium bowl, combine the radicchio, broccoli slaw, and carrot ribbons. Drizzle the reserved honey-mustard mixture over the slaw and toss to coat.
7. Serve the cutlets with the radicchio slaw.

PER SERVING

Calories: 468; Total fat: 22 g; Saturated fat: 3 g; Cholesterol: 123 mg; Sodium: 534 mg; Potassium: 463 mg; Total carbohydrates: 31 g; Fiber: 5 g; Sugars: 21 g; Protein: 36 g

Lemongrass Coconut Curry Chicken

Prep time: 15 minutes | Cook time: 45 minutes| Serves 4

- 1 cup brown jasmine rice
- 2 teaspoons extra-virgin olive oil
- 3 cloves garlic, minced
- 1 medium red bell pepper, sliced
- 3 tablespoons minced fresh ginger
- 1½ tablespoons curry powder
- 1 stalk lemongrass , bottom 6 inches only, outer leaves peeled
- 1 tablespoon honey
- ⅔ cup canned "lite" coconut milk
- ¾ cup low-sodium chicken broth
- 1 pound boneless, skinless chicken breasts, cut into bite-size cubes
- ¼ cup chopped unsalted cashews
- 2 tablespoons unsweetened shredded coconut (optional)
- 2 tablespoons golden raisins
- 4 tablespoons chopped fresh cilantro leaves

1. In a medium saucepan with a tight-fitting lid, combine the rice and 2 cups water, bring to a boil, stir once, cover, and reduce the heat to low. Simmer until all of the liquid is absorbed, 30 to 35 minutes. Do not lift the lid or stir during cooking.
2. Meanwhile, in a large skillet, heat the olive oil over medium-high heat. Add the garlic and sauté for 1 minute. Add the bell pepper and continue cooking for 2 minutes. Add the ginger and curry powder and mix well, cooking for 1 minute.
3. Mash the lemongrass lightly with a kitchen mallet to release the flavors. Add the lemongrass, honey, coconut milk, and broth to the skillet, reduce the heat to medium, and cook for 3 minutes, until the ingredients are combined and simmering.
4. Add the chicken to the pan, stir all of the ingredients, and cover the pan. Simmer over medium-low heat until the chicken is cooked through, about 25 to 30 minutes.
5. Remove and discard the lemongrass stalk and stir in the cashews, shredded coconut (if using), raisins, and cilantro.
6. Fluff the rice with a fork and portion onto 4 serving plates. Serve the chicken over the rice.

PER SERVING

Calories: 426; Total fat: 12 g; Saturated fat: 5 g; Cholesterol: 55 mg; Sodium: 229 mg; Potassium: 153 mg; Total carbohydrates: 52 g; Fiber: 5 g; Sugars: 8 g; Protein: 29 g

Pan-Seared Turkey Cutlets and Pepper Sauté

Prep time: 5 minutes | Cook time: 30 minutes | Serves 4

- Salt and freshly ground black pepper
- 1 pound turkey breast cutlets
- 2 tablespoons extra-virgin olive oil
- 2 cloves garlic, minced
- 1 large yellow bell pepper, cut into strips
- 1 large red bell pepper, cut into strips
- 1 cup button mushrooms, sliced
- 1 tablespoon dried tarragon
- 1 (14.5-ounce) can no-salt-added diced tomatoes, undrained

1. Sprinkle a dash of salt and pepper over the turkey cutlets. In a large skillet, heat 1 tablespoon of the olive oil over medium-high heat. Add the turkey cutlets to the skillet and cook until browned on the bottom, 1 to 3 minutes. Flip and continue cooking until cooked all the way through, 1 to 3 minutes more. The outside should be nicely browned and the inside fully cooked and opaque throughout. Remove the turkey to a plate and cover with foil to keep warm.
2. Add the remaining 1 tablespoon olive oil to the skillet, then add the garlic and sauté for 1 minute, until sizzling. Add the bell peppers and mushrooms and continue cooking until starting to soften, 5 to 7 minutes.
3. Add the tarragon and tomatoes and their juices, cover, and bring to a simmer, stirring often, 3 to 5 minutes, until slightly reduced.
4. Return the turkey cutlets to the skillet and bring to a simmer. Reduce the heat to medium-low and cook for 2 to 3 minutes to warm the turkey through.

PER SERVING

Calories: 225; Total fat: 8 g; Saturated fat: 1 g; Cholesterol: 70 mg; Sodium: 67 mg; Potassium: 180 mg; Total carbohydrates: 10 g; Fiber: 2 g; Sugars: 3 g; Protein: 30 g

Oatmeal-Crusted Chicken Tenders

Prep time: 15 minutes | Cook time: 20 minutes | Serves 4

- 1 cup rolled oats
- ½ cup freshly grated Parmesan cheese
- 2 teaspoons chopped fresh rosemary
- ⅛ teaspoon sweet paprika
- ⅛ teaspoon salt
- ¼ teaspoon freshly ground black pepper
- 1 pound boneless, skinless chicken tenders

1. Preheat the oven to 450°F. Lightly coat a large baking sheet with cooking spray.
2. Place the oats in a food processor or blender and pulse for 30 seconds until coarsely ground. You do not need the oatmeal to be powdered, just a few pulses to break it down. Add the Parmesan, rosemary, paprika, salt, and pepper and pulse to combine. Pour into a shallow bowl.
3. Place each chicken tender between two sheets of plastic wrap and use a meat mallet or small heavy skillet to pound to a ¼-inch thickness. Coat both sides of the tenders with cooking spray, then dredge the tenders in the oat mixture.
4. Place the tenders on the prepared baking sheet and bake until browned and crispy, turning at the halfway point, about 15 minutes.

PER SERVING

Calories: 225; Total fat: 6 g; Saturated fat: 2 g; Cholesterol: 70 mg; Sodium: 493 mg; Potassium: 2 mg; Total carbohydrates: 14 g; Fiber: 2 g; Sugars: <1 g; Protein: 30 g

Spinach-Stuffed Turkey Burgers

Prep time: 15 minutes | Cook time: 20 minutes | Serves 4

- 12 ounces 93% lean ground turkey
- 4 cups fresh baby spinach
- ⅓ cup rolled oats
- 2 garlic cloves, minced
- 2 teaspoons freshly squeezed lemon juice
- ¾ teaspoon freshly ground black pepper
- 1 teaspoon hot sauce (optional)

1. In a medium bowl, combine all of the ingredients, and mix until well incorporated. Using your hands, form the mixture into four 5-inch-wide patties.
2. Spray a large skillet with nonstick cooking spray, and place it over medium heat. Place the patties in the skillet and cook for 7 to 8 minutes on each side, or until well done and browned and an instant-read thermometer registers 165°F.
3. Serve with your favorite toppings.

PER SERVING

Calories: 173; Total Fat: 8g; Saturated Fat: 2g; Cholesterol: 107mg; Sodium: 106mg; Potassium: 196mg; Magnesium: 24mg; Total Carbohydrates: 6g; Fiber: 2g; Sugars: 0g; Protein: 20g

Fresh Rosemary Balsamic Chicken and Brussels Sprouts

Prep time: 15 minutes | Cook time: 35 minutes| Serves 2

CHICKEN

- ½ cup + 2 tablespoons balsamic vinegar
- 1 teaspoon extra-virgin olive oil
- 1 tablespoon chopped fresh rosemary
- 1 clove garlic, minced
- ⅛ teaspoon salt
- Freshly ground black pepper
- 2 boneless, skinless chicken breasts (4 ounces each)

BRUSSELS SPROUTS

- ½ pound Brussels sprouts, trimmed of outer leaves and halved lengthwise
- 2 teaspoons extra-virgin olive oil
- 2 teaspoons balsamic vinegar
- ⅛ teaspoon salt
- ⅛ teaspoon freshly ground black pepper
- 2 tablespoons sliced almonds
- Sprigs fresh rosemary

1. Marinate the chicken: In a small saucepan, combine the balsamic vinegar, olive oil, rosemary, garlic, salt, and pepper. Bring to a boil, reduce the heat to medium, and simmer until reduced by half, about 3 minutes. Place in the refrigerator to cool for 15 minutes or for a quicker chill, place in the freezer for 5 minutes.
2. Coat a 9 × 9-inch baking dish with cooking spray. Place the chicken in the baking dish and pour the cooled marinade over it. Marinate in the refrigerator for 30 minutes.
3. Preheat the oven to 375°F.
4. When the chicken is done marinating, remove from the refrigerator and cover the baking dish with foil.
5. Prepare the Brussels sprouts: In a medium bowl, toss the Brussels sprouts with the olive oil, balsamic vinegar, salt, and pepper. Spread on a nonstick baking sheet.
6. Transfer the chicken and Brussels sprouts to the oven and roast until an instant-read thermometer inserted in a chicken breast reads 165°F and the Brussels sprouts are browned and tender, 30 to 35 minutes. Turn the Brussels sprouts once about halfway through cooking.
7. While the chicken and Brussels sprouts cook, in a small dry skillet, toast the almonds over medium heat, stirring constantly, until golden and fragrant, 3 to 4 minutes.
8. Remove the Brussels and chicken from the oven, mix the almonds with the sprouts, and garnish with rosemary sprigs to serve.

PER SERVING

Calories: 304; Total fat: 12 g; Saturated fat: 1 g; Cholesterol: 55 mg; Sodium: 556 mg; Potassium: 449 mg; Total carbohydrates: 23 g; Fiber: 5 g; Sugars: 3 g; Protein: 28 g

Slow Cooker Pineapple Chicken

Prep time: 15 minutes | Cook time: 4 to 5 hours on low or 1½ to 2 hours on high | Serves 4

- 1 pound frozen boneless, skinless chicken breasts
- 2 medium carrots, sliced
- 1 medium red bell pepper, cut into 1-inch chunks
- 1 (20-ounce) can water- or juice-packed crushed or chopped pineapple, undrained
- ¼ cup balsamic vinegar
- 1 tablespoon reduced-sodium soy sauce
- 2 tablespoons pure maple syrup
- 1 teaspoon red pepper flakes

1. Coat the inside of the slow cooker with cooking spray. Add the chicken, carrots, and bell pepper.
2. Drain the pineapple juice from the can into a small bowl. Add the balsamic vinegar, soy sauce, maple syrup, and pepper flakes and whisk to combine. Pour over the chicken and add the crushed or chopped pineapple.
3. Cover the slow cooker and cook on LOW for 4 to 5 hours or on HIGH for 1½ to 2 hours, until cooked through. The vegetables should be fork-tender and the chicken should register 165°F on an instant-read thermometer and be tender enough to easily tear apart with a fork. Remove the chicken from the slow cooker and shred with two forks. Return the chicken to the slow cooker, stir to mix the ingredients, and set the temperature to warm until ready to serve.

PER SERVING

Calories: 242; Total fat: 2 g; Saturated fat: 0 g; Cholesterol: 55 mg; Sodium: 376 mg; Potassium: 307 mg; Total carbohydrates: 34 g; Fiber: 2 g; Sugars: 27 g; Protein: 24 g

Ground Turkey Brussels Sprouts Skillet

Prep time: 15 minutes | Cook time: 30 minutes| Serves 4

- 2 tablespoons olive oil, divided
- 1 red onion, diced
- 1 pound 93% lean ground turkey
- 4 garlic cloves, minced
- 2 teaspoons chili powder
- ½ pound Brussels sprouts, shredded
- 1 bell pepper, diced

1. In a large skillet over medium heat, warm 1 tablespoon of the olive oil. Add the onion and stir-fry for 5 minutes, or until the onion is soft.
2. Add the ground turkey, garlic, and chili powder, and cook, stirring occasionally, for 15 to 20 minutes, until the meat is completely cooked through and no longer pink, and an instant-read thermometer registers 165°F.
3. Set aside some of the turkey in a bowl to make room for the Brussels sprouts and bell pepper. Add the remaining 1 tablespoon of oil to the skillet, and add the Brussels sprouts and bell pepper. Stir-fry for 5 minutes, or until the vegetables are tender.
4. Add the meat back to the pan and mix well. Serve immediately.

PER SERVING

Calories: 262; Total Fat: 16g; Saturated Fat: 4g; Cholesterol: 80mg; Sodium: 114mg; Potassium: 314mg; Magnesium: 20mg; Total Carbohydrates: 9g; Fiber: 3g; Sugars: 3g; Protein: 25g

Glazed Chicken Skewers

Prep Time: 10 minutes| Cook time: 8 minutes|Serves: 4

- 12 skewers
- 4 (4 ounces, 113g) chicken breasts, cut into 1-inch cubes
- 3 large red bell peppers, cut into 1-inch pieces
- 2 large white onions, cut into 1-inch pieces
- 6 apricots, pitted and cut into 1-inch pieces
- Marinade:
- 1 heaping tablespoon reduced-sugar apricot marmalade
- ½ teaspoon sesame oil
- ¼ cup extra virgin olive oil
- 1½ teaspoon finely chopped fresh ginger
- 1 tablespoon Dijon mustard or brown mustard
- 4 tablespoons apple cider vinegar
- 1 large clove garlic, chopped

1. Mix all marinade ingredients in a large bowl.
2. Place the cubed chicken in a large zip-top bag, pour in the marinade, squeeze the air out of the bag, and seal tightly.
3. Work the mixture into the chicken by hand by moving the bag and contents around. Let the chicken marinate in the refrigerator for at least two hours if you can.
4. Soak 12 large wooden skewers in water, and then chop the peppers, onions and apricots into

similar-sized pieces.
5. Skewer the pieces of chicken, pepper, onion, and apricot, alternating ingredients.
6. Grill the skewers on a hot grill or grill pan, about 4 to 5 minutes per side, or until the chicken is no longer pink in the center.

PER SERVING

Calories 314 ;Fat 16 g ; Sodium 357 mg;Carbs 21 g ;Fiber 4 g ;Sugar 10 g ;Protein 25 g

Chicken Salad with Creamy Tarragon Dressing

Prep time: 15 minutes | Cook time: 10 minutes| Serves 4

- 1 (15-ounce) can white beans, drained and rinsed, divided
- ⅓ cup white balsamic vinegar
- 1 tablespoon olive oil 2 garlic cloves
- 2 teaspoons dried tarragon, divided
- 6 cups salad greens
- ½ red onion, thinly sliced
- 1½ cups chopped cooked chicken breast
- 1 cup English cucumber, thinly sliced
- ¾ teaspoon freshly ground black pepper

1. In a blender, combine ½ cup of the beans, the balsamic vinegar, olive oil, garlic, and 1 teaspoon of tarragon, and purée.
2. Arrange the greens on four serving plates. Top with the remaining beans, onion, chicken, cucumber, black pepper, and remaining tarragon.
3. Serve the dressing on the side.

PER SERVING

Calories: 267; Total Fat: 7g; Saturated Fat: 1g; Cholesterol: 53mg; Sodium: 196mg; Potassium: 484mg; Magnesium: 49mg; Total Carbohydrates: 25g; Fiber: 8g; Sugars: 1g; Protein: 28g

Tandoori Chicken with Rice

Prep time: 15 minutes | Cook time: 30 minutes| Serves 4

- 1 pound boneless, skinless chicken breast or tenderloins, trimmed of visible fat
- ¼ cup lemon juice
- ½ cup plain nonfat Greek yogurt
- 3 garlic cloves, minced
- 1 teaspoon curry powder
- 1 teaspoon ground ginger
- 1 teaspoon paprika
- 1 teaspoon ground cumin
- 1 cup instant brown rice

1. Preheat the oven to 400°F.
2. Place the chicken in a 9-by-9-inch baking dish and pierce the chicken pieces all over with a fork.
3. In a small bowl, whisk together the lemon juice, Greek yogurt, garlic, curry powder, ginger, paprika, and cumin. Pour the spice mixture over the chicken, turning to coat. Let stand for 20 minutes.
4. Place the chicken in the oven and bake for 15 minutes. Turn the chicken, and bake for 15 minutes more, or until an instant-read thermometer registers 165°F.
5. While the chicken bakes, prepare the rice according to the package directions.
6. Divide the rice among four plates, and top each serving with chicken. Serve immediately.

PER SERVING

Calories: 246; Total Fat: 5g; Saturated Fat: 2g; Cholesterol: 66mg; Sodium: 61mg; Potassium: 157mg; Magnesium: 36mg; Total Carbohydrates: 22g; Fiber: 2g; Sugars: 2g; Protein: 30g

Coconut Chicken Curry

Prep time: 15 minutes | Cook time: 45 minutes| Serves 4

- 1 cup brown jasmine rice
- 2 cups water
- 2 teaspoons olive oil
- 2 garlic cloves, minced
- 2 tablespoons minced fresh ginger
- 1 tablespoon curry powder
- 1 medium apple, peel on, cored and diced
- 1 tablespoon honey
- ¼ cup low-fat/light coconut milk
- ¾ cup low-sodium chicken broth
- 1 pound boneless, skinless chicken breast, cut into bite-size cubes
- ¼ cup chopped unsalted cashews
- 2 tablespoons golden raisins
- 4 tablespoons chopped fresh cilantro leaves

1. In a medium saucepan with a tight-fitting lid, combine the rice and water, and bring to a boil. Stir once, cover, and reduce heat to low. Simmer for 30 to 35 minutes. Do not lift the lid or stir.
2. Meanwhile, heat the olive oil in a large skillet over medium heat. Add the garlic and sauté for 1 minute. Add the ginger and curry powder and mix well, cooking for 1 minute.
3. Add the apple, honey, coconut milk, and broth, reduce the heat to medium, and cook for about 3 minutes.
4. Add the chicken to the pan, stir all the ingredients, and cover the pan. Simmer over medium-low heat until the chicken is cooked through and an instant-read thermometer registers 165°F, about 30 minutes.
5. Add the cashews and raisins and stir in the cilantro.
6. Fluff the rice with a fork. Serve the chicken over the rice.

PER SERVING

Calories: 439; Total Fat 12g; Saturated Fat: 4g; Cholesterol: 65mg; Sodium: 69mg; Potassium: 114mg; Magnesium: 8mg; Total Carbohydrates: 51g; Fiber: 4g; Sugars: 11g; Protein: 31g

Turkey Meatballs

Prep Time: 15 minutes|Cook Time: 25 minutes|Serves: 6

- 1 medium onion, chopped
- 1 medium green sweet pepper, chopped
- ½ cup quick-cooking rolled oats
- 1 egg, beaten
- 2 tablespoons fat-free milk
- 2 cloves garlic, minced
- 1 teaspoon dried Italian seasoning, crushed
- 1 teaspoon salt-free seasoning blend
- 1 teaspoon Creole seasoning
- 1 pound uncooked ground turkey

1. Preheat the oven to 375˚F.
2. Grease a 15-inch x 10-inch baking dish.
3. Mix the onion, oats, milk, egg, garlic, sweet pepper, salt, Creole seasoning, and Italian seasoning in a bowl.
4. Add the turkey and mix well to coat.
5. Make small meatballs out of the mixture.
6. Arrange the balls in the greased pan.
7. Bake for 25 minutes.
8. Serve warm.

PER SERVING

Calories 350 ;Fat 8g ;Sodium 61mg;Carbs 21g ;Fiber 0g ;Sugar 4g ;Protein 44g

Turkey Chili

Prep time: 10 minutes | Cook time: 45 minutes| Serves 6

- 1½ teaspoons extra-virgin olive oil
- 1 medium onion, chopped
- 1 red bell pepper, chopped
- 3 garlic cloves, minced
- 1 pound extra-lean ground turkey
- 1½ cups unsalted chicken stock
- 1 (15-ounce) can no-salt-added kidney beans, drained and rinsed
- 1 (15-ounce) can no-salt-added corn kernels
- 1 (28-ounce) can no-salt-added diced tomatoes
- 2 teaspoons chili powder
- 1½ teaspoons ground cumin
- 1 teaspoon dried oregano
- ½ teaspoon paprika
- ½ teaspoon salt
- ½ teaspoon freshly ground black pepper
- ¼ teaspoon cayenne pepper
- Unsalted corn chips, shredded reduced-fat cheese or reduced-fat sour cream, and cubed avocado, for topping (optional)

1. In a large pot, heat the oil over medium heat. Add the onion, bell pepper, and garlic and sauté, stirring regularly, for about 5 minutes, or until softened.
2. Add the turkey and cook, making sure to break up the meat, until it evenly browns. Pour in the chicken stock, beans, corn, and tomatoes. Stir well.
3. Stir in the chili powder, cumin, oregano, paprika, salt, black pepper, and cayenne pepper. Bring to a boil, then reduce the heat to a simmer, cover, and cook for 30 minutes to blend the flavors. Let cool, then divide into 6 storage containers. Top with chips, cheese, and avocado (if using).

PER SERVING (WITHOUT TOPPINGS)

Calories: 257; Total fat: 3g; Carbohydrates: 32g; Fiber: 9.5g; Protein: 27g; Calcium: 97mg; Vitamin D: 11 IU; Potassium: 939mg; Magnesium: 62mg; Sodium: 286mg

Apricot Chicken

Prep time: 5 minutes | Cook time: 30 minutes| Serves 4

- 2 teaspoons olive oil
- 1 pound boneless, skinless chicken breasts, trimmed and cut into 4 pieces
- 8 to 9 ripe apricots, pitted and chopped
- ½ cup dry white wine
- ½ cup no-salt chicken stock
- Juice of 1 orange
- ¼ cup honey
- 1 teaspoon dried thyme
- 1 tablespoon fresh orange zest

1. Heat a large nonstick skillet over medium-high heat, and heat the olive oil. Place the chicken breasts in the pan and cook for 5 to 8 minutes per side, or until an instant-read thermometer registers 165°F. Transfer the chicken breasts to a clean plate and cover with foil to keep warm.
2. In the same skillet, add the apricots, wine, chicken stock, orange juice, and honey. Turn the heat to high and allow the liquid to come to a boil. Boil, uncovered, for about 10 minutes, stirring occasionally. The liquid should reduce by half, and the apricots should break down a little but still be somewhat chunky. The sauce should be on the thick side.
3. Remove the sauce from the heat and stir in the thyme and orange zest. Spoon the sauce over the warm chicken breasts.
4. Serve immediately with a desired side dish.

PER SERVING

Calories: 287; Total Fat: 7g; Saturated Fat: 2g; Cholesterol: 65mg; Sodium: 49mg; Potassium: 256mg; Magnesium: 12mg; Total Carbohydrates: 28g; Fiber: 2g; Sugars: 25g; Protein: 27g

Chicken Stew

Prep Time: 10 minutes| Cook time: 30 minutes|Serves: 5

- 1-pound boneless, skinless chicken breasts, cut into 1-inch cubes (2.5 cm)
- 1 ½ cups peeled, cubed potatoes
- ½ cup sliced celery
- ½ cup chopped onions
- ½ cup thinly sliced carrots
- ¼ teaspoon pepper
- ½ teaspoon paprika
- ¼ teaspoon dried thyme
- ¼ teaspoon rubbed sage
- 3 ounces unsalted tomato paste
- 1 ½ tablespoons corn starch mixed with two tablespoons water
- 1 can (14.5 ounces) low-sodium chicken broth
- Shredded Parmesan cheese, to serve (optional)

1. Place chicken, vegetables, spices, herbs, tomato paste and broth in a soup pot. Stir until well combined.
2. Cook covered over medium flame until chicken and vegetables are tender.
3. Add cornstarch mixture and constantly stir until thick.
4. Ladle into bowls and serve.

PER SERVING

Calories 180 ;Fat 2g ; Sodium 280mg;Carbs 18g ;Fiber 4g ;Sugar 6g ;Protein 21g

Barbecue Turkey Breast

Prep time: 5 minutes | Cook time: 1 hour to 1 hour 15 minutes| Serves 8

- Nonstick cooking spray (optional)
- ¼ cup packed brown sugar
- 2 teaspoons garlic powder
- 2 teaspoons onion powder
- 1 teaspoon paprika
- 1 teaspoon freshly ground black pepper
- 1 teaspoon mustard powder
- ½ teaspoon chili powder (optional)
- ¼ teaspoon cayenne pepper
- 3 pounds boneless turkey breast

1. Preheat the oven to 350°F. Line a roasting pan with aluminum foil or coat with nonstick cooking spray.
2. In a small bowl, mix together the brown sugar, garlic powder, onion powder, paprika, black pepper, mustard powder, chili powder (if using), and cayenne pepper. Season the turkey breast with this rub and transfer to the prepared roasting pan.
3. Cover the turkey with foil to avoid browning. Roast for 40 minutes. Then begin checking the turkey breast every 10 to 15 minutes until the internal temperature of the turkey breast has reached 165°F. Let rest for 5 minutes before slicing. Portion the turkey into 8 storage containers.

PER SERVING

Calories: 233; Total fat: 3g; Carbohydrates: 8g; Fiber: 0.5g; Protein: 41g; Calcium: 21mg; Vitamin D: 13 IU; Potassium: 365mg; Magnesium: 45mg; Sodium: 136mg

Baked Ranch Chicken Thighs

Prep time: 10 minutes | Cook time: 35 minutes| Serves 8

- Nonstick cooking spray (optional)
- 2 tablespoons dried parsley
- 2 teaspoons dried dill
- 2 teaspoons dried basil
- 2 teaspoons garlic powder
- 2 teaspoons onion powder
- 1 teaspoon freshly ground black pepper
- 1 teaspoon dried chives
- ¼ cup dried buttermilk powder
- ½ cup dried unseasoned bread crumbs
- 8 (4-ounce) boneless, skinless chicken thighs
- 1 tablespoon extra-virgin olive oil

1. Preheat the oven to 400°F. Line a sheet pan with aluminum foil or coat with nonstick cooking spray.
2. In a small bowl, mix together the parsley, dill, basil, garlic powder, onion powder, pepper, chives, buttermilk powder, and bread crumbs.
3. Pat the chicken thighs dry with a paper towel. Lightly coat both sides of the chicken thighs with the oil. Dip the chicken in the seasoned bread crumbs to coat both sides. Arrange on the prepared sheet pan.
4. Cook for about 35 minutes, or until the internal temperature of the chicken has reached 165°F. Let cool, then divide among 8 storage containers.

PER SERVING

Calories: 202; Total fat: 8.5g; Carbohydrates: 8g; Fiber: 0.5g; Protein: 22g; Calcium: 69mg; Vitamin D: 6 IU; Potassium: 293mg; Magnesium: 26mg; Sodium: 142mg

Chicken Lettuce Wraps

Prep Time: 15 minutes | Serves: 1

- ½ English cucumber, sliced thinly
- ½ tablespoon fresh mint leaves, minced
- 3 ounces cooked chicken breast, cut into strips
- ¼ cup fresh strawberries, hulled and sliced thinly
- 2 large lettuce leaves

1. Take a bowl and add all the given ingredients except for lettuce leaves and gently toss to coat well.
2. Place the lettuce leaves onto serving plates.
3. Divide the chicken mixture over each leaf evenly.
4. Serve immediately.
5. Enjoy!

PER SERVING

Calories: 147 ;Fat: 2.6g; Sat Fat: 0.1g ;Carbohydrates: 11.8g ;Fiber: 2.4g ;Sugar: 5.4g ;Protein: 19.8g

Grapefruit and Herb Chicken

Prep time: 10 minutes | Cook time: 40 minutes | Serves 4

- Nonstick cooking spray
- ¼ cup extra-virgin olive oil
- 2 tablespoons honey
- 2 garlic cloves, minced
- Zest and juice of 1 large lemon
- Zest and juice of ½ medium grapefruit
- ½ teaspoon dried basil
- ½ teaspoon dried rosemary
- ¼ teaspoon dried thyme
- 2 tablespoons chopped fresh parsley
- 4 (4-ounce) chicken breast cutlets, thinly sliced
- ¼ teaspoon salt
- ½ teaspoon freshly ground black pepper

1. Preheat the oven to 425°F. Coat a 9-by-13-inch baking dish with cooking spray.
2. In a large resealable bag, mix together the oil, honey, garlic, lemon zest, lemon juice, grapefruit zest, grapefruit juice, basil, rosemary, thyme, and parsley. Seal and shake until well combined.
3. Put the chicken cutlets in the bag. Seal and shake until the chicken is well coated with the marinade.
4. Transfer the chicken and the marinade to the prepared baking dish. Sprinkle the chicken with the salt and pepper. Bake for 30 to 40 minutes, or until the chicken is no longer pink in the middle. Let cool, then divide among 4 storage containers (including the juices from the baking dish).

PER SERVING

Calories: 278; Total fat: 16g; Carbohydrates: 10g; Fiber: 0.5g; Protein: 23g; Calcium: 23mg; Vitamin D: 4 IU; Potassium: 218mg; Magnesium: 24mg; Sodium: 202mg

Cheesy Broccoli and Chicken Bake

Prep time: 15 minutes | Cook time: 25 minutes | Serves 6

- Nonstick cooking spray
- 2 tablespoons extra-virgin olive oil
- 1 pound boneless, skinless chicken breasts, cubed
- 4 garlic cloves, minced
- 1 small onion, thinly sliced
- ¼ teaspoon freshly ground black pepper
- 2 cups brown rice
- 4½ cups unsalted chicken stock
- 1½ large heads broccoli, cut into bite-size florets
- 1 cup nonfat plain Greek yogurt
- 1½ teaspoons Dijon mustard
- 1½ cups reduced-fat shredded Cheddar cheese

1. Preheat the oven to 400°F. Coat a 9-by-13-inch baking dish with cooking spray.
2. In a large skillet, heat the oil over medium heat. Add the chicken, garlic, onion, and pepper. Sauté while stirring for about 5 minutes. Add the rice and chicken stock and stir. Increase the heat to high and bring to a boil.
3. Pour the chicken and rice mixture into the prepared baking dish. Arrange the broccoli on top and spread evenly. Do not mix in. Cover with a lid or aluminum foil. Bake for 40 to 45 minutes.
4. Meanwhile, in a small bowl, blend together the yogurt and mustard.
5. Remove the baking dish from the oven. Uncover and stir in the yogurt and mustard mixture. Sprinkle the Cheddar cheese on top. Return to the oven and bake uncovered for 5 to 10 minutes, or until the cheese has melted. Let cool, then divide among 6 storage containers.

PER SERVING

Calories: 531; Total fat: 19g; Carbohydrates: 52g; Fiber: 3.5g; Protein: 39g; Calcium: 341mg; Vitamin D: 4 IU; Potassium: 600mg; Magnesium: 115mg; Sodium: 347mg

Pistachio-Crusted Chicken

Prep time: 15 minutes | Cook time: 30 minutes| Serves 4

- ½ cup finely chopped pistachio nuts (shelled)
- ½ teaspoon freshly ground black pepper
- 1 pound boneless, skinless chicken breasts, trimmed and cut into 4 pieces
- 2 tablespoons olive oil

1. Preheat the oven to 350°F.
2. In a small bowl or bag, combine the pistachio nuts and black pepper.
3. Brush the chicken breasts with olive oil, then roll them in the bowl or shake them in the bag to cover both sides with the nut mixture.
4. Place the chicken breasts in a greased 9-by-13-inch pan. Bake for 25 to 35 minutes, or until juices run clear and an instant-read thermometer registers 165°F.
5. Serve immediately.

PER SERVING

Calories: 286; Total Fat: 18g; Saturated Fat: 3g; Cholesterol: 65mg; Sodium: 40mg; Potassium: 3mg; Magnesium: 4mg; Total Carbohydrates: 5g; Fiber: 2g; Sugars: 1g; Protein: 28g

Stuffed Chicken Breasts with Garlic Mushrooms and Zesty Spinach

Prep time: 15 minutes | Cook time: 35 minutes| Serves 4

- Nonstick cooking spray (optional)
- 2 (8-ounce) boneless, skinless chicken breasts
- 3 tablespoons extra-virgin olive oil, divided
- 2 garlic cloves, chopped
- 12 small cremini mushrooms, sliced
- 2 cups baby spinach, chopped
- ¼ teaspoon freshly ground black pepper
- ¼ cup grated Parmesan cheese
- Zest of 1 large lemon, divided
- 3 teaspoons fresh lemon juice, divided

1. Preheat the oven to 375°F. Line a sheet pan with aluminum foil or coat with nonstick cooking spray.
2. Working from the thickest part of each breast, cut an opening about 3 inches wide, then cut three-quarters of the way through the breast to create a pocket. Do not cut all the way through the chicken or the stuffing will spill out.
3. In a skillet, heat 2 tablespoons of oil over medium-high heat. Add the garlic and stir frequently for 30 seconds to 1 minute. Add the mushrooms and cook for about 2 minutes, or until tender. Add the spinach and stir for about 1 minute, or until wilted. Season with the pepper.
4. Transfer the cooked vegetables to a medium bowl. Add the Parmesan cheese, half of the lemon zest, and 1½ teaspoons of lemon juice. Divide the filling into 2 portions and stuff each chicken breast.
5. In a small bowl, stir together the remaining 1

tablespoon of oil and the remaining 1½ teaspoons of lemon juice. Brush on top of each chicken breast.

6. Bake for about 35 minutes, or until the internal temperature of the chicken reaches 165°F. Let cool, top with remaining lemon zest, then cut each stuffed breast in half and divide into 4 storage containers.

PER SERVING

Calories: 254; Total fat: 14g; Carbohydrates: 5g; Fiber: 1g; Protein: 27g; Calcium: 94mg; Vitamin D: 6 IU; Potassium: 473mg; Magnesium: 49mg; Sodium: 170mg

Chicken Kebabs

Prep Time: 10 minutes|Cook time: 8 minutes|Serves: 2

- 1 tablespoon olive oil
- ⅛ teaspoon Cayenne pepper
- ½ garlic clove, pepper
- 6 tablespoons fat-free plain Greek yogurt
- 1 tablespoon ground cumin
- 1 tablespoon fresh lemon juice
- 2 boneless chicken-breasts, cut into 1-inch chunks
- Pinch of salt
- Fresh ground black pepper according to your flavor

1. Take a bowl and add all the ingredients except for chicken chunks and mix them until well combined.
2. Add the chicken chunks and coat with the yogurt mixture generously.
3. Refrigerate overnight.
4. Preheat the grill to medium-high heat and grease the grill grate finely.
5. Thread the chicken chunks onto pre-soaked wooden skewers.
6. Arrange chicken kebabs onto the grill and cook for about three to four minutes per side.
7. Serve hot and enjoy!

PER SERVING

Calories: 221 ;Fat: 9.3g ;Sat Fat: 1.1g ; Carbohydrates: 3.7g ;Fiber: 0.4g ;Sugar: 1.9g ;Protein: 31.2g

Breaded and Baked Chicken Tenders

Prep time: 10 minutes | Cook time: 20 minutes| Serves 4

- Nonstick cooking spray
- ¼ cup whole wheat flour
- ¼ teaspoon salt
- 2 large eggs
- 1 cup dried unseasoned bread crumbs
- ¼ cup grated Parmesan cheese
- ¼ teaspoon paprika
- ¼ teaspoon garlic powder
- 1 pound chicken tenders

1. Preheat the oven to 400°F. Line a large sheet pan with foil and coat with nonstick cooking spray.
2. Set up a dredging station: In a shallow dish, mix together the flour and salt. In a small bowl, beat the eggs. In a second shallow dish, mix the bread crumbs, Parmesan, paprika, and garlic.
3. Dip each tender in the flour mixture, then the egg wash, then the bread crumb mixture until covered on both sides. Try to use one hand for dry dipping, and one for dipping in the egg to prevent a gummy mess. Arrange the tenders on the prepared sheet pan.
4. Bake for 15 to 20 minutes, or until the coating is golden brown and the chicken is no longer pink in the center, turning once halfway through. Divide among 4 storage containers.

PER SERVING

Calories: 328; Total fat: 14g; Carbohydrates: 21g; Fiber: 1.5g; Protein: 31g; Calcium: 103mg; Vitamin D: 22 IU; Potassium: 258mg; Magnesium: 36mg; Sodium: 419mg

Chicken Legs with Rice and Peas

Prep time: 5 minutes | Cook time: 45 minutes| Serves 4

- 4 chicken drumsticks
- 3 tablespoons olive oil
- 4 garlic cloves, chopped
- 1 tablespoon paprika
- 1 teaspoon dried oregano
- 1 cup instant brown rice
- 2¾ cup frozen peas

1. Preheat the oven to 425°F.
2. Place the drumsticks in a 9-by-13-inch baking dish.
3. In a small skillet, heat the olive oil over medium heat. Add the garlic, paprika, and oregano. Cook for 1 minute, and remove from the heat.
4. Pour the mixture over the drumsticks and turn to coat evenly. Bake for about 45 minutes, or until an instant-read thermometer reads 180°F.
5. While the chicken bakes, cook the rice according to the package directions. When the rice has 7 minutes of cook time remaining, stir in the peas and re-cover.
6. Divide the rice among four plates and top each with a drumstick, skin removed.

PER SERVING

Calories: 345; Total Fat: 15g; Saturated Fat: 2g; Cholesterol: 48mg; Sodium: 96mg; Potassium: 279mg; Magnesium: 88mg; Total Carbohydrates: 40g; Fiber: 4g; Sugars: 2g; Protein: 18g

Chicken Pesto Pasta with Asparagus

Prep Time: 30 minutes|Cook Time: 15 minutes|Serves: 6

- 8 oz. whole-wheat penne
- 1 lb. fresh asparagus, trimmed and cut into 2-inch pieces
- 3 cups shredded cooked chicken breast
- 1 (7 oz.) container refrigerated basil pesto
- 1 tsp. salt
- ¼ tsp. ground pepper
- 1 oz. parmesan cheese, grated (about ¼ cup)
- Small fresh basil leaves for garnish

1. Cook the pasta in a large pot according to package directions.
2. Add the asparagus to the pot during the final 2 minutes of cooking time. Drain, reserving ½ cup of the cooking water.
3. Return the pasta mixture to the pot. Stir in the chicken, pesto, salt, and pepper. Stir in the reserved cooking water 1 tbsp. at a time to reach the desired consistency.

PER SERVING

Calories 422 ;Protein 31.4g ;Carbohydrates 32.2g ; Dietary fiber 0.8g ;Sugars 3.5g ;Fat 18.4g; Sodium 714.1mg

Chapter 7
Beef, Lamb & Pork

Fiery Beer-Basted Grilled Steaks

Prep time: 5 minutes | Cook time: 20 minutes| Serves 8

- 1 tsp. extra-virgin olive oil
- Splash of hot sauce
- 1 tsp. cayenne pepper
- 2 tsp. crushed garlic
- 1 tbsp. low-sodium soy sauce
- 1 tsp. crushed ginger
- 2 tbsp. dry sherry
- 2 tbsp. dark brown sugar
- 4 medium spring onions, chopped
- 12 oz. light beer
- 2 lbs. boneless sirloin steak, fat removed

1. In a large bowl, whisk together the oil, hot sauce, cayenne pepper, garlic, soy sauce, ginger, sherry, dark brown sugar, spring onions, and beer.
2. Once all of the sugar granules have disappeared, add the steak and toss to coat.
3. Seal the bowl with cling wrap and chill for a minimum of 1 hour and no more than 24 hours, turning every few hours to ensure even marination. (Note: The longer the meat stands in the beer mixture the better the taste.)
4. Set the oven grill to preheat on high.
5. Remove the meat from the beer mixture. Throw away the remaining sauce.
6. Place the meat on a lightly coated baking tray and bake in the oven for 8-12 minutes per side, or until the meat reaches the desired rarity.

PER SERVING

Calories: 135; Sodium: 95mg; Total Fat: 4½g; Saturated Fat: 1½g; Cholesterol: 59mg; Total Carbohydrates: 0g; Fiber: 0g; Protein: 22g

Herb-Encrusted Lamb Chops

Prep time: 5 minutes | Cook time: 25 minutes| Serves 4

- 1 tsp. crushed thyme
- 1 tsp. fresh parsley, chopped
- 1 tsp. fresh rosemary, chopped
- 1 lemon, zested
- 2 tbsp. crushed garlic
- Pinch of white pepper
- 1 lb. small lamb chops (approx. 12 chops)
- 1 tbsp. extra-virgin olive oil

1. In a small glass bowl, whisk together the thyme, parsley, rosemary, zested lemon peel, garlic, and white pepper.
2. Use your fingers to massage the herb mixture evenly into the chops before transferring the lamb to a covered bowl and chilling for 1 hour.
3. In a large frying pan over medium-high heat, heat the oil before adding six of the chops to start with. Fry the chops for about 12 minutes, flipping halfway through the frying time to ensure even browning. Transfer the cooked chops to a clean

plate and keep warm.
4. Repeat the process with the remaining chops.
5. Serve immediately while hot. (Note: Any leftover chops can be refrigerated in an airtight container for no more than 3 days.)

PER SERVING

Calories: 228; Sodium: 81mg; Total Fat: 14g; Saturated Fat: 4g; Cholesterol: 75mg; Total Carbohydrates: 2g; Fiber: 0g; Protein: 23g

Mint Spiced Lamb Skewers

Prep time: 5 minutes | Cook time: 15 minutes| Serves 4

- ¼ tsp. ground allspice
- ¼ tsp. ground cinnamon
- ½ tsp. ground cilantro seeds
- 1 tbsp. fresh parsley, finely chopped
- 1 tbsp. fresh mint, finely chopped
- 1 tbsp. crushed garlic
- 1 large free-range egg
- ½ small shallot, shredded
- 1 lb. extra-lean ground lamb

1. Place all the ingredients in a large mixing bowl and use a wooden spoon to combine properly.
2. Use clean hands to form the lamb mince into eight sausages that run the length of eight wooden skewers that have been soaked in cold water to prevent charring.
3. Carefully slip the formed sausages onto the skewers, firmly compacting the meat with your hand. Be sure to leave a few inches at the bottom of the skewer as a handle.
4. Chill the lamb skewers for about 30 minutes, or until completely cold. Set the oven grill to preheat on medium while you wait.
5. Place the chilled skewers on a lightly coated baking sheet and grill in the oven for about 15 minutes, turning occasionally, or until the skewers are properly cooked and lightly browned on the outside.

PER SERVING

Calories: 300; Sodium: 67mg; Total Fat: 14g; Saturated Fat: 7g; Cholesterol: 80mg; Total Carbohydrates: 2g; Fiber: 1g; Protein: 19g

Quick & Easy Pork Wraps

Prep time: 5 minutes | Cook time: 25 minutes| Serves 4

- Extra-virgin olive oil
- 1 lb. pork tenderloin, sliced into strips
- 2 tsp. crushed garlic
- 1 medium yellow bell pepper, cut into strips
- 1 medium red bell pepper, cut into strips
- 1 medium shallot, cut into strips
- 1 tsp. smoked paprika
- 1 tsp. ground cumin
- 1 tsp. chili powder
- Pinch of cayenne pepper
- Freshly ground black pepper
- Himalayan salt
- 4 whole-wheat wraps (heated for serving)
- 1 Hass avocado, sliced
- Fresh coriander leaves, chopped
- 1 lime, quartered

1. Heat ½ tbsp. olive oil in a large frying pan over medium-high heat. When the oil is nice and hot, toss the pork in the pan and fry for 5-10 minutes, or until the pork is properly cooked. Transfer to a covered platter and set aside.
2. In the same pan, add another ½ tbsp. oil. Add the garlic, bell peppers, and shallot strips to the pan when the oil is hot. Toss for about 1 minute before adding the paprika, cumin, chili powder, cayenne pepper, and a small pinch each of salt and pepper. Continue to toss and cook the vegetables for 4-5 minutes, or until the shallot strips are translucent and beginning to crisp around the edges.
3. Add the cooked pork back to the pan and toss until heated (approx. 1-2 additional minutes). Remove the pan from the heat.
4. Build the wraps by dividing the pork filling between the heated wraps and topping with sliced avocado and chopped coriander. Drizzle with the lime juice. Fold and serve.

PER SERVING

Calories: 366; Sodium: 203mg; Total Fat: 16g; Saturated Fat: 3g; Cholesterol: 67mg; Total Carbohydrates: 29g; Fiber: 8g; Protein: 29g

Pasta-less Beef Lasagna

Prep time: 5 minutes | Cook time: 45 minutes| Serves 4

- 1 tbsp. extra-virgin olive oil
- 1 lb. extra-lean ground beef
- 2 tsp. crushed garlic
- 1½ tbsp. dried dill weed, crushed
- 1½ medium shallots, chopped
- Pinch of white pepper
- 1 medium eggplant, sliced (⅛-inches thick)
- 2 cups plain, non-fat, unsweetened Greek yogurt

1. Lightly coat a deep baking dish with cooking spray and set the oven to preheat at 350°F with the wire rack in the center of the oven.
2. In a large frying pan, heat the oil before adding the ground beef and frying for about 8-10 minutes, or until the pork is properly cooked and browned. The beef will break up as you stir and fry.
3. Toss in the garlic, dill weed, shallots, and pepper. Toss for about 30 seconds until the beef is evenly seasoned. Remove from the heat.
4. Begin layering your dish with eggplant topped with the cooked beef. Continue the layers until you have used all of the ingredients. Scrape the yogurt over the top and use an offset spatula to smooth out the surface.
5. Place the dish in the oven for 45-60 minutes, or until the eggplant is fork-tender.
6. Serve hot.

PER SERVING

Calories: 274; Sodium: 187mg; Total Fat: 6g; Saturated Fat: 2½g; Cholesterol: 65mg; Total Carbohydrates: 23g; Fiber: 5g; Protein: 33g

Beefy Whole-Wheat Pasta

Prep time: 5 minutes | Cook time: 30 minutes| Serves 4

- 8 oz. whole-wheat pasta
- 2 tsp. extra-virgin olive oil
- 1 lb. extra-lean ground beef
- 1 tbsp. smoked paprika
- 1 tbsp. balsamic vinegar
- 1 tbsp. crushed garlic
- 1 small shallot, chopped
- 2 red bell peppers, chopped
- 2 cups button mushrooms, sliced
- 2 tsp. fresh oregano, chopped
- 2 tbsp. no-salt-added tomato paste
- 2 cups tomatoes, chopped
- ¼ cup sour cream

1. Prepare the pasta in a large pot of boiling water – leave out the salt. Drain and set aside.
2. While the pasta is still boiling, add the oil to a large frying pan over medium-high heat. Once the oil is nice and hot, cook the beef for about 6 minutes, or until properly browned.
3. Stir in the paprika, vinegar, garlic, shallots, peppers, and mushrooms. Fry for about 7 minutes, or until the shallots are translucent.
4. Add the oregano, tomato paste, and chopped tomatoes to the pan and gently stir until the sauce begins to bubble. Lower the heat and allow the sauce to simmer for 10 minutes. Stir occasionally to prevent burning.
5. Stir in the sour cream and cooked pasta until properly combined and heated through (approx. 4 minutes).
6. Serve hot.

PER SERVING

Calories: 442; Sodium: 96mg; Total Fat: 11g; Saturated Fat: 4g; Cholesterol: 66mg; Total Carbohydrates: 56g; Fiber: 12g; Protein: 35g

Lamb & Vegetable Couscous

Prep time: 5 minutes | Cook time: 65 minutes| Serves 4

- ¼ cup seedless raisins
- 1 tbsp. extra-virgin olive oil
- ¾lbs. boneless lamb stew meat
- 1 medium shallot, chopped
- 1 cup baby carrots
- ¼ tsp. ground turmeric
- ½ tsp. ground ginger
- 1 tsp. ground cumin
- 1 tsp. smoked paprika
- 2 tsp. crushed garlic
- 1 whole cinnamon stick
- ¼ cup black olives, pips removed
- 1 medium lemon, quartered, seeds removed
- 1 cup low-sodium chicken stock
- 15½ oz. no-salt-added chickpeas, rinsed and drained
- ½ cup fresh coriander leaves, chopped
- 1 cup raw whole-wheat couscous

1. In a large bowl, cover the raisins in warm water and soak for 1 hour. Pour the raisins through a colander set over the sink and allow to drain while you prepare the rest of the dish.
2. Heat the oil in a large pot over medium-high heat. When the oil is nice and hot, add the lamb and brown for 4-5 minutes.
3. Toss in the shallot and baby carrots. Fry until the carrots are fork-tender and the shallot is translucent (approx. 2-3 minutes).
4. Add the turmeric, ginger, cumin, paprika, garlic, cinnamon, olives, lemon, chicken stock, and chickpeas to the pot. Stir until the broth begins to simmer.
5. Lower the heat and allow the sauce to simmer for 1 hour with the lid on the pot. After 1 hour, add in the coriander leaves and raisins. Gently stir to combine. Simmer for an additional 20-30 minutes, or until the lamb is soft.
6. While the lamb is simmering, cook the couscous according to the packaging – leave out the salt.
7. When the lamb is soft, serve the stew over a bed of fluffed couscous. (Note: Throw away the lemon wedges and cinnamon stick before serving.)

PER SERVING

Calories: 513; Sodium: 232mg; Total Fat: 9½g; Saturated Fat: 2.2g; Cholesterol: 46mg; Total Carbohydrates: 81g; Fiber: 14g; Protein: 30g

Oregano Baked Beef & Beans

Prep time: 5 minutes | Cook time: 45 minutes | Serves 4

- 1 tsp. extra-virgin olive oil
- 1 lb. extra-lean ground beef
- 2 tsp. crushed oregano
- 2 tsp. crushed garlic
- 2 celery stalks, chopped
- 1 small shallot, chopped
- ½ cup no-salt-added beef stock
- 1 yellow bell pepper, diced
- 1 red bell pepper, diced
- 2 cups green beans, chopped
- 2 cups cherry tomatoes, halved

1. Set the oven to preheat at 400°F with the wire rack in the center of the oven.
2. In a large frying pan over medium-high heat, heat the olive oil before adding the ground beef. Cook for about 7 minutes, or until properly browned.
3. Stir in the oregano, garlic, celery, and shallot pieces for about 5 minutes, or until the shallot pieces are translucent. Transfer the pan to a wooden chopping board.
4. Stir in the beef stock, bell peppers, green beans, and tomatoes.
5. Scrape the beef and vegetables into an oven-safe casserole dish.
6. Place the dish in the oven for about 30 minutes, or until the vegetables are fork-tender.
7. Serve immediately.

PER SERVING

Calories: 203; Sodium: 81mg; Total Fat: 6g; Saturated Fat: 2g; Cholesterol: 59mg; Total Carbohydrates: 15g; Fiber: 5g; Protein: 24g

Caffeinated Beef Roast

Prep time: 5 minutes | Cook time: 1 hour 25 minutes | Serves 12

- 1 tsp. smoked paprika
- 1 tsp. white pepper
- 1 tsp. onion powder
- 1 tsp. garlic powder
- 2 tsp. crushed thyme
- 2 tsp. instant espresso granules
- Himalayan salt
- 3 lbs. eye-of-round beef roast, fat removed
- Extra-virgin olive oil

1. Set the oven to preheat at 325°F with the wire rack in the center of the oven. Fit a wire rack over a rimmed baking sheet and lightly spray both with cooking spray.
2. In a small glass bowl, whisk together the smoked paprika, white pepper, onion powder, garlic powder, thyme, espresso granules, and ½ tsp. salt.
3. with the beef roast on the sprayed rack, use a basting brush to coat the beef in 1 tbsp. oil. Use your fingers to rub the espresso mixture into the meat. Press the spices down to form a crust.
4. Heat 1 tbsp. oil in a large frying pan over medium-high heat. When the oil is nice and hot, seer the roast on all sides (approx. 2 minutes per side). Carefully place the seared roast back on the coated wire rack.
5. Place the rack in the oven for 1 hour 20 minutes, or until a candy thermometer measures 135°F at the center of the roast. Remove the roast from the oven at this point. (Note: The meat will not yet be properly cooked.)
6. Allow the roast to rest for 10 minutes on a wooden chopping board. (Note: The meat will continue to cook as it stands.) After 10 minutes, carve the meat and season with ¼ tsp. salt.
7. Serve hot or cooled.

PER SERVING

Calories: 144; Sodium: 186mg; Total Fat: 3½g; Saturated Fat: 1g; Cholesterol: 48mg; Total Carbohydrates: 1g; Fiber: 0g; Protein: 25g

Creamy Beef & Lentils in Mushroom Sauce

Prep time: 5 minutes | Cook time: 25 minutes | Serves 6

- 1 tsp. extra-virgin olive oil
- 1 lb. extra-lean ground beef
- ½ tsp. Himalayan salt
- 3 tsp. crushed garlic
- 1 small shallot, chopped
- 1 tbsp. crushed oregano
- 2 tbsp. tomato paste
- ⅔ cups warm water
- 1 lb. button mushrooms, sliced
- 28 oz. whole no-salt-added tomatoes
- ½ cup raw split red lentils, rinsed

1. Heat the oil in a large frying pan over medium heat before browning the beef with ¼ tsp. Himalayan salt. After about 2-3 minutes, stir in the garlic and shallot pieces.
2. Cook the beef for an additional 5-7 minutes or until the blood has completely cooked away.
3. Raise the heat to medium-high and stir in the oregano, tomato paste, water, mushrooms, tomatoes with sauce, and lentils. Gently stir until the sauce begins to simmer. Lower the heat and allow the pot to simmer for about 15 minutes until the lentils are tender. Stirring at regular intervals to prevent burning.
4. Season the dish with the remaining salt if necessary and serve.

PER SERVING

Calories: 225; Sodium: 266mg; Total Fat: 6g; Saturated Fat: 2g; Cholesterol: 48mg; Total Carbohydrates: 21g; Fiber: 5g; Protein: 24g

Apple-Cinnamon Roasted Pork Chops

Prep time: 5 minutes | Cook time: 45 minutes| Serves 4

- 2 Granny Smith apples, peeled and sliced
- 1 tsp. ground cinnamon
- 1 medium sweet onion, thinly sliced
- 4 boneless pork chops with fat trimmed (½-inch thick)
- White pepper
- ¾ cups warm water
- 1 tbsp. extra-virgin olive oil
- 3 tbsp. light brown sugar

1. Set the oven to preheat at 375° F with the wire rack in the center of the oven.
2. In a deep casserole dish, arrange the apple slices in a single layer. Sprinkle evenly with the cinnamon.
3. Place the sweet onion slices on top of the apples in a single layer, followed by the pork chops. Season the chops with 1\8 tsp. salt and a pinch of pepper to taste.
4. In a medium glass bowl, whisk together the warm water, olive oil, and brown sugar until all of the sugar granules have dissolved. Pour the sauce over everything in the casserole dish.
5. Bake in the oven for 30-45 minutes, or until the chops are properly cooked and the apples are tender.
6. Allow the chops to cool on the counter for 3 minutes before serving.

PER SERVING

Calories: 325; Sodium: 126mg; Total Fat: 16g; Saturated Fat: 5g; Cholesterol: 66mg; Total Carbohydrates: 24g; Fiber: 3g; Protein: 24g

Creamy Beef & Mushroom Macaroni

Prep time: 5 minutes | Cook time: 25 minutes| Serves 4

- 8 oz. uncooked elbow macaroni
- 1½ tsp. dried basil
- 1½ tsp. dried Italian seasoning
- 3 tsp. crushed garlic
- 1 medium shallot, diced
- 8 oz. button mushrooms, sliced
- 8 oz. extra-lean ground beef
- ¼ tsp. Himalayan salt
- 1 tsp. low-sodium Worcestershire sauce
- 2 tbsp. fresh parsley, chopped
- 6 oz. no-salt-added tomato paste
- 1 cup warm water

1. Cook the pasta by following the directions on the packaging – leave out the salt. Drain and set aside.
2. In a large frying pan over medium-high heat, combine the basil, Italian seasoning, garlic, shallot pieces, mushrooms, and ground beef. Cook the beef for about 8-10 minutes, or until nicely browned. The mushrooms and shallot pieces should be nice and tender.
3. Add the sauce to the pan, along with the cooked pasta, and simmer for 5 minutes.

4. Serve immediately.

PER SERVING

Calories: 246; Sodium: 182mg; Total Fat: 3g; Saturated Fat: 1g; Cholesterol: 22mg; Total Carbohydrates: 39g; Fiber: 3g; Protein: 17g

Cumin Marinated Pork & Beans

Prep time: 5 minutes | Cook time: 25 minutes| Serves 4

PORK MARINADE:

- ¼ tsp. Himalayan salt
- 1 tsp. cayenne pepper
- 1 tsp. dried oregano
- 2 tsp. extra-virgin olive oil
- ¼ cup freshly squeezed orange juice
- 2 tbsp. freshly squeezed lime juice
- 2 tbsp. lime zest, grated
- 1 lb. pork tenderloin

BEANS:

- 1 tbsp. extra-virgin olive oil
- 1 small shallot, chopped
- 2 tsp. dried oregano
- 1 tbsp. ground cumin
- 1 medium red bell pepper
- 2 large heirloom tomatoes, chopped
- ½ cup low-sodium chicken stock
- 15 oz. black turtle beans, rinsed and drained
- ¼ cup fresh coriander leaves, chopped

1. In a large bowl, whisk together the salt, cayenne pepper, oregano, cumin, 1 tsp. olive oil, orange juice, lime juice, and lime zest. Add the pork and toss to coat. Cover the bowl with cling wrap and chill for at least 1 hour, but no longer than 24 hours, stirring occasionally.
2. Once the pork is properly chilled. Heat 1 tsp. oil in a large frying pan over medium-high heat. When the oil is hot, remove the pork from the marinade, keeping the marinade for later, and fry for 5-6 minutes. Turn the pork and add the marinade. Cook for an additional 5-7 minutes, or until the pork is properly cooked. Turn off the heat and keep the pork warm.
3. Use a second frying pan to heat 1 tbsp. olive oil over medium-high heat. When the oil is nice and hot, fry the shallot pieces for 3-4 minutes, or until translucent. Stir in the oregano, cumin, peppers, and chopped tomatoes. Fry for an additional 3-4 minutes, or until the peppers are soft.
4. Stir in the chicken stock and black beans. When the stock begins to boil, lower the heat and simmer for 3-4 minutes.
5. Serve the pork on a bed of beans and garnish with the fresh coriander leaves.

PER SERVING

Calories: 310; Sodium: 228mg; Total Fat: 11g; Saturated Fat: 2g; Cholesterol: 45mg; Total Carbohydrates: 25g; Fiber: 6g; Protein: 31g

Thyme-Baked Pork Tenderloin

Prep time: 5 minutes | Cook time: 35 minutes| Serves 6 \

- ¼ tsp. white pepper
- ¼ tsp. Himalayan salt
- ½ tsp. onion powder
- ½ tsp. ground cumin
- 1 tsp. dried thyme
- 1½ lbs. pork tenderloin
- 1 tbsp. avocado oil
- 3 tsp. crushed garlic

1. Set the oven to preheat at 400°F with the wire rack in the center of the oven.
2. In a small glass bowl, mix together the pepper, salt, onion powder, cumin, and thyme.
3. Place the pork tenderloin on a wooden chopping board. Massage the spice mixture evenly into the pork using your fingers.
4. Heat the oil in an oven-proof pan over medium-high heat before frying the garlic for 30 seconds. Sear the pork on all sides (approx. 2-3 minutes per side).
5. Place the pan in the oven and bake for 15-20 minutes, or until properly cooked.
6. Slice and serve.

PER SERVING

Calories: 160; Sodium: 157mg; Total Fat: 6g; Saturated Fat: 2g; Total Carbohydrates: 1g; Fiber: 0g; Protein: 24g

Citrus Beef Stir Fry

Prep Time: 10 minutes| Cook time: 10 minutes|Serves: 2

- ½ pound boneless beef sirloin steak, cut into thin strips
- 2 teaspoons olive oil, divided
- ¼ cup orange juice
- 1 tablespoon reduced-sodium soy sauce
- 1 tablespoon corn starch
- ¼ cup cold water
- 3 cups frozen stir-fry vegetable blend
- 1 garlic clove, minced

1. Mix the cornstarch, water, orange juice and soy sauce until smooth in a small bowl. Set the mixture aside.
2. In a large wok or skillet, heat one teaspoon of olive oil over medium-high heat.
3. Stir-fry the beef for 3 to 4 minutes, until no longer pink.
4. Remove to a plate or bowl and cover to keep warm.
5. Add the remaining olive oil to the wok and allow to heat. Stir-fry the vegetable blend and garlic for 3 minutes.
6. Stir the cornstarch mixture, then add it to the cooking vegetables and bring to a boil. Stir for 2 minutes, until thickened.
7. Add the beef and stir until heated through.

PER SERVING

Calories 268 ;Fat 10g ; Sodium 376mg;Carbs 8g ;Fiber 3g ;Sugar 8g ;Protein 26g

Garlic Beef Brisket

Prep Time: 10 minutes|Cook Time: 3 hours and 10 minutes|Serves: 4

- 1 tablespoon olive oil
- 2½ pounds beef brisket, cut into pieces
- Ground black pepper, to taste
- 1½ cups onions, chopped
- 4 garlic cloves, smashed and peeled
- 1 teaspoon dried thyme
- 1 can (14½ ounces) tomatoes (with its liquid)
- ¼ cup red wine vinegar
- 1 cup low-sodium beef stock

1. Preheat the oven to 350°F.
2. Grease a Dutch oven with 1 tablespoon of oil and heat on a medium flame.
3. Add the ground pepper to the brisket for seasoning and sauté in the Dutch oven until it turns brown.
4. Transfer the seared brisket to a plate.
5. Add the onions to the same pot and sauté until golden brown.
6. Stir in the thyme and garlic and cook for 1 minute.
7. Add the vinegar, stock, and tomatoes.
8. Bring the mixture to a boil and return the brisket to the pot.
9. Reduce the heat to a simmer and cook for 3 hours or more until the meat is tender.
10. Serve warm.

PER SERVING

Calories 209 ;Fat 9g ;Sodium 72mg;Carbs 21.4g ;Fiber 1.3g ;Sugar 1.2g ;Protein 10.2g

Tender & Creamy Beef Noodles

Prep time: 5 minutes | Cook time: 25 minutes| Serves 4

- 6 oz. dried egg noodles
- 1 lb. boneless sirloin steak, cubed (fat discarded)
- ½ tsp. freshly ground black pepper
- 1 tsp. extra-virgin olive oil
- 1 medium shallot, diced
- 1 lb. button mushrooms, sliced
- ¼ cup fresh parsley, chopped
- ¼ cup fat-free sour cream
- 1 tbsp. fresh dill chopped

1. Cook the noodles by following the directions on the packaging – leave out the salt. Strain and set aside.
2. Place the cubed pork in a large bowl and season with the pepper.
3. Heat the oil in a large frying pan over medium-high heat before adding the beef. Fry for 4-6 minutes, or until the cubes reach the desired rarity. Scrape into a bowl and cover.
4. Add the shallot pieces and mushrooms to the frying pan used to fry the beef and fry over medium-high heat for about 8 minutes, or until the shallot pieces are translucent and the mushrooms have darkened in color.
5. Stir in the parsley and cooked beef cubes.
6. Serve the beef over a bed of the cooked noodles topped with sour cream and fresh dill.

PER SERVING

Calories: 346; Sodium: 87mg; Total Fat: 6g; Saturated Fat: 1½g; Cholesterol: 58mg; Total Carbohydrates: 41g; Fiber: 4g; Protein: 31g

Beef Fennel Stew

Prep Time: 25 minutes | Cook Time: 1 hour and 30 minutes | Serves: 4

- 3 tablespoons all-purpose flour
- 1 pound lean boneless beef, cut into cubes
- 2 tablespoons olive oil
- ½ fennel bulb, sliced vertically
- 3 large shallots, chopped
- ¾ teaspoon ground black pepper
- 2 fresh thyme sprigs
- 1 bay leaf
- 3 cups vegetable stock
- ½ cup red wine, optional
- 4 carrots, peeled and cut into 1-inch pieces
- 4 large white potatoes, peeled and cubed
- 18 small boiling onions, halved crosswise
- 3 portobello mushrooms, diced
- ⅓ cup fresh flat-leaf parsley, chopped

1. Spread the flour in a shallow container or plate.
2. Add the beef cubes and dredge them in the flour to coat well, then shake off the excess.
3. Take a large saucepan and add the oil to it. Heat over medium flame.
4. Add the beef and sauté for 5 minutes, then transfer it to a plate using a slotted spoon.
5. Add the shallots and fennel to the same saucepan and sauté for 7 minutes.
6. Stir in the thyme, bay leaf, and pepper. Cook for 1 minute.
7. Add the beef to the pan along with the wine and stock.
8. Bring to a boil and then reduce it to a simmer. Cover it and cook for 45 minutes.
9. Now add the mushrooms, onions, potatoes, and carrots.
10. Cook for 30 minutes until the vegetables are soft.
11. Remove the bay leaf and thyme sprigs.
12. Garnish with parsley.
13. Serve warm.

PER SERVING

Calories 384 ;Fat 2g ;Sodium 60mg;Carbs 26g ;Fiber 0.4g ;Sugar 2g ;Protein 32g

Roasted Pork Loin and Potatoes

Prep Time: 10 minutes| Cook time: 1 hour|Serves: 4

- 1 (1-pound/454-gram) pork loin, trimmed
- 8 garlic cloves
- ¼ cup olive oil, divided
- Black pepper, to taste
- 1 cup cubed raw sweet potato
- 1 cup small gold potatoes, quartered
- 8 fresh thyme sprigs, chopped

1. Preheat the oven to 350° F.
2. Rub the pork with garlic and 2 tablespoons of olive oil.
3. Season with black pepper. Coat a 9-by-13-inch baking dish with nonstick cooking spray.
4. Place the pork in the prepared baking dish.
5. Bake for an hour, or until an instant-read thermometer inserted in the center registers 145° F.
6. Twenty minutes into the cooking time, place the cubed and sliced sweet potatoes and gold potatoes on a rimmed baking dish, drizzle with the remaining olive oil, sprinkle with the thyme, and place in the oven.
7. The potatoes should be finished roasting about the same time as the pork and should be tender and slightly browned.
8. Once the pork is finished cooking, remove it from the oven and let the meat stand for 15 minutes before carving.
9. Cut into eight slices.

PER SERVING

Calories 426 ;Fat 22 g ; Sodium 56 mg;Carbs 21 g ;Fiber 4 g ;Sugar 3 g ;Protein 27 g

Classic Beef & Bean Chili

Prep Time: 15 minutes|Cook Time: 25 minutes| Serves 8

- 1 tablespoon canola oil
- 1 yellow onion, peeled and diced
- 1½ pounds lean ground beef
- 5 to 6 garlic cloves, peeled and minced
- 3 tablespoons chili powder
- 1 teaspoon kosher or sea salt
- ½ teaspoon ground black pepper
- 2 tablespoons no-salt-added tomato paste
- 1 (32-ounce) can no-salt-added crushed tomatoes
- 2 (15-ounce) cans no-salt-added dark red kidney beans, rinsed and drained
- 2 cups unsalted beef stock
- 2 avocados, peeled and diced
- ½ cup shredded sharp Cheddar cheese

1. Heat the oil in a Dutch oven or stockpot over medium heat. Add the onion and sauté for 3 to 4 minutes, until the onion is starting to soften. Add the ground beef and cook, breaking it up into smaller pieces, until the beef is browned. Stir in the garlic, chili powder, salt, black pepper, and tomato paste and cook for 1 minute.
2. Add the crushed tomatoes, kidney beans, and beef stock and bring to a simmer. Cook for 15 minutes. Taste and adjust the seasoning, if necessary.
3. Divide the chili evenly into bowls and top with the diced avocados and shredded Cheddar cheese.
4. Transfer leftover chili into microwaveable airtight containers, top with shredded Cheddar cheese, and refrigerate for up to 5 days. Reheat in the microwave on high for 1 to 3 minutes, until heated through, and top with avocado.

PER SERVING

Calories: 363; Total Fat: 17g; Saturated Fat: 5g; Cholesterol: 59mg; Sodium: 526mg; Potassium: 344mg; Total Carbohydrate: 29g; Fiber: 10g; Sugars: 6g; Protein: 26g

Baked Lamb Meatballs

Prep Time: 10 minutes| Cook time: 20 minutes|Serves: 4

- 1 pound ground lamb
- Olive oil cooking spray
- 1 large egg, beaten
- 1 garlic clove, chopped
- ¼ cup fresh mint, chopped
- ¼ cup shallot, chopped
- ¼ teaspoon ground cinnamon
- ½ teaspoon Kosher salt
- ¼ teaspoon red pepper flakes
- 1 teaspoon ground coriander
- 1 teaspoon ground cumin

1. Preheat the oven to 400° F. Grease a 12-cup muffin tin with olive oil cooking spray.

2. Mix the lamb, mint, egg, garlic, shallot, salt, coriander, cinnamon, cumin and red pepper flakes; stir well.
3. Shape the batter into 12 balls and put one in each cup of the prepared muffin tin.
4. Air-fry for 20 minutes, or until the meatballs are golden brown.
5. Remove from the oven and serve on plates.

PER SERVING

Calories 350 ; Fat 28g ; Sodium 227mg; Carbs 2g ; Fiber 1g ; Sugar 0g ; Protein 21g

Grilled Flank Steak with Peach Compote

Prep Time: 10 minutes| Cook time: 25 minutes|Serves: 6

PEACH COMPOTE:

- 2 peaches, cored and diced
- 1 tablespoon honey
- ½ tablespoon apple cider vinegar
- ¼ teaspoon ground cinnamon
- ¼ teaspoon ground ginger
- ¼ teaspoon ground nutmeg
- ¼ teaspoon Kosher or Sea salt

GRILLED FLANK STEAK:

- 1½ pounds flank steak
- 2 tablespoons canola oil
- ½ teaspoon Kosher or Sea salt
- ¼ teaspoon ground black pepper

MAKE THE PEACH COMPOTE:

1. Place the peaches, honey, apple cider vinegar, cinnamon, ginger, nutmeg and salt in a saucepan and bring to a simmer.
2. Stirring frequently, cook for 7 to 10 minutes, until the peaches are tender and the mixture has thickened. Remove from the heat and reserve.

MAKE THE GRILLED FLANK STEAK:

1. Heat a grill or grill pan over medium-high heat. Coat the steak with canola oil, salt and black pepper.
2. Grill for 6 minutes per side until the internal temperature reaches 155° F.
3. Let rest for 10 minutes on a cutting board, then thinly slice across the grain.
4. Divide the steak and serve.

PER SERVING

Calories 236 ; Fat 12 g | Sodium 356 mg; Carbs 7 g ; Fiber 1 g ; Sugar 5 g ; Protein 24 g

Pulled Pork

Prep time: 5 minutes | Cook time: 8 hours | Serves 4

- 1 small onion, diced
- 2 garlic cloves, minced
- 1 cup unsalted chicken stock
- Juice of ½ orange
- 1 tablespoon paprika
- 1 teaspoon dried oregano
- 1 teaspoon freshly ground black pepper
- ½ teaspoon ground cumin
- ½ teaspoon salt
- 2 pounds boneless pork shoulder or pork butt

1. In a slow cooker, combine the onion, garlic, chicken stock, and orange juice.
2. In a small bowl, mix together the paprika, oregano, pepper, cumin, and salt.
3. Trim any excess fat from the pork and rub the spice mix all over until it is well coated. Place it in the slow cooker on top of the onion and liquids.
4. Cover and cook on low for 8 hours, or until the meat can be pulled apart in shreds with a fork.
5. Remove the pork to a cutting board and use 2 forks to shred it. Portion the pork into 4 storage containers. Add some of the cooking liquids to each container to add moisture to the pork (good for both reheating and serving).

PER SERVING

Calories: 394; Total fat: 25g; Carbohydrates: 2g; Fiber: 0.5g; Protein: 37g; Calcium: 49mg; Vitamin D: 66 IU; Potassium: 462mg; Magnesium: 35mg; Sodium: 391mg

Honey Garlic Pork Chops

Prep time: 5 minutes | Cook time: 25 minutes | Serves 4

- 2½ tablespoons honey
- 4 garlic cloves, minced
- 1 tablespoon reduced-sodium soy sauce
- 1 tablespoon no-salt-added ketchup
- ½ teaspoon freshly ground black pepper
- ½ teaspoon dried oregano
- 4 (6-ounce) bone-in loin pork chops, fat trimmed
- 1 tablespoon extra-virgin olive oil
- 1 tablespoon unsalted butter

1. Preheat the oven to 400°F.
2. In a small bowl, mix together the honey, garlic, soy sauce, ketchup, pepper, and oregano.
3. Put the pork chops in a large bowl and pour the sauce over them. Mix until fully coated.
4. In a large oven-safe skillet, heat the oil over medium-high heat. Add the pork chops with sauce to the skillet. Sear for about 2 minutes per side, until they brown slightly. Remove from the heat.
5. Add ¾ teaspoon of butter to the top of each pork chop. Transfer to the oven and bake for 15 to 18 minutes, or until the pork reaches an internal temperature of 145°F. Let cool, then place a chop in each of 4 storage containers. Divide the pan sauce evenly over the portions.

PER SERVING

Calories: 271; Total fat: 14g; Carbohydrates: 13g; Fiber: 0g; Protein: 22g; Calcium: 56mg; Vitamin D: 31 IU; Potassium: 330mg; Magnesium: 22mg; Sodium: 211mg

Savory Pork Loin

Prep time: 5 minutes | Cook time: 25 to 30 minutes | Serves 6

- Nonstick cooking spray (optional)
- 1½ tablespoons fresh rosemary, chopped
- 1½ tablespoons fresh thyme, chopped
- 2 garlic cloves, minced
- ¼ teaspoon freshly ground black pepper
- 2 pounds boneless pork loin

1. Preheat the oven to 350°F. Line a roasting pan with aluminum foil or coat with nonstick cooking spray.
2. In a small bowl, mix together the rosemary, thyme, garlic, and pepper. Season the pork loin with this rub.
3. Transfer to the prepared roasting pan and bake for 25 to 30 minutes, or until the internal temperature of the pork loin has reached 145°F. Let rest for 5 minutes before slicing. Portion the pork into 6 storage containers.

PER SERVING

Calories: 216; Total fat: 11g; Carbohydrates: 0g; Fiber: 0g; Protein: 29g; Calcium: 15mg; Vitamin D: 24 IU; Potassium: 477mg; Magnesium: 25mg; Sodium: 72mg

Sheet Pan Steaks with Roasted Vegetables

Prep time: 15 minutes | Cook time: 35 minutes| Serves 4

- Nonstick cooking spray (optional)
- 6 medium carrots
- 2 medium zucchini, cut into 2-inch sections
- 2 medium sweet potatoes, peeled and cut into 1-inch cubes
- 1 tablespoon extra-virgin olive oil
- ¼ teaspoon garlic salt, divided
- ¼ teaspoon lemon pepper, divided
- 4 (4-ounce) sirloin steaks

1. Preheat the oven to 350°F. Line a 12-by-17-inch sheet pan with aluminum foil or coat with nonstick cooking spray.
2. Peel the carrots and cut into 2-inch sections where thin and 1-inch sections where thick. In a large bowl, toss together the carrots, zucchini, and sweet potatoes with the oil, ⅛ teaspoon of garlic salt, and ⅛ teaspoon of lemon pepper.
3. Spread the vegetables onto the prepared sheet pan and bake for 35 minutes, turning once.
4. Season both sides of the steaks with the remaining ⅛ teaspoon of garlic salt and ⅛ teaspoon of lemon pepper.
5. Add the steaks to the sheet pan. Turn the oven to broil and broil the steaks for 4 minutes per side, or until the internal temperature reaches 145°F for medium-rare.
6. Place a steak in each of 4 storage containers. Divide the vegetables into 4 separate storage containers.

PER SERVING

Calories: 311; Total fat: 12g; Carbohydrates: 24g; Fiber: 5g; Protein: 27g; Calcium: 78mg; Vitamin D: 6 IU; Potassium: 975mg; Magnesium: 59mg; Sodium: 277mg

Greek-Style Top Round Steaks

Prep time: 5 minutes | Cook time: 12 to 15 minutes| Serves 4

- 1½ teaspoons garlic powder
- 1½ teaspoons dried basil
- 1½ teaspoons dried oregano
- ⅛ teaspoon salt
- ⅛ teaspoon freshly ground black pepper
- 4 (4-ounce) top round steaks
- Nonstick cooking spray
- Zest of ½ large lemon
- 1 tablespoon fresh lemon juice
- 2 tablespoons crumbled feta cheese

1. In a small bowl, mix together the garlic powder, basil, oregano, salt, and pepper. Season the steaks on both sides.
2. Coat the grill grates with cooking spray. Preheat the grill to medium-high heat (350°F to 400°F).
3. Grill the steaks for 6 minutes on each side, or until the internal temperature reaches 135°F for

medium-rare. Add a few more minutes for medium.

4. Let the steaks cool, then store them in 4 storage containers. Store the lemon zest, lemon juice, and feta cheese separately.
5. To serve, after reheating the steaks, sprinkle with lemon zest and lemon juice and top with the cheese.

PER SERVING

Calories: 214; Total fat: 12g; Carbohydrates: 1g; Fiber: 0.5g; Protein: 27g; Calcium: 33mg; Vitamin D: 2 IU; Potassium: 382mg; Magnesium: 16mg; Sodium: 225mg

Beef Tenderloin Medallions with Horseradish Yogurt Sauce

Prep time: 10 minutes | Cook time: 5 minutes| Serves 4

FOR THE HORSERADISH SAUCE

- ¾ cup whole-milk Greek yogurt
- 2 tablespoons prepared horseradish
- 1 garlic clove, minced
- ¼ teaspoon freshly ground black pepper
- 2 teaspoons 1% milk

FOR THE MEDALLIONS

- 12 ounces beef tenderloin, flattened and cut into 4 pieces
- ½ teaspoon freshly ground black pepper
- ½ teaspoon garlic powder
- 1 tablespoon unsalted butter

TO MAKE THE HORSERADISH SAUCE

- In a small bowl, whisk together the yogurt, horseradish, garlic, pepper, and milk until well mixed. Divide the sauce among 4 condiment cups.

TO MAKE THE MEDALLIONS

1. 2.Season the tenderloin with the pepper and garlic powder.
2. In a large skillet, melt the butter over medium-high heat. Add the beef and sauté for about 2 minutes on each side, or until the outside is browned and the inside is very pink, medium-rare. Remove from the heat. When cool, portion the beef into 4 storage containers.
3. To serve, reheat the beef and top with horseradish sauce.

PER SERVING

Calories: 185; Total fat: 9g; Carbohydrates: 3g; Fiber: 0.5g; Protein: 23g; Calcium: 72mg; Vitamin D: 3 IU; Potassium: 332mg; Magnesium: 18mg; Sodium: 87mg

Chapter 8
Seafood

Seared Lime-Basil Scallops

Prep time: 10 minutes | Cook time: 10 minutes | Serves 4

- 1 pound sea scallops, cleaned
- Freshly ground black pepper
- 1 tablespoon olive oil
- Juice of 1 lime
- 1 tablespoon chopped fresh basil
- 2 tablespoons unsalted butter, at room temperature
- Lightly season the scallops with pepper.

1. Heat the oil in a large skillet over medium-high heat. Sear the scallops, cooking undisturbed for about 3 minutes on each side, until just cooked through and browned.
2. Add the lime juice, basil, and butter to the skillet and heat until the butter melts.
3. Turn the scallops to coat. Serve warm.
4. Store any leftover scallops in a covered container in the refrigerator for up to 1 day.

PER SERVING

Sodium: 224mg; Calories: 184; Total Fat: 11g; Saturated Fat: 4g; Total Carbohydrates: 4g; Net Carbs: 3g; Fiber: 0g; Protein: 19g; Potassium: 382mg; Cholesterol: 53mg

Shrimp and Avocado Salad

Prep time: 5 minutes | Cook time: 10 minutes | Serves 4

- 1 pound cooked salad shrimp
- 2 avocados, peeled, pitted, and cubed
- 2 tomatoes, diced
- 2 tablespoons diced red onion
- 8 cups fresh baby spinach
- FOR THE DRESSING
- 2 tablespoons olive oil
- ¼ cup red wine vinegar
- 1 teaspoon parsley, chopped
- 1 teaspoon Dijon mustard
- ½ teaspoon garlic powder

1. In a large bowl, toss together the shrimp, avocados, tomatoes, and onion.
2. In a 2-cup measuring cup, mix together ingredients for the dressing. Whisk until well combined.
3. Pour the dressing over the shrimp to lightly coat as desired.
4. Divide the spinach among four serving plates, and top with the shrimp salad. Serve additional dressing on the side.

PER SERVING

Calories: 347; Total Fat: 21g; Saturated Fat: 3g; Cholesterol: 138mg; Sodium: 309mg; Potassium: 925mg; Magnesium: 80mg; Total Carbohydrates: 13g; Fiber: 9g; Sugars: 1g; Protein: 29g

Shrimp and Mushroom Fried Rice

Prep time: 10 minutes | Cook time: 25 minutes | Serves 4

- 2 teaspoons olive oil
- 1 teaspoon sesame oil
- 1 pound peeled and deveined shrimp, chopped
- 1 leek, white and green parts, finely chopped
- 1 tablespoon minced garlic
- 2 teaspoons grated peeled fresh ginger
- 2 pounds sliced cremini or white mushrooms
- 3 cups cooked basmati rice
- 2 tablespoons reduced-sodium soy sauce
- 2 tablespoons chopped fresh cilantro
- 1 scallion, green and white parts, thinly sliced on the bias

1. Heat the oils in a large skillet over medium-high heat. Sauté the shrimp until just cooked through, about 4 minutes. Use a slotted spoon to remove the shrimp to a plate and set aside.
2. Add the leeks, garlic, and ginger to the skillet and sauté until softened, about 6 minutes.
3. Stir in the mushrooms and sauté until lightly caramelized, about 10 minutes.
4. Stir in the shrimp, rice, soy sauce, cilantro, and scallion until heated through, about 5 minutes. Serve warm.
5. Store any leftover fried rice in a sealed container in the refrigerator for up to 3 days.

PER SERVING

Sodium: 555mg; Calories: 241; Total Fat: 5g; Saturated Fat: 1g; Total Carbohydrates: 30g; Net Carbs: 26g; Fiber: 4g; Protein: 26g; Potassium: 287mg; Cholesterol: 80mg

Halibut with Greens and Ginger
Prep time: 5 minutes | Cook time: 10 minutes| Serves 4

- 4 (4-ounce) halibut fillets, rinsed and patted dry
- ½ teaspoon freshly ground black pepper
- 3 teaspoons olive oil, divided
- 4 cups baby spinach
- 1 tablespoon minced peeled ginger
- 2 garlic cloves, minced
- 1 tablespoon balsamic vinegar
- 1 tablespoon freshly squeezed lime juice

1. Sprinkle the fish with the black pepper. Using your fingertips, gently press in the seasoning so it adheres to the fish.
2. In a large nonstick skillet, heat 2 teaspoons of the olive oil over medium-high heat, swirling to coat the bottom. Cook the fish for 2 minutes, or until browned on the bottom. Turn over, and cook for 2 minutes more, or until the fish flakes easily when tested with a fork. Transfer to a plate and cover to keep warm.
3. In the same skillet, heat the remaining 1 teaspoon of olive oil, swirling the bottom to coat. Add the spinach, ginger, and garlic, and cook, stirring constantly, for 2 minutes, or until the spinach begins to wilt. Remove the skillet from the heat.
4. Add the balsamic vinegar and lime juice to the spinach and stir. Divide the spinach among four plates and top each serving with a halibut fillet. Serve immediately.

PER SERVING

Calories: 162; Total Fat: 6g; Saturated Fat: 1g; Cholesterol: 35mg; Sodium: 84mg; Potassium: 672mg; Magnesium: 120mg; Total Carbohydrates: 3g; Fiber: 1g; Sugars: 0g; Protein: 24g

Angel Hair Pasta with Fresh Tomatoes, Fennel, and Shrimp
Prep time: 15 minutes | Cook time: 25 minutes | Serves 4

- 1 tablespoon olive oil
- ½ pound shrimp, peeled and deveined
- ½ sweet onion, chopped
- ¼ fennel bulb, chopped
- 1 tablespoon minced garlic
- 6 large tomatoes, chopped
- ¼ cup chopped fresh basil
- ¼ cup no-salt-added vegetable broth
- ⅛ teaspoon red pepper flakes
- 8 ounces angel hair pasta

1. In a large skillet, heat the olive oil over medium-high heat. Sauté the shrimp until cooked through, about 5 minutes. Use a slotted spoon to remove the shrimp to a plate and set aside.
2. Add the onion, fennel, and garlic and sauté until softened, about 8 minutes.
3. Stir in the tomatoes, basil, broth, and pepper flakes. Bring the sauce to a boil. Continue cooking, stirring frequently, until slightly thickened, about 5 minutes.
4. Reduce the heat to low and let the sauce simmer.
5. Meanwhile, fill a large saucepan three-quarters full with water and bring to a boil over high heat.
6. Cook the pasta according to package instructions.
7. Drain the pasta and add it to the skillet along with the shrimp, tossing to combine.
8. Serve immediately. Store any leftover pasta and shrimp in a covered container in the refrigerator for up to 3 days.

PER SERVING

Sodium: 149mg; Calories: 352; Total Fat: 7g; Saturated Fat: 1g; Total Carbohydrates: 54g; Net Carbs: 48g; Fiber: 6g; Protein: 21g; Potassium: 641mg; Cholesterol: 88mg

Baked Flounder Packets with Summer Squash
Prep time: 5 minutes | Cook time: 10 minutes| Serves 4

- 4 (6-ounce) flounder fillets, or other white fish
- Freshly ground black pepper
- 2 medium zucchini, sliced into thin rounds
- 2 medium yellow summer squash, sliced into thin rounds
- 1 medium red onion, sliced
- 2 tablespoons olive oil
- 2 tablespoons freshly squeezed lemon juice
- 1 lemon, thinly sliced
- 2 teaspoons dried basil

1. Preheat the oven to 450°F. Prepare four 12-by-18-inch sheets of aluminum foil. Spray the center of each sheet of foil with nonstick cooking spray.
2. Season the fish with the black pepper. Place one fish fillet on each piece of foil.
3. Arrange the zucchini, squash, and onion slices around each fillet. Drizzle ½ tablespoon of olive oil and ½ tablespoon of lemon juice onto the vegetables and fish.
4. Arrange a few lemon slices on top of each fillet and top each piece with ½ teaspoon of dried basil.
5. Bring up the sides of the foil and fold the tops over twice. Seal the ends, leaving room for air to circulate inside the packet. Set the packets on a rimmed baking sheet, and bake for 8 minutes. Carefully open one packet to check the fish and test with a fork to see if it flakes easily.
6. Serve immediately, using caution when opening the packets as the steam will be very hot.

PER SERVING

Calories: 233; Total Fat: 9g; Saturated Fat: 1g; Cholesterol: 98mg; Sodium: 130mg; Potassium: 273mg; Magnesium: 24mg; Total Carbohydrates: 10g; Fiber: 4g; Sugars: 3g; Protein: 32g

Salmon and Asparagus in Foil

Prep time: 5 minutes | Cook time: 20 minutes| Serves 4

- 4 (5-ounce) salmon fillets
- 1 pound fresh asparagus, ends trimmed, divided
- 2 teaspoons dried dill, divided
- Freshly squeezed lemon juice
- Freshly ground black pepper (optional)
- Lemon wedges for serving

1. Preheat the oven to 450°F.
2. Prepare four 12-by-18-inch sheets of aluminum foil. Spray the center of each sheet of foil with nonstick cooking spray.
3. Place one salmon fillet in the center of each sheet, top with a quarter of the asparagus, ½ teaspoon of dill, and a squeeze of lemon juice. Sprinkle with black pepper (if using).
4. Bring up the sides of the foil and fold the top over twice. Seal the ends, leaving room for air to circulate inside the packet. Repeat with the remaining fillets.
5. Place the packets on a baking sheet and bake for 15 to 18 minutes, or until the salmon is opaque.
6. Use caution when opening the packets, as the steam is very hot. Serve with lemon wedges on the side.

PER SERVING

Calories: 202; Total Fat: 7g; Saturated Fat: 1g; Cholesterol: 63mg; Sodium: 110mg; Potassium: 326mg; Magnesium: 24mg; Total Carbohydrates: 5g; Fiber: 3g; Sugars: 0g; Protein: 31g

Salmon Shrimp Burgers

Prep time: 10 minutes, plus 1 hour to chill | Cook time: 20 minutes | Serves 4

- 2 (5.3-ounce) cans water-packed salmon
- ½ cup chopped cooked shrimp
- ½ cup bread crumbs
- 1 large egg white
- ¼ red bell pepper, finely chopped
- 1 scallion, white and green parts, finely chopped
- 1 tablespoon chopped fresh parsley
- Juice of ½ lime
- Olive oil nonstick cooking spray
- 4 hamburger buns, whole-grain
- 4 tablespoons mayonnaise or tartar sauce

1. In a large bowl, combine the salmon, shrimp, bread crumbs, egg white, bell pepper, scallion, parsley, and lime juice until well mixed. Add more bread crumbs if the mixture is still too wet.
2. Shape the mixture into 4 patties, cover, and place them in the refrigerator for 1 hour.
3. Preheat the oven to 400°F. Line a baking sheet with parchment paper.
4. Place the patties on the lined baking sheet and lightly coat with olive oil spray.
5. Bake the patties until heated through, turning once, about 18 minutes.
6. Serve the burgers on a bun with 1 tablespoon of mayonnaise and your favorite low-sodium toppings.
7. Store any cooled leftover burgers in a sealed container in the refrigerator for up to 2 days.

PER SERVING

Sodium: 625mg; Calories: 351; Total Fat: 17g; Saturated Fat: 2g; Total Carbohydrates: 26g; Net Carbs: 24g; Fiber: 2g; Protein: 28g; Potassium: 309mg; Cholesterol: 80mg

Salmon Veggie Kebabs

Prep time: 15 minutes, plus 30 minutes to marinate | Cook time: 15 minutes | Serves 4

- ¼ cup olive oil
- 3 tablespoons apple cider vinegar
- ½ teaspoon chopped fresh thyme
- Freshly ground black pepper
- 16 white mushrooms
- 2 red bell peppers, cut into 8 pieces each
- 2 small red onions, cut into quarters
- ½ small eggplant, cut into 1-inch cubes
- 1 pound boneless, skinless salmon, cut into 2-inch chunks

1. In a medium bowl, stir the olive oil, vinegar, thyme, and black pepper. Pour half of the marinade into a plastic bag and set aside.
2. Add the mushrooms, bell peppers, onions, and eggplant to the bowl, tossing to coat with the marinade. Set aside at room temperature.
3. Add the salmon to the bag with the remaining marinade, squeeze the air out of the bag, and seal it. Place the fish in the refrigerator for 30 minutes.
4. Preheat the oven to broil and place an oven rack about 6 inches from the heat.
5. Thread the salmon and vegetables onto 8 metal or soaked wooden skewers, alternating ingredients and leaving ½ inch between them.
6. Place the skewers on a baking sheet or broiler pan and broil, turning once, until the fish is cooked through and the vegetables are tender, 12 to 15 minutes.
7. Serve two skewers to each person.
8. Store any leftover kebabs in a covered container in the refrigerator for up to 3 days.

PER SERVING

Sodium: 74mg; Calories: 374; Total Fat: 23g; Saturated Fat: 4g; Total Carbohydrates: 14g; Net Carbs: 9g; Fiber: 5g; Protein: 26g; Potassium: 533mg; Cholesterol: 65mg

Pecan-Crusted Catfish

Prep time: 5 minutes | Cook time: 20 minutes| Serves 4

- 4 catfish fillets (approximately 1 pound)
- ½ teaspoon freshly ground black pepper
- ½ teaspoon garlic powder
- 2 teaspoons dried rosemary
- 2 egg whites, beaten
- ¾ cup pecans, chopped
- Lemon wedges for serving

1. Preheat the oven to 400°F.
2. Line a baking sheet with foil and coat the foil with nonstick cooking spray.
3. Sprinkle the catfish fillets with the black pepper, garlic, and rosemary, then dip each fillet into the egg whites to coat.
4. Place the chopped pecans on a plate and press the egg-coated fillets firmly into the pecans, turning to coat both sides. Place the fillets on the baking sheet.
5. Bake for 20 minutes or until the fish flakes easily with a fork.
6. Serve with lemon wedges and enjoy.

PER SERVING

Calories: 263; Total Fat: 20g; Saturated Fat: 2g; Cholesterol: 47mg; Sodium: 228mg; Potassium: 104mg; Magnesium: 28mg; Total Carbohydrates: 4g; Fiber: 3g; Sugars: 1g; Protein: 18g

Crispy Fish Sandwiches with Creamy Coleslaw

Prep Time: 20 minutes|Cook Time: 10 minutes| Serves 8

FOR THE COLESLAW:

- ¼ cup plain nonfat Greek yogurt
- 2 tablespoons mayonnaise
- 1 tablespoon dried minced onion
- 1 tablespoon granulated sugar
- 1 tablespoon white wine vinegar
- ½ tablespoon dry mustard powder
- ½ tablespoon celery seed
- 4 ounces green cabbage, diced
- 4 ounces carrots, peeled and diced

FOR THE SANDWICHES:

- ⅓ cup all-purpose flour
- 1 large egg, beaten
- 2 tablespoons milk
- 2₃ cup panko bread crumbs
- ½ teaspoon ground black pepper
- 3 tablespoons canola oil
- 2 pounds whitefish (cod, haddock, tilapia) fillets, cut into 4-ounce pieces
- 8 whole-wheat sandwich buns, toasted

TO MAKE THE COLESLAW:

In a bowl, whisk together the Greek yogurt, mayonnaise, onion, sugar, white wine vinegar, dry mustard, celery

seed, salt, and black pepper. Fold in the green cabbage and carrots until combined. Refrigerate until use.

TO MAKE THE SANDWICHES:

1. Set up a breading station: one with the flour, one with the mixed beaten egg and milk, and one with the bread crumbs. Evenly distribute the salt and black pepper into each bowl and whisk each to thoroughly combine.
2. Heat the canola oil in a large skillet over medium heat.
3. Dip each fish fillet in the flour, egg mixture, then bread crumbs and place in the hot oil. Repeat with the remaining fish fillets, working in batches if needed. Cook the fish until all sides are crispy and browned and the fish flakes easily with a fork. Place the fish fillets on the whole-wheat buns and top with the coleslaw.
4. You can prep the crispy fish in advance. For reheating, it is recommended to broil fish in the oven set on low for 2 to 3 minutes per side. The coleslaw should be stored in an airtight container in the refrigerator for up to 3 days.

PER SERVING

Calories: 396; Total Fat: 12g; Saturated Fat: 1g; Cholesterol: 28mg; Sodium: 504mg; Potassium: 109mg; Total Carbohydrate: 45g; Fiber: 6g; Sugars: 10g; Protein: 33g

Louisiana-Style Seafood Stew

Prep time: 20 minutes | Cook time: 35 minutes | Serves 4

- 1 tablespoon olive oil
- 1 sweet onion, chopped
- 2 red bell peppers, diced
- 3 celery stalks, sliced
- 1 large carrot, shredded
- 1 tablespoon minced garlic
- 2 cups low-sodium chicken broth
- 2 cups diced fresh tomatoes
- 1 teaspoon smoked paprika
- 1 teaspoon dried oregano
- ¼ teaspoon red pepper flakes
- ¼ teaspoon freshly ground black pepper
- 1 pound tilapia, cut into 2-inch chunks
- ¼ cup chopped fresh parsley
- Juice of 1 lemon

1. Heat the oil in a large saucepan over medium-high heat. Sauté the onion, bell pepper, celery, carrot, and garlic until softened, about 6 minutes.
2. Stir in the broth, tomatoes, paprika, oregano, pepper flakes, and black pepper and bring to a boil. Reduce the heat to low and simmer until the vegetables are tender, about 20 minutes.
3. Add the fish and simmer another 10 minutes.
4. Stir in the parsley and lemon juice and serve.
5. Store any leftover stew in a covered container in the refrigerator for up to 3 days.

PER SERVING

Sodium: 247mg; Calories: 201; Total Fat: 12g; Saturated Fat: 1g; Total Carbohydrates: 14g; Net Carbs: 10g; Fiber: 4g; Protein: 26g; Potassium: 431mg; Cholesterol: 68mg

Oven-Roasted Halibut and Root Vegetables

Prep time: 15 minutes | Cook time: 25 minutes | Serves 4

- 4 (3-ounce) boneless, skinless halibut fillets
- 6 teaspoons olive oil, divided
- 3 beets, peeled and quartered
- 2 parsnips, cut into 2-inch chunks
- 2 carrots, cut into 2-inch chunks
- 1 sweet potato, cut into eighths
- 1 red onion, cut into eighths
- 2 teaspoons chopped fresh rosemary
- Freshly ground black pepper

1. Preheat the oven to 400°F. Line a baking sheet with parchment paper.
2. Place the halibut on one-quarter of the sheet. Drizzle the fish with 2 teaspoons of olive oil.
3. Arrange the vegetables on the remaining three-quarters of the baking sheet. Drizzle the vegetables with the remaining 4 teaspoons of oil and sprinkle everything with the rosemary.
4. Season the fish and vegetables with pepper.
5. Roast until the fish is cooked through and the vegetables are lightly caramelized, turning the vegetables once, 22 to 25 minutes. Serve.
6. Store any leftover halibut and vegetables in a covered container in the refrigerator for up to 3 days.

PER SERVING

Sodium: 96mg; Calories: 218; Total Fat: 8g; Saturated Fat: 1g; Total Carbohydrates: 31g; Net Carbs: 23g; Fiber: 8g; Protein: 21g; Potassium: 657mg; Cholesterol: 21mg

Crispy Cashew Fish Sticks

Prep time: 15 minutes | Cook time: 20 minutes | Serves 4

- ½ cup ground unsalted roasted cashews
- ¼ cup low-sodium bread crumbs
- 1 teaspoon chopped fresh thyme
- 1 egg white
- 2 tablespoons water
- 4 (3-ounce) skinless haddock fillets
- Freshly ground black pepper
- Olive oil nonstick cooking spray
- 1 lemon, quartered, for serving

1. Preheat the oven to 400°F. Line a baking sheet with parchment paper and set aside.
2. In a small bowl, stir the cashews, bread crumbs, and thyme.
3. In a small bowl, whisk the egg white with the water.
4. Lightly season a fish fillet with pepper and dredge it in the egg white mixture.
5. Shake off the excess liquid and dredge the fish in the bread crumb mixture until coated. Lay it on the lined baking sheet. Repeat with the remaining fillets.
6. Coat them lightly with the olive oil spray. Bake until the fish is just cooked through and the breading is golden, about 20 minutes. Serve with

lemon wedges.
7. These are best enjoyed immediately; however, you can store any leftover fish sticks in a covered container in the refrigerator for up to 1 day.

PER SERVING

Sodium: 82mg; Calories: 140; Total Fat: 5g; Saturated Fat: 1g; Total Carbohydrates: 3g; Net Carbs: 2g; Fiber: 1g; Protein: 18g; Potassium: 60mg; Cholesterol: 41mg

Roasted Cajun Blackened Salmon with Asparagus

Prep time: 15 minutes | Cook time: 15 minutes| Serves 4

- 2 teaspoons dried parsley
- 1 teaspoon ground cumin
- 1 teaspoon garlic powder
- 1 teaspoon onion powder
- 1 teaspoon sweet paprika
- 1 teaspoon dark brown sugar
- ¼ teaspoon chili powder
- ¼ teaspoon salt, plus more to taste
- ¼ teaspoon freshly ground black pepper, plus more to taste
- 4 skinless salmon fillets (6 ounces each); see Tip
- 1 pound asparagus, tough ends trimmed
- 1 tablespoon extra-virgin olive oil
- 1 lemon, quartered

1. Preheat the oven to 425°F. Line two large baking sheets with foil and lightly coat with cooking spray.
2. In a shallow bowl, combine the parsley, cumin, garlic powder, onion powder, paprika, brown sugar, chili powder, and ¼ teaspoon each salt and black pepper and mix the blackened seasoning thoroughly.
3. Place the salmon on a plate and coat with cooking spray. Season with 1 teaspoon of the blackened seasoning, flip, coat with more cooking spray and season with another 1 teaspoon of the seasoning. Place on one of the prepared baking sheets.
4. Place the asparagus in a small bowl and drizzle with the olive oil and sprinkle with salt and pepper, if desired. Place on the second prepared baking sheet.
5. Transfer the salmon and asparagus to the oven and roast until the asparagus is tender and slightly browned and the salmon flakes easily with a fork, is blackened and crispy on the outside, and an instant-read thermometer reads 145°F, 12 to 15 minutes, depending on the thickness of the salmon and the asparagus.
6. Portion onto 4 plates and squeeze fresh lemon juice over each.

PER SERVING

Calories: 280; Total fat: 11 g; Saturated fat: 2 g; Cholesterol: 75 mg; Sodium: 227 mg; Potassium: 369 mg; Total carbohydrates: 10 g; Fiber: 4 g; Sugars: 3 g; Protein: 38 g

Tuna Stuffed Avocados

Prep Time: 15 minutes|Serves: 1

- ½ tablespoon red onion, chopped finely
- 4 tablespoons cooked tuna
- ½ tablespoon fresh cilantro, minced
- ½ large avocado, halved and pitted
- 1 tablespoon fresh lime juice
- Pinch of Cayenne pepper
- Fresh ground black pepper to taste

1. Draw out the flesh from the center of the avocado and transfer into a bowl.
2. Add chopped onion and lemon juice and mash until well combined.
3. Add tuna, cayenne pepper and black pepper and stir to combine everything well.
4. Divide the tuna mixture in both avocado halves evenly.
5. Serve immediately and enjoy!

PER SERVING

Calories: 1543 ;Fat: 77.2g ; Sat Fat: 15.9g ;Carbohydrates: 13g ;Fiber: 7.1g ;Sugar: 1.5g ;Protein: 191.1g

Orange-Thyme Salmon and Summer Squash in a Packet

Prep time: 15 minutes | Cook time: 25 minutes| Serves 4

- Juice of 1 lemon
- 1 tablespoon extra-virgin olive oil
- 2 teaspoons dried thyme
- ¼ teaspoon salt
- ¼ teaspoon freshly ground black pepper
- 2 cups sliced yellow summer squash (about 2 medium)
- 2 cups sliced zucchini (about 2 medium)
- 1 small red onion, thinly sliced
- 2 blood oranges, peeled and thinly sliced
- 4 skinless salmon fillets (6 ounces each)
- 4 sprigs fresh thyme

1. Preheat the oven to 400°F. Tear off 4 pieces of foil or parchment that are 2 inches longer than the salmon fillets.
2. In a medium bowl, combine the lemon juice, olive oil, dried thyme, salt, and pepper.
3. Place the foil/parchment pieces on your work surface and on one side of each piece of foil/parchment, layer one-quarter of the yellow squash, zucchini, red onion, and blood orange. Top each stack of vegetables with a salmon fillet and drizzle each stack with the lemon juice mixture. Place a thyme sprig on top of each piece of fish.
4. Fold the other half of the foil/parchment over the ingredients. To seal the packets, begin at one corner and tightly fold the edges over about ½ inch all around, overlapping the folds. The foil/parchment should not come undone.
5. Place the packets on a baking sheet. Transfer to the oven and bake until the salmon turns opaque throughout, about 20 minutes.

6. Serve the pouches on a plate or remove the contents to a plate, being very careful of the escaping steam when opening as it will be very hot. Spoon any liquid remaining in the foil/parchment over the salmon and vegetables.

PER SERVING

Calories: 309; Total fat: 11 g; Saturated fat: 2 g; Cholesterol: 75 mg; Sodium: 279 mg; Potassium: 615 mg; Total carbohydrates: 18 g; Fiber: 6 g; Sugars: 10 g; Protein: 37 g

Coriander-and-Lemon-Crusted Salmon with Asparagus Salad and Poached Egg

Prep Time: 45 minutes|Cook Time: 20 minutes|Serves: 4

- 1 tbsp. coriander seeds
- 1 tsp. lemon zest
- ¾ tsp. fine sea salt, divided
- ½ tsp. crushed red pepper
- 1 lb. wild salmon, skin-on, cut into 4 portions
- 1 lb. asparagus, trimmed
- 2 tbsp. extra-virgin olive oil
- 1 tbsp. lemon juice
- 1 tbsp. chopped fresh mint
- 1 tbsp. chopped fresh tarragon
- ¼ tsp. ground pepper, plus more for garnish
- 8 cups water
- 1 tbsp. white vinegar
- 4 large eggs

1. Position a rack in the upper third of the oven and preheat the broiler to high. Coat a rimmed baking sheet with cooking spray.
2. Toast the coriander in a small skillet over medium heat, shaking the pan frequently until fragrant (about 3 minutes).
3. Pulse the coriander, lemon zest, ½ tsp. of salt, and the crushed red pepper in a spice grinder until finely ground.
4. Coat the salmon flesh with the spice mixture (about 1½ tsp. per portion) and place the salmon on the prepared baking sheet.
5. Cut off the asparagus tips and very thinly slice the stalks on the diagonal. Toss the tips and slices with oil, lemon juice, mint, tarragon, pepper, and the remaining salt. Let the mixture stand while you cook the salmon and eggs.
6. Meanwhile, broil the salmon until just cooked through (3 to 6 minutes), depending on thickness. Tent the salmon with foil to keep it warm.
7. Reduce the boiling water to barely a simmer. Gently stir in a circle, so the water is swirling around the pot. Crack the eggs, one at a time, into the water. Cook until the whites are set, but the yolks are still runny (3 to 4 minutes).

PER SERVING

Calories 288 ;Protein 30.5g ; Carbohydrates 4.2g ;Dietary fiber 1.9g ;Sugars 1g ;Fat 16.3g ;Sodium 360.1mg

One-Pot Shrimp Pasta Primavera
Prep time: 15 minutes | Cook time: 15 minutes| Serves 4

- 8 ounces whole-grain angel hair pasta
- 2 tablespoons extra-virgin olive oil
- 1 cup broccoli florets
- 1 large red bell pepper, chopped
- 1 cup sliced yellow squash (about 1 medium)
- 1 cup green peas (if frozen, slightly thawed)
- 8 ounces frozen peeled and deveined cooked shrimp
- 2 teaspoons dried basil
- 2 teaspoons dried oregano
- ¼ teaspoon red pepper flakes
- Salt and freshly ground black pepper (optional)
- 1 lemon, halved
- 4 tablespoons grated Parmesan cheese

1. Cook the pasta according to the package directions. Drain and cover to keep warm.
2. In a large nonstick skillet, heat the olive oil over medium heat. Add the garlic and sauté for 1 minute. Add the broccoli, bell pepper, and squash and sauté until crisp-tender, 3 to 4 minutes.
3. Add the peas and shrimp and sauté until just heated through. Season with the basil, oregano, pepper flakes, and salt and black pepper, if desired. Squeeze the lemon over the shrimp and vegetables. Continue to cook for 2 to 3 minutes, until the liquid has been reduced by half. Remove from the heat.
4. Toss the shrimp and vegetables with the pasta. Portion onto 4 plates and top each serving with 1 tablespoon Parmesan.

PER SERVING

Calories: 405; Total fat: 11 g; Saturated fat: 2 g; Cholesterol: 115 mg; Sodium: 243 mg; Potassium: 388 mg; Total carbohydrates: 54 g; Fiber: 10 g; Sugars: 5 g; Protein: 24 g

Haddock Tacos with Cabbage Slaw
Prep time: 15 minutes | Cook time: 5 minutes| Serves 2

- 1 teaspoon ground cumin
- ½ teaspoon chili powder
- ⅛ teaspoon salt
- ⅛ teaspoon freshly ground black pepper
- 8 ounces skinless haddock fillets, cut into 1-inch chunks
- 2 cups angel hair cabbage
- ½ avocado, chopped
- 2 tablespoons fresh lime juice
- 3 teaspoons extra-virgin olive oil
- 2 (6-inch) whole-wheat tortillas, warmed
- Fresh cilantro

1. In a small bowl, combine the cumin, chili powder, salt, and pepper. Add the haddock and toss to coat.
2. In a separate small bowl, mix together the cabbage, avocado, lime juice, and 1 teaspoon of the olive oil.
3. In a medium skillet, heat the remaining 2 teaspoons olive oil over medium-high heat. Add the haddock and cook, turning, until the fish is just opaque and flakes easily with a fork, 4 to 5 minutes.
4. Divide the fish between the warmed tortillas and top with the cabbage avocado mixture. Serve garnished with fresh cilantro.

PER SERVING

Calories: 368; Total fat: 16 g; Saturated fat: 2 g; Cholesterol: 84 mg; Sodium: 408 mg; Potassium: 261 mg; Total carbohydrates: 22 g; Fiber: 7 g; Sugars: 2 g; Protein: 32 g

Sheet Pan Flounder with White Beans, Tomatoes, and Basil
Prep time: 5 minutes | Cook time: 30 minutes| Serves 4

- 2 (15-ounce) cans cannellini beans or other white bean, rinsed and drained
- 1 medium red onion, sliced
- 1 large red bell pepper, sliced
- 1 pint cherry tomatoes, halved (a pint of mixed colors provides a striking dish)
- 4 cloves garlic, minced
- 2 teaspoons dried marjoram
- 2 tablespoons extra-virgin olive oil
- Salt and freshly ground black pepper
- ¼ cup white wine
- 4 flounder fillets (4 ounces each)
- 1 lemon, halved
- 4 tablespoons coarsely chopped fresh basil

1. Preheat the oven to 400°F. Line a rimmed baking sheet with foil.
2. Spread the beans, onion, and bell pepper over the baking sheet and nestle the cherry tomatoes cut side up among them. Sprinkle with half of the minced garlic and all the marjoram. Drizzle with 1 tablespoon of the olive oil and season with a dash each of salt and black pepper. Transfer to the oven and roast for 10 minutes.
3. Remove the baking sheet from the oven and drizzle with the white wine. Move the vegetables to the sides and place the flounder on the baking sheet. Sprinkle with the remaining garlic and 1 tablespoon olive oil. Season lightly with salt and pepper, if desired, and squeeze the lemon over the top. Roast until the fish is cooked through, opaque, and flakes easily with a fork, about 15 minutes.
4. Place a fillet on each of 4 serving plates. Portion the vegetables onto the plates and sprinkle each serving with 1 tablespoon fresh basil.

PER SERVING

Calories: 368; Total fat: 8 g; Saturated fat: 1 g; Cholesterol: 65 mg; Sodium: 89 mg; Potassium: 316 mg; Total carbohydrates: 40 g; Fiber: 10 g; Sugars: 3 g; Protein: 32 g

Lemon-Ginger Cod with Roasted Cauliflower and Carrots

Prep time: 15 minutes | **Cook time:** 25 minutes | **Serves 4**

- 6 medium carrots, sliced
- 3 cups or about 1 medium head cauliflower, trimmed into small florets
- 3 tablespoons extra-virgin olive oil
- Salt and freshly ground pepper
- 2 cups instant brown rice
- 1 tablespoon grated fresh ginger
- 2 cloves garlic, grated
- 2 lemons, sliced
- 4 cod fillets (4 ounces each)
- ½ cup dry white wine
- ¼ cup chopped fresh chives, plus more for garnish

1. Preheat the oven to 400°F. Coat a rimmed baking sheet with cooking spray.
2. Arrange the vegetables on the baking sheet and drizzle with 1 tablespoon of the olive oil and, if desired, lightly season with salt and pepper. Bake until tender and golden brown, about 25 minutes.
3. Meanwhile cook the rice according to the package directions.
4. In a small bowl, combine 1 tablespoon of the olive oil, the ginger, garlic, lemon slices, and salt and pepper, if desired. Set aside.
5. In a large skillet, heat the remaining 1 tablespoon olive oil over medium-high heat. When the oil is shimmering, add the fish and sear for 5 minutes, then move to the side leaving extra room in the pan. Add the ginger/garlic/lemon slice mixture to the pan and sauté until the lemon slices have turned golden brown, 3 to 4 minutes.
6. Add the white wine and chives and cook until a sauce begins to form, about 3 minutes. Scoop some of the sauce over the fish.
7. Add the cooked rice to the pan and simmer until the sauce is fully absorbed, 3 to 5 minutes.
8. Place a cod fillet on each of 4 serving plates. Portion the rice and sauce mixture next to the fish. Remove the vegetables from the oven and portion onto each plate. Garnish with additional chives, if desired.

PER SERVING

Calories: 450; Total fat: 13 g; Saturated fat: 2 g; Cholesterol: 62 mg; Sodium: 187 mg; Potassium: 959 mg; Total carbohydrates: 53 g; Fiber: 9 g; Sugars: 6 g; Protein: 32 g

Lemon-Garlic Tilapia with Roasted Vegetables and Arugula

Prep time: 5 minutes | **Cook time:** 15 minutes | **Serves 4**

- 3 cups broccoli florets
- 1 cup sliced yellow squash (about 1 medium)
- 2 tablespoons + 2 teaspoons extra-virgin olive oil
- Salt and freshly ground black pepper
- 2 tablespoons fresh lemon juice
- 2 tablespoons minced shallot
- 2 tablespoons chopped fresh parsley
- 1 tablespoon minced garlic
- 4 tilapia fillets (4 ounces each)
- 5 ounces baby arugula
- 2 tablespoons grated Parmesan cheese

1. Preheat the oven to 400°F. Coat a rimmed baking sheet with cooking spray.
2. Place the broccoli and squash on the baking sheet, drizzle with 1 tablespoon of the olive oil and season with salt and pepper, if desired. Push the vegetables to the sides of the pan.
3. In a small bowl, mix together 1 tablespoon of the olive oil, the lemon juice, shallot, parsley, garlic, ¼ teaspoon pepper, and ⅛ teaspoon salt. Place the tilapia fillets on the baking sheet in between the vegetables and season with the lemon/shallot/parsley mixture, gently pressing into the fish, turning, and seasoning the other side.
4. Transfer the baking sheet to the oven and bake until the fish flakes easily with a fork, 12 to 15 minutes.
5. Meanwhile, in a medium bowl, toss together the arugula, remaining 2 teaspoons olive oil, the Parmesan, and salt and pepper, if desired. Toss to combine.
6. Place a tilapia fillet on each of 4 plates. Portion the roasted vegetables and the arugula salad onto the plates.

PER SERVING

Calories: 244; Total fat: 13 g; Saturated fat: 2 g; Cholesterol: 57 mg; Sodium: 208 mg; Potassium: 828 mg; Total carbohydrates: 9 g; Fiber: 3 g; Sugars: 3 g; Protein: 29 g

Crispy Coconut Shrimp

Prep Time: 10 minutes| Cook time: 15 minutes|Serves: 4

- ¼ cup unsweetened coconut
- ¼ cup Panko bread crumbs
- ½ teaspoon Kosher salt
- ½ cup coconut milk
- 12 large shrimp, peeled and deveined

1. Switch on the oven and set it to 375° F to preheat.
2. Grease a baking pan with cooking spray and set it aside. Grind Panko with salt and coconut in a food processor.
3. Add this mixture to a bowl and pour coconut milk into another bowl.
4. First, dip each shrimp in coconut milk, then coat it with Panko mixture.
5. Place the coated shrimp in the baking pan. Cover them with a light layer of cooking spray.
6. Bake for 15 minutes.
7. Serve warm.

PER SERVING

Calories 249 ;Fat 11.9 g ; Sodium 77 mg;Carbs 1.8 g ;Fiber 1.2 g ;Sugar 0.3 g ;Protein 35 g

Hazelnut-Parsley Roast Tilapia

Prep Time: 30 minutes|Cook Time: 20 minutes|Serves: 4

- 2 tbsp. olive oil, divided
- 4 (5 oz.) tilapia fillets (fresh or frozen, thawed)
- ⅓ cup finely chopped hazelnuts
- ¼ cup finely chopped fresh parsley
- 1 small shallot, minced
- 2 tsp. lemon zest
- ⅛ tsp. salt plus ¼ tsp., divided
- ¼ tsp. ground pepper, divided
- 1½ tbsp. lemon juice

1. Preheat the oven to 450˚F. Line a large rimmed baking sheet with foil and brush with 1 tbsp. of oil.
2. Bring the fish to room temperature by leaving it on the counter for 15 minutes.
3. Meanwhile, stir together the hazelnuts, parsley, shallot, lemon zest, 1 tsp. of oil, $1/_8$ tsp. salt, and $1/_8$ tsp. pepper in a small bowl.
4. Pat both sides of the fish dry with a paper towel. Place the fish on the prepared baking sheet. Brush both sides of the fish with lemon juice and the remaining 2 tsp. of oil. Season both sides of the fish evenly with the remaining ¼ tsp. salt and $1/_8$ tsp. pepper.
5. Divide the hazelnut mixture evenly among the tops of the fillets and pat gently to adhere.
6. Roast the fish until it is opaque, firm, and just beginning to flake (7 to 10 minutes).

PER SERVING

Calories 262 ;Protein 30.2g ; Carbohydrates 3.3g ; Dietary fiber 1.2g ;Sugars 0.8g ;Fat 15g ;Sodium 294.7mg.

Easy Scallop Quinoa Paella

Prep time: 10 minutes | Cook time: 35 minutes| Serves 4

- 1 tablespoon extra-virgin olive oil
- 1 cup chopped onion
- 3 cloves garlic, minced
- 1 medium red bell pepper, chopped
- 1 cup chopped baby bella mushrooms (5 to 6 mushrooms)
- 1 (14.5-ounce) can no-salt-added diced tomatoes, undrained
- 1 (14.5-ounce) can water-packed artichoke hearts, drained and rinsed
- 1 cup quinoa, rinsed
- 1 teaspoon smoked paprika
- 1 teaspoon ground turmeric
- Salt and freshly ground black pepper (optional)
- 2 cups low-sodium vegetable broth
- 1 cup frozen green peas, thawed
- 1 pound scallops
- 1 lemon, halved
- Fresh parsley

1. In a large skillet, heat the olive oil over medium heat. Add the onions and garlic and cook until translucent, 3 to 4 minutes. Add the bell pepper and mushrooms and sauté until they start to soften and the mushrooms begin to brown, an additional 3 to 4 minutes.
2. Add the tomatoes and their juices, the artichoke hearts, quinoa, smoked paprika, turmeric, and salt and black pepper, if desired, mixing well to combine. Add the broth and stir again to incorporate. Bring the mixture to a boil, then cover, reduce the heat, and simmer until most of the liquid has been absorbed, about 15 minutes.
3. Add the peas and scallops, cover, and continue cooking until the scallops are cooked through, about 5 minutes.
4. Remove the lid and squeeze the lemon over the top. Serve garnished with fresh parsley.

PER SERVING

Calories: 431; Total fat: 8 g; Saturated fat: <1 g; Cholesterol: 37 mg; Sodium: 339 mg; Potassium: 913 mg; Total carbohydrates: 62 g; Fiber: 15 g; Sugars: 10 g; Protein: 31 g

Curried Cod

Prep Time: 10 minutes| Cook time: 25 minutes|Serves: 2

- ½ tablespoon oil
- 1 tablespoon curry powder
- 2 cloves garlic, crushed
- ½ can (from 14.1 ounces can) chickpeas
- Zest of ½ lemon, grated
- ½ onion, chopped
- 1 inch (2.5 cm) ginger, peeled, finely grated
- 1 can (14.1 ounces) chopped tomatoes
- 2 cod fillets (about 5 ounces)
- Chopped cilantro to garnish
- Lemon wedges to serve
- Salt to taste

1. Place a pan (that has a fitting lid) over medium flame. Pour oil into the pan and let it heat.
2. Once the oil is heated, stir in onions and cook until translucent.
3. Add ginger, garlic and curry powder and cook for a couple of minutes until you get a nice aroma.
4. Add tomatoes and mix well. Cook for a couple of minutes, stirring often.
5. Stir in chickpeas and salt. Cook until slightly thick. Place Cod in the pan and cover the pan with a fitting lid.
6. Once the fish is cooked, turn off the heat.
7. Serve and enjoy.

PER SERVING

Calories 296 ;Fat 6g | Sodium 757mg;Carbs 22g ;Fiber10.5g ;Sugar 1.4g;Protein 34g

Orecchiette with Broccoli Rabe

Prep Time: 30 minutes|Cook Time: 15 minutes|Serves: 6

- 2 tsp. salt
- 12 oz. orecchiette pasta (about 3½ cups)
- 2 lbs. broccoli rabe (about 2 bunches)
- ¼ cup extra-virgin olive oil
- 3 cloves garlic, chopped
- ½ tsp. crushed red pepper
- 8 anchovy fillets, chopped
- 1 pint cherry tomatoes, halved

1. Bring 2 quarts of water to a boil in a large pot. Stir in salt, add the pasta, and cook until just tender. Drain, reserving ½ cup of the water.
2. Meanwhile, thoroughly wash the broccoli rabe and trim off the tough ends. Chop the rabe into 2-inch lengths. Leave some water clinging to the leaves and stems (this will help create a sauce).
3. Heat the oil in a large skillet over medium heat until it starts to shimmer. Add the garlic, crushed red pepper, and anchovies, mashing the fillets until they dissolve.
4. Add the broccoli rabe (you may have to do this in batches, stirring each batch a little until it wilts enough to add more). Cook, stirring, until almost

tender (6 to 10 minutes).
5. Add the tomatoes and toss until they begin to soften (about 2 minutes).
6. Add the pasta and toss to coat. If it's too dry, add a little of the reserved pasta water.

PER SERVING

Calories 359 ;Protein 14.9g ; Carbohydrates 49.5g ;Dietary fiber 6.9g ;Sugars 2.6g ;Fat 12.1g ; Sodium 388.5mg

Garlicky Shrimp

Prep Time: 8 minutes|Cook time: 7 minutes|Serves: 1

- 1 garlic clove, minced
- ½ tablespoon fresh cilantro, chopped
- ¼ pound shrimp, peeled and deveined
- ½ tablespoon olive oil
- ½ teaspoon fresh lemon juice
- ½ Serrano pepper, seeded and chopped finely

1. Take a large frying-pan and heat the oil over medium heat and fry garlic and Serrano pepper for about one minute.
2. Include the shrimp and let it cook for about four to five minutes.
3. Stir in lemon juice and remove the pan from the heat.
4. Serve hot with the topping of cilantro.

PER SERVING

Calories: 201 ;Fat: 9g ;Sat Fat: 1.6g ; Carbohydrates: 3g ;Fiber: 0.2g ;Sugar: 0.2g ;Protein: 26.1g

Tomato Basil Halibut

Prep Time: 15 minutes|Cook Time: 12 minutes|Serves: 4

- 2 tomatoes, diced
- 2 tablespoons fresh basil, chopped
- 1 teaspoon fresh oregano, chopped
- 1 tablespoon garlic, minced
- 2 teaspoons olive oil
- 4 halibut fillets

1. Preheat the oven to 350˚F.
2. Layer a 9-inch x 13-inch baking pan with cooking spray.
3. Toss the tomato with basil, olive oil, garlic, and oregano in a bowl.
4. Place the halibut fillets in the baking pan and pour the tomato mixture on top.
5. Bake for 12 minutes until the fish is done.
6. Serve.

PER SERVING

Calories 205 ;Fat 20g ;Sodium 41mg;Carbs 6.1g ;Fiber 0.9g ;Sugar 0.9g ;Protein 22g

Chapter 9
Vegetarian and Vegan Mains

Roasted Red Pepper and Spinach Falafel

Prep time: 15 minutes | Cook time: 30 minutes| Serves 4

FALAFEL

- 1 (15-ounce) can chickpeas, rinsed and drained
- ⅓ cup chopped red onion
- 4 cloves garlic, coarsely chopped
- ½ cup packed fresh parsley, destemmed
- ½ cup jarred roasted red peppers , drained
- 1 cup baby spinach
- 2 teaspoons ground cumin
- 2 teaspoons sweet paprika
- 1 teaspoon ground coriander
- 1 teaspoon freshly ground black pepper
- ⅛ teaspoon cayenne pepper
- ⅛ teaspoon salt
- 2 teaspoons extra-virgin olive oil
- 1 tablespoon fresh lemon juice
- About ¼ cup chickpea flour (or other flour)
- 2 tablespoons black or white sesame seeds (optional)

TZATZIKI

- ½ cup nonfat (0%) plain Greek yogurt
- ⅓ cup peeled and grated cucumber
- 1 tablespoon minced fresh dill
- 1 teaspoon fresh lemon juice
- ¼ teaspoon minced garlic

1. Make the falafel: Preheat the oven to 375°F. Line a baking sheet with parchment paper.
2. In a food processor, combine the chickpeas, onion, garlic, parsley, roasted red peppers, spinach, cumin, paprika, coriander, black pepper, cayenne, salt, olive oil, and lemon juice. Pulse several times, then blend until fully incorporated but not entirely smooth, as you want a bit of texture.
3. Scoop out the falafel mixture into a large bowl and add the chickpea flour 1 tablespoon at a time until you have a workable dough that isn't too sticky but is still a bit wet.
4. Place the sesame seeds (if using) in a small bowl.
5. Using a large spoon, measure out portions of the mixture and form into golf ball-size balls (I usually get 12 balls but you can make as many or few as you like). If you are using the optional sesame seeds, roll the balls in the seeds. Place the falafel on the lined baking sheet and flatten them a bit with the palm of your hand.
6. Transfer to the oven and bake until browned, about 30 minutes, turning halfway through.
7. While the falafel are baking, make the tzatziki: In a small bowl, stir together the yogurt, cucumber, dill, lemon juice, and garlic. Refrigerate until ready to use.
8. Serve the falafel with the tzatziki sauce. These also make a great appetizer.

PER SERVING

Calories: 192; Total fat: 4 g; Saturated fat: 1 g; Cholesterol: 1 mg; Sodium: 73 mg; Potassium: 411 mg; Total carbohydrates: 29 g; Fiber: 8 g; Sugars: 7 g; Protein: 11 g

Coconut Rice and White Beans

Prep time: 15 minutes | Cook time: 30 minutes| Serves 2

- 1 stalk lemongrass, bottom 6 inches only, outer leaves peeled
- 1 teaspoon extra-virgin olive oil
- 2 cloves garlic, minced
- 2 tablespoons minced shallot
- ½ cup chopped red bell pepper
- 1 cup cubed and peeled eggplant
- 1 teaspoon ground cardamom
- 1 teaspoon ground coriander
- ½ teaspoon ground cinnamon
- ½ cup canned no-salt-added diced tomatoes and their juices
- ½ cup black rice
- ⅔ cup canned "lite" coconut milk
- 1 (15-ounce) can small white beans, rinsed and drained
- 2 cups chopped baby kale
- ½ lime
- hot sauce (optional)
- Salt and freshly ground black pepper (optional)

1. Lightly pound the lemongrass stalk with a kitchen mallet.
2. In a large pot, heat the olive oil over high heat. Add the garlic and shallot and cook until soft, 3 to 5 minutes. Add the bell pepper and eggplant and continue cooking until softened, 3 to 5 minutes.
3. Add the cardamom, coriander, and cinnamon and cook for 1 more minute, stirring occasionally to prevent the spices from burning.
4. Add the tomatoes, black rice, coconut milk, 1½ cups water, and beans and stir to combine. Cover, bring to a boil, then reduce the heat to low and allow to simmer for 20 minutes.
5. Stir in the kale, cover, and continue cooking until the kale is wilted, the rice is done, and most of the liquid is absorbed, 5 to 8 minutes longer.
6. To serve, remove the lemongrass stalk and squeeze in the lime juice. If desired, season with hot sauce and a dash of salt and black pepper.

PER SERVING

Calories: 433; Total fat: 9 g; Saturated fat: 5 g; Cholesterol: 0 mg; Sodium: 32 mg; Potassium: 474 mg; Total carbohydrates: 75 g; Fiber: 16 g; Sugars: 6 g; Protein: 19 g

Creamy Cauliflower Butternut Squash Mac and Cheese

Prep time: 5 minutes | Cook time: 20 minutes | Serves 2

- 8 ounces chickpea pasta elbows
- 2 cups cubed peeled butternut squash
- 2 cups cauliflower florets
- 2 cups fat-free milk
- ½ teaspoon freshly ground black pepper
- Dash of salt
- ½ tablespoon extra-virgin olive oil
- ½ medium red onion, minced
- 2 cloves garlic, minced
- 2 teaspoons Dijon mustard
- 2 teaspoons sweet paprika
- 1 cup shredded low-fat cheddar cheese
- ½ cup part-skim ricotta cheese

1. Cook the pasta according to the package directions. Drain and set aside.
2. In a medium saucepan, combine the butternut squash, cauliflower, and 1 cup of the milk. Season with the pepper and salt. Bring to a simmer over medium-high heat, then reduce the heat to low, cover, and cook until fork-tender, 8 to 10 minutes. Transfer the cooked vegetables to a food processor or blender and puree until smooth.
3. Meanwhile, in a large saucepan, heat the olive oil over medium-high heat. Add the onion and garlic and sauté until tender, 3 to 5 minutes.
4. Add the vegetable puree, the remaining 1 cup milk, the mustard, and paprika to the saucepan and bring to a simmer. Cook until starting to thicken, about 5 minutes.
5. Add the cheddar and ricotta cheese and stir to combine. Add the drained pasta to the pan and stir to combine.
6. Serve immediately.

PER SERVING

Calories: 372; Total fat: 9 g; Saturated fat: 2 g; Cholesterol: 15 mg; Sodium: 405 mg; Potassium: 616 mg; Total carbohydrates: 53 g; Fiber: 13 g; Sugars: 13 g; Protein: 28 g

Two-Pea Jollof Rice

Prep time: 15 minutes | Cook time: 55 minutes | Serves 2

- 2 teaspoons extra-virgin olive oil
- ½ cup chopped onion
- 2 cloves garlic, minced
- 1 teaspoon minced peeled fresh ginger
- 2 fresh Thai chili peppers or Scotch bonnet peppers, sliced
- ¼ teaspoon salt
- ½ cup brown basmati rice
- 1 teaspoon ground coriander
- 1 teaspoon dried thyme
- ½ teaspoon ground cumin
- ½ teaspoon sweet paprika
- 1 cup canned no-salt-added diced tomatoes with their juices
- 2 tablespoons tomato paste
- 1 cup low-sodium vegetable broth
- ⅔ cup frozen green peas
- 1 cup canned black-eyed peas, drained and rinsed
- ¼ cup chopped fresh parsley (optional)

1. In a large soup pot or Dutch oven, heat the olive oil over medium-high heat. Add the onion and cook, stirring frequently, until starting to turn translucent, 4 to 5 minutes. Mix in the garlic, ginger, and chili peppers and cook for 30 seconds, until the spices turn fragrant. Add the salt and basmati rice and stir. Continue toasting the rice for 2 minutes.
2. Add the coriander, thyme, cumin, paprika, diced tomatoes, tomato paste, vegetable broth, green peas, and black-eyed peas and stir until well combined. Cover, reduce the heat to medium-low, and simmer until all of the liquid is absorbed and the stew has thickened, 35 to 40 minutes. Don't lift the lid during cooking.
3. Remove the pan from the heat and let sit for 8 to 10 minutes to let the rice finish cooking.
4. Fluff with a fork and serve immediately, sprinkled with fresh parsley, if desired.

PER SERVING

Calories: 407; Total fat: 6 g; Saturated fat: <1 g; Cholesterol: 0 mg; Sodium: 536 mg; Potassium: 586 mg; Total carbohydrates: 74 g; Fiber: 14 g; Sugars: 11 g; Protein: 15 g

Tofu, Carrot, and Walnut "Meatballs" over Butternut Squash Noodles

Prep time: 25 minutes | Cook time: 30 minutes | Serves 4

- 1 (14-ounce) block firm tofu
- 1½ tablespoons extra-virgin olive oil
- 4 cloves garlic, minced
- 1 cup coarsely chopped red onion
- 1 cup grated carrot
- ½ cup walnuts, chopped
- ¼ cup frozen shelled edamame
- 1 tablespoon Bragg liquid aminos
- 2 teaspoons dried oregano
- 1½ teaspoons fennel seeds
- 1 teaspoon red pepper flakes
- ¼ cup coconut flour
- 3 tablespoons nutritional yeast
- 1 to 2 tablespoons fresh lemon juice
- 1 (10-ounce) package butternut squash noodles
- ½ cup chopped fresh basil leaves
- Salt and freshly ground black pepper (optional)

1. Use a tofu press or pat the tofu dry and roll in a clean absorbent towel and place something heavy on top such as a heavy skillet or plates with a can on top, for at least 15 minutes (up to 1 hour) in order to remove excess water.
2. Preheat the oven to 350°F. Coat a large baking sheet with cooking spray or line with parchment paper.
3. In a medium skillet, heat 1 tablespoon of the olive oil over medium-high heat. Add the garlic, onion, and carrot and sauté until soft, 3 to 5 minutes. Remove from the heat and set aside.
4. In a food processor, pulse the walnuts until they are coarsely ground.
5. To the food processor, add the tofu, edamame, Bragg aminos, oregano, fennel seeds, pepper flakes, coconut flour, nutritional yeast, and sautéed vegetables and blend slowly until combined, adding the lemon juice 1 tablespoon at a time until the mixture is moist enough to hold together.
6. Form the mixture into 12 balls (a little bigger than a golf ball) and place on the prepared baking sheet. Bake for 15 minutes, then flip over and continue baking until lightly browned, about 15 minutes more.
7. During the last 10 minutes of baking, heat the remaining ½ tablespoon olive oil in the skillet over medium-high heat. Add the butternut squash noodles and lightly sauté until warmed through, 3 to 5 minutes.
8. Divide the squash noodles among 4 serving plates, top each plate with 3 meatballs, garnish with fresh basil, and season with salt and pepper, if desired.

PER SERVING

Calories: 369; Total fat: 22 g; Saturated fat: 2 g; Cholesterol: 0 mg; Sodium: 520 mg; Potassium: 527 mg; Total carbohydrates: 31 g; Fiber: 10 g; Sugars: 5 g; Protein: 21 g

Bean Pasta with Arugula Avocado Walnut Pesto

Prep Time: 10 minutes | Cook Time: 8 minutes | Serves 4

- 2 cups packed arugula
- 1 cup packed fresh basil leaves
- ¼ cup chopped walnuts
- ⅔ cup green peas (thawed if frozen)
- ½ medium avocado
- 3 cloves garlic, coarsely chopped
- 2 tablespoons fresh lemon juice
- ¼ cup nutritional yeast (see Tips)
- Pinch of salt
- 3 tablespoons extra-virgin olive oil
- 8 ounces bean pasta
- Fresh parsley (optional)

1. Fill a large saucepan three-quarters full with water and bring to a rolling boil over high heat.
2. Meanwhile, in a food processor, combine the arugula, basil, walnuts, peas, avocado, garlic, lemon juice, nutritional yeast, and salt and pulse until finely chopped. Add the olive oil and continue to process the pesto until creamy or the desired consistency is reached.
3. Add the pasta to the boiling water and cook to al dente, according to the package directions, being certain not to overcook. Drain the pasta and transfer to a bowl. Add the pesto and toss to combine.
4. Portion onto 4 serving plates and garnish with fresh parsley, if desired.

PER SERVING

Calories: 417; Total fat: 22 g; Saturated fat: 2 g; Cholesterol: 0 mg; Sodium: 122 mg; Potassium: 289 mg; Total carbohydrates: 43 g; Fiber: 13 g; Sugars: 7 g; Protein: 21

Lentil Sloppy Joes

Prep Time: 15 minutes | Cook Time: 20 minutes | Serves 4

- 1 cup green or brown lentils, rinsed
- ¼ cup unsweetened dried apricots, chopped
- 2 tablespoons tomato paste
- ½ teaspoon yellow mustard
- ½ tablespoon extra-virgin olive oil
- ½ medium yellow onion, diced
- 1 medium green bell pepper, diced
- 1 large stalk celery, diced
- ½ cup grated carrot
- 3 cloves garlic, minced
- 1 (15-ounce) can tomato sauce
- 1 tablespoon red wine vinegar
- 1 tablespoon vegetarian Worcestershire sauce (see Tip)
- 2 teaspoons chili powder
- 1 teaspoon ground cumin
- 1 teaspoon smoked or sweet paprika
- Lettuce leaves or whole-grain buns

1. In a small saucepan, combine the lentils and 2 cups water. Bring to a boil, reduce the heat, and simmer, covered, until tender but not falling apart, 20 to 25 minutes. Drain and set aside.
2. Meanwhile, in a food processor or blender, combine the dried apricots, tomato paste, and mustard and process/blend until the apricots are blended into a paste. Transfer the apricot paste to a small bowl and set aside.
3. Heat a large skillet over medium-high heat. Add the olive oil, onion, bell pepper, celery, carrot, and garlic and stir to combine. Cook, stirring frequently, until the vegetables are slightly browned and tender, 4 to 5 minutes.
4. Add the apricot paste, tomato sauce, vinegar, Worcestershire sauce, chili powder, cumin, and paprika to the skillet. Stir to combine and cook until the spices are fragrant, 2 minutes.
5. Add the drained lentils to the pan and stir well to combine. Continue cooking over medium-low heat until the sauce thickens, stirring occasionally, 5 to 10 minutes. Taste and adjust seasonings before serving.
6. Ladle the mixture onto lettuce leaves or toasted buns.

PER SERVING (WITHOUT BUN)

Calories: 269; Total fat: 3 g; Saturated fat: <1 g; Cholesterol: 0 mg; Sodium: 559 mg; Potassium: 804 mg; Total carbohydrates: 50 g; Fiber: 17 g; Sugars: 13 g; Protein: 15 g

Lentil-Walnut Mushroom Tacos

Prep Time: 15 minutes | Cook Time: 30 minutes | Serves 2

- ¼ cup green or brown lentils, rinsed
- 4 portobello mushrooms
- ¼ cup unsalted pistachios
- ¼ cup walnut halves
- 2 tablespoons chopped canned chipotle peppers in adobo sauce
- 2 cups riced cauliflower
- 1 teaspoon chili powder
- 1 teaspoon ground coriander
- 1 teaspoon ground cumin
- 1 teaspoon garlic powder
- 1 teaspoon dried oregano
- 1 teaspoon smoked paprika
- Juice of 1 lime

1. In a small saucepan, cook the lentils in water to cover over medium-high heat until tender, 20 to 25 minutes. Drain and set aside.
2. Meanwhile, preheat the oven to 375°F. Line a large baking sheet with parchment paper.
3. Remove the stems and carefully scrape out the gills from the mushrooms using a small paring knife. Transfer to a food processor.
4. In a dry medium skillet, toast the pistachios and walnuts, stirring constantly, until lightly golden, 2 to 3 minutes.
5. Scrape the nuts into the food processor. Add the chipotle peppers in adobo sauce and the drained lentils. Pulse lightly until the ingredients are combined, being careful not to overprocess as you want there to be some texture.
6. In a medium bowl, combine the riced cauliflower, chili powder, coriander cumin, garlic powder, oregano, and paprika. Add the contents of the food processor to the bowl and mix until everything is combined.
7. Spread the mixture on the parchment and drizzle with lime juice. Bake for 15 minutes. Use a spatula to turn the mixture, and also make room for the portobello mushroom caps. Coat both sides of the caps lightly with cooking spray. Return to the oven and bake until the mushroom caps are lightly browned and the lentil mixture is lightly browned and crumbly but not overly dry, 15 minutes to 20 minutes longer.
8. Remove the pan from the oven and give the lentil mixture a good stir.
9. To serve, place 2 mushroom caps on each of 2 serving plates and top with the lentil-nut "meat."

PER SERVING

Calories: 346; Total fat: 19 g; Saturated fat: 2 g; Cholesterol: 0 mg; Sodium: 141 mg; Potassium: 1,212 mg; Total carbohydrates: 33 g; Fiber: 15 g; Sugars: 16 g; Protein: 19 g

The Best Black Bean and Beet Burger

Prep Time: 15 minutes | Cook Time: 30 minutes| Serves 6

- 1 tablespoon chia seeds
- 1 (15-ounce) can black beans, rinsed and drained
- ¼ pound cooked and peeled beets, quartered (2 medium)
- ½ cup steel-cut oats
- 1 cup sliced mushrooms
- 1 teaspoon dry mustard
- 1 teaspoon ground cumin
- ½ teaspoon smoked paprika
- 1 teaspoon Bragg liquid aminos or reduced-sodium soy sauce
- 1 teaspoon vegan Worcestershire sauce
- 1 teaspoon minced garlic
- Pinch of salt
- 2 tablespoons chickpea flour or other whole-grain flour, plus more as needed
- Lettuce leaves or whole-grain buns

1. In a small bowl, combine the chia seeds and 3 tablespoons water to make a chia "egg." Set aside for 5 minutes, until the mixture forms a gel.
2. Meanwhile, in a medium bowl, coarsely mash ½ cup of the black beans with a fork, leaving some texture.
3. In a food processor, combine the remaining black beans, the chia "egg," beets, oats, mushrooms, mustard, cumin, paprika, liquid aminos, Worcestershire sauce, garlic, and salt. Pulse until the ingredients are combined but not completely pulverized. You want the burgers to have some texture.
4. Add the contents of the food processor to the bowl with the mashed beans. Add the chickpea flour and mix (it might be easier to use your hands) until the ingredients hold together, adding more flour as needed. Refrigerate to chill for 10 minutes while you preheat the oven. Chilling helps the burgers hold together better.
5. Preheat the oven to 375°F. Coat a baking sheet with cooking spray.
6. Remove the mixture from the fridge and form it into 6 evenly sized balls, then use the palm of your hand to gently flatten into patties.
7. Arrange the burgers on the baking sheet and lightly spray the tops with cooking spray. Bake for 30 minutes to heat through, until lightly browned, gently turning halfway through cooking.
8. Serve on lettuce leaves or toasted whole-grain buns.

PER SERVING (WITHOUT BUN)

Calories: 132; Total fat: 1 g; Saturated fat: <1 g; Cholesterol: 0 mg; Sodium: 89 mg; Potassium: 103 mg; Total carbohydrates: 24 g; Fiber: 6 g; Sugars: 2 g; Protein: 7 g

Cauliflower "Fried Rice" and Mixed Vegetables

Prep Time: 15 minutes | Cook Time: 20 minutes| Serves 4

- 1 tablespoon + 1 teaspoon sesame oil
- 1 cup chopped scallions, white and green parts separated
- 2 cloves garlic, minced
- 1 teaspoon grated fresh ginger
- 1 red bell pepper, chopped
- 1 cup frozen shelled edamame, thawed
- 1 cup mushrooms, sliced
- 4 cups fresh or frozen riced cauliflower
- 2 egg whites, whisked
- 1 large egg, beaten
- 1 tablespoon reduced-sodium soy sauce
- 1 tablespoon balsamic vinegar
- Pinch of red pepper flakes
- ¼ cup chopped peanuts or cashews

1. In a large wok or nonstick skillet, heat 1 tablespoon of the sesame oil over medium-high heat. Add the scallion whites, garlic, and ginger and cook, stirring often, until fragrant but not browned, 2 to 3 minutes.
2. Add the bell pepper, edamame, and mushrooms and cook until the pepper is softened, about 2 minutes. Add the cauliflower rice, stir to combine, and stir-fry quickly to cook the cauliflower to a soft but not mushy texture, 5 to 7 minutes.
3. Make a well in the center of the vegetables. Reduce the heat, add the remaining 1 teaspoon sesame oil to the center, and add the egg whites and whole egg. Stir gently and constantly until the eggs are fully cooked, then stir together with the cauliflower rice.
4. Stir in the scallion greens, the soy sauce, balsamic vinegar, and pepper flakes and cook for 1 minute.
5. Serve garnished with chopped nuts.

PER SERVING

Calories: 219; Total fat: 12 g; Saturated fat: 2 g; Cholesterol: 46 mg; Sodium: 219 mg; Potassium: 497 mg; Total carbohydrates: 17 g; Fiber: 6 g; Sugars: 4 g; Protein: 15 g

Crustless Vegan Mushroom and Sweet Potato Mini Quiches

Prep Time: 5 minutes | Cook Time: 35 minutes| Serves 2

- 1 cup chickpea flour
- ¼ cup nutritional yeast
- 1 teaspoon baking powder
- 2 teaspoons ground sage
- 1 teaspoon dried thyme
- 1 teaspoon ground turmeric
- Pinch of salt
- Freshly ground black pepper
- 1 cup unsweetened cashew milk (or fat-free dairy milk if you are not vegan)
- ⅔ cup frozen green peas, slightly thawed
- 1 cup riced cauliflower and sweet potato (see Tip)
- 1 cup finely chopped button mushrooms
- 1 teaspoon minced garlic
- 1 tablespoon minced shallot

1. Preheat the oven to 375°F. For a main course, lightly coat four 1-cup ramekins with cooking spray; for a snack or side, spray 8 cups of a muffin tin.
2. In a medium bowl, stir together the chickpea flour, nutritional yeast, baking powder, sage, thyme, turmeric, salt, and black pepper to taste. Stir in the milk.
3. Add the peas, riced cauliflower and sweet potato, mushrooms, garlic, and shallot and mix to combine. The batter will be thin.
4. Divide the batter evenly among the prepared ramekins or muffin cups. Transfer to the oven and bake until firm to the touch and lightly browned, about 35 minutes.
5. Remove from the oven and let sit for an additional 10 minutes (they will continue to firm up), then transfer to a wire rack and allow to cool slightly if eating immediately or completely if storing for later. Store in an airtight container in the refrigerator for up to 1 week.

PER MAIN-COURSE SERVING

Calories: 356; Total fat: 1 g; Saturated fat: <1 g; Cholesterol: 0 mg; Sodium: 178 mg; Potassium: 506 mg; Total carbohydrates: 57 g; Fiber: 16 g; Sugars: 11 g; Protein: 23 g

PER SNACK/SIDE SERVING

Calories: 178; Total fat: <1 g; Saturated fat: <1 g; Cholesterol: 0 mg; Sodium: 89 mg; Potassium: 253 mg; Total carbohydrates: 29 g; Fiber: 8 g; Sugars: 5 g; Protein: 12 g

Couscous with Veggies

Prep Time: 8 minutes|Cook time: 15 minutes|Serves: 2

- 1 garlic clove, minced
- ½ cup pearl couscous
- ½ shallot, chopped
- ½ teaspoon Balsamic vinegar
- 1 tablespoon olive oil, divided
- ½ tablespoon fresh lemon juice
- 1 cup cauliflower florets
- 3/2 tablespoon dates, pitted and chopped
- 1 tablespoon fresh parsley, chopped
- ⅝ cup low-sodium vegetable broth
- Fresh ground black pepper to taste

1. For couscous: Take a large pan and heat one tablespoon of oil over medium-heat and fry the garlic for about one minute.
2. Add the broth and couscous to the pan and continue stirring.
3. Reduce the heat to medium and gently cook for about eight to ten minutes.
4. Stir in the lemon juice and remove the pan from the heat.
5. Take a pan and heat the remaining oil over medium heat and fry the shallot for about two minutes.
6. Stir in the cauliflower and cook for about five to six minutes.
7. Stir in the dates and cook for about another two minutes.
8. Add vinegar and black pepper and remove the pan from the heat.
9. Transfer the cauliflower mixture into the pan with couscous and stir to combine everything very well.

PER SERVING

Calories: 266 ;Fat: 7.5g ; Sat Fat: 1g ; Carbohydrates: 43g ;Fiber: 2g ;Sugar: 6.6g ;Protein: 7.4g

Veggie Ratatouille

Prep Time: 15 minutes|Cook time: 45 minutes|Serves: 2

- 1½ tablespoons olive oil, divided
- 6 tablespoons garlic, minced
- ½ zucchini, sliced into thin circles
- ½ eggplant, thinly sliced into circles
- ½ tablespoon fresh thyme leaves, minced
- ½ tablespoon fresh lemon juice
- ¾ cup water
- ½ yellow squash, thinly sliced into circles
- ¼ onion, chopped
- ⅜ cup salt-free tomato paste
- Pinch of salt
- Fresh ground black pepper to taste

1. Preheat the oven to 375° F.
2. Take a bowl, add the tomato paste, oil, onion, garlic, salt and black pepper and blend them well all together.
3. In the base of a baking dish, spread the tomato paste mixture evenly.
4. Arrange alternating vegetable slices, starting at the outer edge of the baking dish and working concentrically towards the center.
5. Drizzle the vegetables with the remaining oil and sprinkle with salt and black pepper.
6. Arrange a piece of parchment paper over the vegetables.
7. Bake them about 45 minutes.
8. Serve them hot.
9. Enjoy!

PER SERVING

Calories: 239 ;Fat: 1.6g ;Sat Fat: 1.6g ;Carbohydrates: 34.1g ;Fiber: 9.1g ;Sugar: 14.9g ;Protein: 6.6g

Veggie Pita Rolls

Prep Time: 15 minutes|Serves: 1

- ½ bell pepper, seeded and chopped
- ½ tomato, seeded and chopped
- ½ garlic clove, minced finely
- ¼ tablespoon fresh lime juice
- 1 whole-wheat pita bread, warmed
- ½ cup romaine lettuce, shredded
- ½ red onion, chopped
- ¼ cup cucumber, chopped
- ½ tablespoon olive oil
- Fresh ground black pepper to flavor

1. Take a bowl and include all the above ingredients except for pita bread and gently toss to coat well.
2. Place pita bread onto the serving plate.
3. Top it with salad and roll the pita bread.
4. Serve and enjoy!

PER SERVING

Calories: 340 ;Fat: 11.8g ;Sat Fat: 1.7g;Carbohydrates: 53.5g ;Fiber: 9.3g ;Sugar: 7.6g ;Protein: 10.6g

Tofu Scramble with Broccoli and Sun-Dried Tomatoes

Prep Time: 15 minutes | Cook Time: 20 minutes| Serves 4

- 1 (14-ounce) block extra-firm tofu
- SAUCE
- 1 teaspoon ground cumin
- 1 teaspoon ground turmeric
- ½ teaspoon chili powder
- ½ teaspoon freshly ground black pepper
- ½ tablespoon reduced-sodium soy sauce or Bragg liquid aminos
- SCRAMBLE
- 1 tablespoon extra-virgin olive oil
- 1 red bell pepper, thinly sliced
- ½ medium onion, thinly sliced
- 2 cloves garlic, minced
- 1 cup broccoli florets
- 1 (15-ounce) can black beans, rinsed and drained
- ¼ cup julienned dry-packed sun-dried tomatoes
- OPTIONAL TOPPINGS
- avocado slices
- Chopped fresh cilantro
- hot sauce

1. Pat the tofu dry and roll it in a clean absorbent towel; place something heavy on top such as a skillet or plates with a can on top for at least 15 minutes (up to 1 hour) in order to remove excess water.
2. While the tofu is draining, prepare the sauce: In a small bowl, whisk together the cumin, turmeric, chili powder, black pepper, and soy sauce. The sauce should have some body and not be too runny.
3. Make the scramble: In a large skillet, heat the olive oil over medium heat. Add the bell pepper and onion and cook until softened, about 5 minutes. Add the garlic and cook for 1 minute.
4. Add the broccoli; cover and steam for 2 minutes.
5. Meanwhile, unwrap the tofu and use a fork to crumble into bite-size pieces.
6. Use a spatula and move the vegetables to one side of the skillet. Add the crumbled tofu and sauté for 2 to 3 minutes, until lightly browned, then combine with the vegetables, pour in the sauce, and cook for another 3 minutes, until the tofu is evenly coated and has absorbed some of the sauce.
7. Add the beans and sun-dried tomatoes and continue cooking until the tofu is lightly browned, another 5 to 7 minutes.
8. Serve with the optional toppings, if desired.

PER SERVING

Calories: 251; Total fat: 8 g; Saturated fat: 1 g; Cholesterol: 0 mg; Sodium: 98 mg; Potassium: 358 mg; Total carbohydrates: 28 g; Fiber: 7 g; Sugars: 3 g; Protein: 18 g

Spinach Ginger Lentils

Prep Time: 10 minutes|Cook Time: 16 minutes|Serves: 4

- 1 tablespoon olive oil
- 1 shallot, minced
- 1 teaspoon ground ginger
- ½ teaspoon curry powder
- ½ teaspoon ground turmeric
- 1 cup yellow lentils, drained
- 1½ cups vegetable stock
- ½ cup light coconut milk
- 2 cups baby spinach leaves, chopped
- ½ teaspoon salt

GARNISH:

- 1 teaspoon white sesame seeds
- 1 tablespoon fresh cilantro, chopped

1. Add the olive oil to a saucepan, then heat it over medium flame.
2. Stir in the ginger, shallot, turmeric, and curry powder.
3. Sauté for 1 minute, then add the stock, coconut milk, and lentils.
4. Let the lentils boil, then reduce the heat to a simmer.
5. Partially cover the pan, then cook for 12 minutes.
6. Meanwhile, toast the sesame seeds in a dry skillet until they turn brown.
7. Add the spinach to the lentils and cook for 3 minutes.
8. Adjust the seasoning with salt.
9. Garnish with the toasted sesame seeds and cilantro.
10. Serve warm.

PER SERVING

Calories 263 ;Fat 7.5g ;Sodium 55mg;Carbs 36g ;Fiber 0.4g ;Sugar 0.4g ;Protein 14g

Almond Butter Tofu and Roasted Asparagus

Prep Time: 15 minutes | Cook Time: 40 minutes| Serves 3

- 1 (14-ounce) block extra-firm tofu
- 1 tablespoon sesame oil
- 1 tablespoon pure maple syrup
- 2 tablespoons reduced-sodium tamari
- 2 tablespoons almond butter
- 2 tablespoons fresh lime juice
- 1 tablespoon balsamic vinegar
- 3 cloves garlic, minced
- 1 pound asparagus, tough ends trimmed
- 1 tablespoon extra-virgin olive oil
- Freshly ground black pepper (optional)
- Chili hot sauce (e.g. Sriracha) (optional)

1. Pat tofu dry and roll in a clean absorbent towel and place something heavy on top such as a heavy skillet or plates with a can on top, for at least 15 minutes (up to 1 hour) in order to remove excess water.
2. Preheat the oven to 400°F. Coat two large baking sheets with cooking spray.
3. Unwrap the tofu and cut into 1-inch cubes. Arrange on one of the prepared baking sheets in an even layer and bake until puffy and slightly browned, 20 to 25 minutes.
4. Meanwhile, in a small bowl, combine the sesame oil, maple syrup, tamari, almond butter, lime juice, balsamic vinegar, and two-thirds of the minced garlic. Whisk to combine. Set the marinade aside.
5. In a medium bowl, drizzle the asparagus with the olive oil, then toss to coat. Sprinkle with the remaining garlic and season with black pepper, if desired. Arrange the asparagus in a single layer on the second baking sheet.
6. Remove the tofu from the oven and place the asparagus in the oven in its place. Add the baked tofu to the marinade and toss to coat. Let marinate for 5 minutes, stirring occasionally.
7. Heat a large skillet over medium heat. Once hot, add the tofu (reserve the marinade) and cook, stirring occasionally, until browned on all sides, about 5 minutes.
8. Remove the roasted asparagus from the oven and add to the skillet with the tofu along with the reserved marinade. Cook for an additional 2 minutes, stirring frequently.
9. Garnish with hot sauce, if desired.

PER SERVING

Calories: 337; Total fat: 21 g; Saturated fat: 3 g; Cholesterol: 0 mg; Sodium: 496 mg; Potassium: 528 mg; Total carbohydrates: 21 g; Fiber: 6 g; Sugars: 8 g; Protein: 21 g

Curried Veggies

Prep Time: 10 minutes|Cook time: 20 minutes|Serves: 3

- ½ medium yellow squash, chopped
- ½ medium zucchini, chopped
- ½ onion, thinly sliced
- 1 bell peppers, seeded and cubed
- 1 tablespoon curry powder
- 1 tablespoon olive oil
- Fresh ground black pepper to taste
- 2 tablespoons low-sodium vegetable broth
- 2 tablespoons fresh cilantro, chopped

1. Preheat oven to 375° F and evenly grease large baking dish.
2. Take a bowl and add all the ingredients except cilantro.
3. Now, mix them until well combined.
4. Transfer the vegetable mixture into the prepared baking dish.
5. Bake it for about 15-20 minutes.
6. Serve and enjoy!

PER SERVING

Calories: 78 ;Fat: 5.1g ; Sat Fat: 0.7g ; Carbohydrates: 8.3g ;Fiber: 2.4g ;Sugar: 3.9g ;Protein: 1.6g

Vegetable Polenta

Prep Time: 10 minutes|Cook Time: 20 minutes|Serves: 6

- 1 eggplant, peeled, cut into slices
- 1 yellow zucchini, cut into slices
- 1 green zucchini, cut into slices
- 6 mushrooms, sliced
- 1 cored sweet red pepper, chopped
- 2½ tablespoons olive oil
- 6 cups water
- 1½ cups coarse polenta
- 2 teaspoons margarine
- ¼ teaspoon cracked black pepper
- 10 ounces frozen spinach, thawed
- 2 plum (Roma) tomatoes, sliced
- 6 dry-packed sun-dried tomatoes, drained and chopped
- 10 ripe olives, chopped
- 2 teaspoons oregano

1. Preheat the broiler and set its rack 4 inches below the heat source.
2. Toss the eggplant, mushrooms, red pepper, and zucchini with 1 tablespoon of the oil.
3. Add the veggies to a baking sheet and broil, flipping them every few minutes.
4. Brush the veggies with more oil if needed and cook until they turn brown.
5. Preheat the oven to 350˚F.
6. Layer a 12-inch quiche pan with cooking spray.
7. Boil the water with the polenta in a saucepan, then reduce the heat to a simmer.
8. Cook the polenta for 5 minutes, then add the

margarine and black pepper to taste.

9. Spread the cooked polenta in the quiche pan and top it with the spinach, tomatoes, sun-dried tomatoes, and olives.
10. Add the remaining roasted vegetables on top.
11. Sprinkle the oregano and black pepper over it.
12. Bake for 10 minutes, then slice.
13. Serve.

PER SERVING

Calories 215 ;Fat 9.4g ;Sodium 189mg;Carbs 23g ;Fiber 0.3g ;Sugar 18.2g ;Protein 37g

Veggies Stuffed Bell Peppers

Prep Time: 10 minutes|Cook time: 25 minutes|Serves: 2

- ¼ pound fresh shiitake mushrooms
- 1 tablespoon olive oil
- 1 garlic cloves, peeled
- 2 bell peppers, halved and seeded
- ½ cup celery stalk
- ¼ cup unsalted walnuts
- Pinch of salt
- Fresh ground black pepper to taste

1. Preheat oven to 400° F.
2. Evenly grease the baking sheet.
3. Remove stem and seeds from bell peppers.
4. In a food processor, add mushrooms, celery, garlic, walnuts, oil, salt, pepper and pulse until everything is chopped finely.
5. Stuff the prepared mushroom mixture into the bell peppers.
6. Arrange the bell peppers onto the baking sheet.
7. Bake them about 20-25 minutes or until they are slightly brown.
8. Serve warm.

PER SERVING

Calories: 138 ;Fat: 7.8g ; Sat Fat: 1.1g; Carbohydrates: 18.2g ;Fiber: 3.3g ;Sugar: 8.4g ;Protein: 2.4g

Masala Chickpeas
Prep Time: 10 minutes| Cook time: 25 minutes|Serves: 4

- 1½ teaspoon garam masala powder
- 1 teaspoon smoked paprika
- 1 teaspoon jeera powder
- 1 teaspoon ground coriander
- 1 teaspoon turmeric powder
- ¼ teaspoon Cayenne pepper
- 1 tablespoon canola oil
- ½ teaspoon black mustard seeds
- 2 tablespoons jeera seeds 1 white onion, diced
- 4 tablespoons finely chopped garlic
- 1 large sweet red pepper, diced
- 2 rosa tomatoes, roughly chopped
- ½ cup broccoli florets
- 1 medium carrot, peeled and cut into cubes
- 2 cups water
- 30 ounces cooked chickpeas, rinsed and drained
- 1 tablespoon tomato paste
- 10 ounces frozen kale, thawed
- Black pepper to taste
- 2 tablespoons finely chopped fresh coriander, plus extra to garnish

1. In a small bowl, make the spice blend by mixing all the dried spices, except for the jeera seeds and mustard seeds. Set aside.
2. Heat the oil in a medium pot, then add in the mustard seeds and jeera seeds.
3. Cook for 10 seconds before adding in the onion and garlic. Fry for 3 minutes.
4. Add in the following vegetables: red pepper, tomatoes, broccoli, and carrots. Then cook the mixture on medium heat for about 6 minutes.
5. Pour in two cups of water, then add the chickpeas, tomato paste, kale, and black pepper to taste.
6. Bring to a slow boil and cook for about 15-20 minutes, or until the vegetables are cooked through and the stew smells aromatic.
7. Enjoy.

PER SERVING

Calories 309 ;Fat 7g ;Sodium 134mg;Carbs 50g ;Fiber 14g ;Sugar 17g ;Protein 15g

Tofu & Oats Burgers
Prep Time: 8 minutes|Cook time: 16 minutes|Serves: 2

- 6 tablespoons rolled oats
- 2 garlic cloves, minced
- ½ medium onion, finely chopped
- 1 cup frozen spinach, thawed
- 2 tablespoons flaxseeds
- ½ teaspoon red pepper flakes, crushed
- 1 tablespoon olive oil
- Fresh ground black pepper to taste
- ½ teaspoon ground cumin
- 3 cups fresh salad greens

1. Take a bowl and include all the above ingredients except for olive-oil and salad greens and mix them all together until well combined.
2. Set aside the bowl for about ten minutes.
3. Make patties from the prepared mixture.
4. Now, take a non-stick frying pan and heat the oil over medium heat.
5. Cook the patties for about six to eight minutes each side.
6. Serve and enjoy!

PER SERVING

Calories: 309 ;Fat: 15.2g ;Sat Fat: 2.5g ; Carbohydrates: 29.4g ;Fiber: 10.1g ;Sugar: 2.3g ;Protein: 18.2g

Stuffed Eggplant Shells

Prep Time: 15 minutes|Cook Time: 25 minutes|Serves: 2

- 1 medium eggplant
- 1 cup water
- 1 tablespoon olive oil
- 4 ounces cooked white beans
- ¼ cup onion, chopped
- ½ cup red, green, or yellow bell peppers, chopped
- 1 cup canned unsalted tomatoes
- ¼ cup tomato liquid
- ¼ cup celery, chopped
- 1 cup fresh mushrooms, sliced
- ¾ cup whole-wheat bread crumbs
- Black pepper, to taste

1. Preheat the oven to 350°F.
2. Grease a baking dish with cooking spray and set it aside.
3. Trim and cut the eggplant in half, lengthwise.
4. Scoop out the pulp using a spoon and leave the shell about ¼-inch thick.
5. Place the shells in the baking dish with their cut side up.
6. Add water to the bottom of the dish.
7. Dice the eggplant pulp into cubes and set them aside.
8. Add oil to an iron skillet and heat it over medium heat.
9. Stir in the onions, peppers, chopped eggplant pulp, tomatoes, celery, mushrooms, and tomato juice.
10. Cook for 10 minutes on simmering heat, then stir in the beans, black pepper, and breadcrumbs.
11. Divide this mixture into the eggplant shells.
12. Cover the shells with a foil sheet and bake for 15 minutes.
13. Serve warm.

PER SERVING

Calories 305 ;Fat 12.7g ;Sodium 82mg;Carbs 36g ;Fiber 1.4g ;Sugar 0.9g ;Protein 15.2g

Quinoa and Red Lentil Stuffed Peppers

Prep Time: 15 minutes | Cook Time: 70 minutes| Serves 4

- ½ cup quinoa, rinsed
- ½ cup red lentils, rinsed
- ½ cup raw cashews
- ¼ cup fresh lemon juice
- 3 to 4 teaspoons minced garlic
- 1 cup fresh basil leaves
- Pinch of salt
- ¼ teaspoon freshly ground black pepper
- 1 cup riced cauliflower
- 2 cups baby spinach or baby kale, chopped
- ¼ cup nutritional yeast
- 2 teaspoons dried thyme
- Pinch of cayenne pepper
- 4 large bell peppers, any color, halved lengthwise
- Fresh chives (optional)

1. In a saucepan, combine the quinoa, lentils, and 2 cups water and bring to a boil over high heat. Reduce the heat, cover, and simmer until the liquid is absorbed, the quinoa is fluffy, and the lentils are tender, 15 to 20 minutes.
2. Preheat the oven to 375°F. Pour ½ inch water into a baking dish big enough to hold the pepper halves in a single layer.
3. Meanwhile, in a food processor or high-powered blender, combine the cashews, ½ cup water, the lemon juice, garlic to taste, basil, salt, and black pepper and process until creamy and smooth. Pour into a medium bowl.
4. To the bowl, add the cooked quinoa and lentils, riced cauliflower, spinach, nutritional yeast, thyme, and cayenne. Mix thoroughly to combine.
5. Lightly spray the halved peppers with nonstick cooking spray and place cut side up in the baking dish. Dividing evenly, spoon the filling into each bell pepper cavity until full. Cover with foil and bake for 30 minutes. Remove the foil and bake until the peppers are soft and slightly golden brown, another 15 to 20 minutes.
6. Garnish with fresh chives, if desired, and serve immediately.

PER SERVING

Calories: 326; Total fat: 9 g; Saturated fat: 0 g; Cholesterol: 0 mg; Sodium: 73 mg; Potassium: 575 mg; Total carbohydrates: 47 g; Fiber: 14 g; Sugars: 8 g; Protein: 17 g

Chapter 10
Soups

Broccoli Chard Soup

Prep time: 15 minutes | Cook time: 25 minutes | Serves 4

- 1 tablespoon olive oil
- 1 sweet onion, chopped
- 2 celery stalks, sliced
- 2 teaspoons minced garlic
- 1½ broccoli heads, chopped
- 1 cup chopped Swiss chard
- 6 cups low-sodium vegetable broth
- 1 tablespoon chopped fresh basil
- 1 teaspoon chopped fresh oregano
- ½ cup plain Greek yogurt
- Freshly ground black pepper

1. Heat the oil in a large saucepan over medium-high heat. Sauté the onion, celery, and garlic until softened, about 5 minutes.
2. Add the broccoli, chard, and vegetable broth and bring the soup to a boil.
3. Reduce the heat to low and simmer until the broccoli is tender, about 20 minutes.
4. Stir in the basil and oregano, transfer the soup to a food processor, and carefully blend until smooth.
5. Transfer the soup back to the saucepan, stir in the yogurt, and season with black pepper.
6. Serve warm.
7. Store any cooled leftover soup in a sealed container in the refrigerator for up to 3 days.

PER SERVING

Sodium: 306mg; Calories: 115; Total Fat: 4g; Saturated Fat: 1g; Total Carbohydrates: 17g; Net Carbs: 12g; Fiber: 5g; Protein: 6g; Potassium: 554mg; Cholesterol: 0mg

Baharat-Spiced Root Vegetable Soup

Prep time: 15 minutes | Cook time: 30 minutes

- 1 tablespoon olive oil
- 1 sweet onion, chopped
- 2 celery stalks, chopped
- 1 tablespoon minced garlic
- 6 cups no-salt-added vegetable broth
- 1 small celeriac, peeled and diced
- 2 cups diced pumpkin or butternut squash
- 2 carrots, diced
- 2 parsnips, diced
- 2 tablespoons Baharat Spice Mix

1. Heat the oil in a saucepan over medium-high heat. Sauté the onion, celery, and garlic until softened, about 5 minutes.
2. Stir in the vegetable broth, celeriac, pumpkin, carrots, parsnips, and spice mix.
3. Bring the soup to a boil, reduce the heat to low, and simmer until the vegetables are tender, about 20 minutes.
4. Use a slotted spoon to scoop out about half the cooked vegetables to a bowl. Use an immersion blender or food processor to puree the remaining soup.

5. Add the reserved vegetables back to the pureed soup and serve.
6. Store any cooled leftover soup in a sealed container in the refrigerator for up to 3 days, or in the freezer for up to 1 month.

PER SERVING

Sodium: 127mg; Calories: 187; Total Fat: 4g; Saturated Fat: 1g; Total Carbohydrates: 38g; Net Carbs: 30g; Fiber: 8g; Protein: 4g; Potassium: 865mg; Cholesterol: 0mg

Chickpea Soup with Harissa

Prep time: 15 minutes | Cook time: 30 minutes | Serves 4

- 1 tablespoon olive oil
- 1 sweet onion, chopped
- 1 tablespoon minced garlic
- 6 cups no-salt-added vegetable broth
- 2 (15-ounce) cans no-salt-added chickpeas, drained and rinsed
- 1 sweet potato, diced
- 1 carrot, diced
- 1 teaspoon ground cumin
- 1 teaspoon ground coriander
- ¼ teaspoon ground cinnamon
- Juice of 1 lemon
- Freshly ground black pepper
- ¼ cup Harissa or hot pepper sauce, for garnish
- 1 cup shredded fresh spinach

1. Heat the oil in a large saucepan over medium-high heat. Sauté the onion and garlic until softened, about 3 minutes.
2. Add the broth, chickpeas, sweet potato, carrot, cumin, coriander, and cinnamon and bring to a boil.
3. Reduce the heat to low and simmer until the vegetables and chickpeas are tender, about 25 minutes.
4. Transfer the soup to a food processor or blender and puree until smooth.
5. Return the soup to the saucepan, stir in the lemon juice, and season with black pepper.
6. Serve topped with the harissa and spinach. The heat from the soup will wilt the spinach.
7. If not serving right away, store the soup, harissa, and spinach separately until ready to serve. Store any cooled leftover soup in a sealed container in the refrigerator for up to 4 days, or in the freezer for up to 1 month.

PER SERVING

Sodium: 240mg; Calories: 346; Total Fat: 29g; Saturated Fat: 2g; Total Carbohydrates: 46g; Net Carbs: 32g; Fiber: 14g; Protein: 20g; Potassium: 617mg; Cholesterol: 38mg

Cabbage and Salsa Soup

Prep time: 15 minutes | Cook time: 30 minutes | Serves 4

- 2 teaspoons olive oil
- 1 sweet onion, chopped
- 2 celery stalks, chopped
- 2 teaspoons minced garlic
- 3 cups shredded cabbage
- 6 carrots, diced
- 6 cups no-salt-added chicken broth
- 1 (15-ounce) can no-salt-added diced tomatoes
- 1 cup Red and Green Salsa
- 2 tablespoons chopped fresh cilantro (optional)

1. Heat the oil in a large saucepan over medium-high heat. Sauté the onion, celery, and garlic until the vegetables are tender, about 5 minutes.
2. Add the cabbage and carrots and sauté for 5 minutes.
3. Stir in the chicken broth and tomatoes and bring the soup to a boil.
4. Reduce the heat to low and simmer until the vegetables are tender, about 20 minutes.
5. Stir in the salsa and serve topped with cilantro (if using).
6. Store any cooled leftover soup in a sealed container in the refrigerator for up to 4 days.

PER SERVING

Sodium: 242mg; Calories: 160; Total Fat: 25g; Saturated Fat: 1g; Total Carbohydrates: 18g; Net Carbs: 11g; Fiber: 7g; Protein: 10g; Potassium: 665mg; Cholesterol: 38mg

Hot and Sour Soup

Prep time: 15 minutes | Cook time: 15 minutes | Serves 4

- 6 cups no-salt-added chicken broth, divided
- 2 tablespoons corn starch
- 2 tablespoons rice vinegar
- 2 teaspoons coconut aminos
- 2 teaspoons minced garlic
- 1 teaspoon grated peeled fresh ginger
- Pinch red pepper flakes
- 1 cup sliced shiitake mushrooms
- 3 baby bok choy, julienned
- 2 large eggs, beaten
- 1 cup cubed (½-inch) firm tofu
- 2 scallions, thinly sliced on the bias
- 1 teaspoon sesame oil

1. In a small bowl, stir ½ cup of chicken broth and the cornstarch until well blended. Set aside.
2. In a large saucepan over medium-high heat, stir the remaining 5½ cups of broth, the vinegar, coconut aminos, garlic, ginger, and pepper flakes and bring to a boil.
3. Add the mushrooms and bok choy, reduce the heat to medium-low, and simmer until the vegetables are tender, 5 to 6 minutes.
4. Stir in the cornstarch mixture and simmer until thickened, about 1 minute.

5. Drizzle the beaten egg into the simmering soup in thin streams to create distinct ribbons and simmer until the egg is cooked, about 2 minutes.
6. Add the tofu and simmer 3 minutes more.
7. Stir in the scallions and serve immediately, drizzled with sesame oil. This dish is best enjoyed right away; however, leftovers can be stored in a covered container in the refrigerator for up to 2 days.

PER SERVING

Sodium: 269mg; Calories: 168; Total Fat: 26g; Saturated Fat: 2g; Total Carbohydrates: 9g; Net Carbs: 7g; Fiber: 2g; Protein: 15g; Potassium: 227mg; Cholesterol: 131mg

Wild Mushroom Thyme Soup

Prep time: 15 minutes | Cook time: 30 minutes | Serves 4

- 1 tablespoon olive oil
- 1 sweet onion, chopped
- 1 tablespoon minced garlic
- 2 pounds cremini mushrooms, sliced
- 1 pound shiitake, oyster, or any other mushroom, sliced
- 5 cups no-salt-added vegetable broth
- Juice of 1 lemon
- 2 teaspoons chopped fresh thyme
- ½ cup plain Greek yogurt
- Freshly ground black pepper

1. Heat the oil in a large saucepan over medium-high heat. Sauté the onion and garlic until softened, about 4 minutes.
2. Add the mushrooms and sauté, stirring frequently, until lightly caramelized, about 10 minutes.
3. Add the broth, lemon juice, and thyme and bring the soup to a boil. Reduce the heat to low and simmer until the vegetables are tender, about 15 minutes.
4. Remove the soup from the heat, stir in the yogurt, season with pepper, and serve.
5. Store cooled leftover soup in a sealed container in the refrigerator for up to 4 days.

PER SERVING

Sodium: 128mg; Calories: 196; Total Fat: 22g; Saturated Fat: 1g; Total Carbohydrates: 17g; Net Carbs: 13g; Fiber: 4g; Protein: 17g; Potassium: 1204mg; Cholesterol: 31mg

Cauliflower Leek Soup

Prep Time: 15 minutes|Cook Time: 25 minutes| Serves 6

- 1 tablespoon canola oil
- 1 yellow onion, peeled and diced
- 1 leek, trimmed and thinly sliced
- 1 head cauliflower, trimmed and cut into florets
- 2 to 3 garlic cloves, peeled and minced
- 2 tablespoons fresh thyme leaves, chopped
- 1¼ teaspoons kosher or sea salt
- 1 teaspoon smoked paprika
- ½ teaspoon ground black pepper
- ¼ teaspoon ground cayenne pepper
- 3 cups unsalted vegetable stock
- 1 tablespoon heavy cream or olive oil
- Zest and juice of ½ lemon

1. Heat the canola oil in a Dutch oven or stockpot over medium heat. Add the onion, leek, and cauliflower and sauté for 4 to 5 minutes, until the onion is starting to soften. Stir in the garlic, thyme, salt, smoked paprika, black pepper, and cayenne pepper. Add the vegetable stock and bring to a simmer for about 15 minutes, until the cauliflower is very soft.
2. Remove from the heat and stir in the cream or olive oil and lemon zest and juice. Use an immersion blender to purée the soup until smooth, or transfer the soup to a blender and purée in batches until smooth. Taste and adjust the seasoning, if necessary.
3. If you are not eating the soup right away, transfer it into microwaveable airtight containers and refrigerate for up to 5 days. Reheat in the microwave on high for 1 to 3 minutes, until heated through.

PER SERVING

Calories: 92; Total Fat: 4g; Saturated Fat: 1g; Cholesterol: 3mg; Sodium: 556mg; Potassium: 526mg; Total Carbohydrate: 13g; Fiber: 4g; Sugars: 4g; Protein: 5g

Linguini Chicken Soup

Prep Time: 10 minutes | Cook Time: 20 minutes | Serves: 6

- 1 teaspoon olive oil
- 1 cup onion, chopped
- 3 garlic cloves, minced
- 1 cup celery, chopped
- 1 cup carrots, sliced and peeled
- 4 cups chicken broth
- 4 ounces dried linguini, broken
- 1 cup cooked chicken breast, cut into the desired size
- 2 tablespoons fresh parsley

1. Add the olive oil to a saucepan, then heat it on medium flame.
2. Stir in the garlic and onion. Sauté until soft.
3. Add the carrots and celery. Stir and cook for 3 minutes.
4. Pour in the broth and cook until it boils, then reduce it to a simmer.
5. Cook for 5 minutes, then add the linguini.
6. Bring to a boil and then reduce the heat to a simmer.
7. Cook for 10 more minutes.
8. Add the chicken and parsley.
9. Cook for a minute, then serve warm.

PER SERVING

Calories 381 ;Fat 15g ;Sodium 42mg;Carbs 9.7g ;Fiber 0.4g ;Sugar 1g ;Protein 25.2g

Silky Corn Chowder

Prep time: 15 minutes | Cook time: 25 minutes | Serves 4

- 1 tablespoon olive oil
- 1 sweet onion, chopped
- 1 jalapeño or poblano pepper, chopped
- 1 tablespoon minced garlic
- 2 teaspoons chili powder
- 1 teaspoon ground cumin
- 4 cups low-sodium vegetable broth
- 3 cups fresh or frozen corn kernels
- 2 cups unsweetened almond milk or regular milk
- Juice of 1 lime
- Freshly ground black pepper
- ½ cup Red and Green Salsa
- 1 tablespoon chopped fresh cilantro, for garnish

1. Heat the oil in a large saucepan over medium-high heat. Sauté the onion, jalapeño, garlic, chili powder, and cumin until the vegetables are softened, about 4 minutes.
2. Stir in the broth, corn, milk, and lime juice. Bring the soup to a boil, reduce the heat to low, and simmer until the vegetables are tender, about 20 minutes.
3. Remove the soup from the heat and season with black pepper. Puree the soup with an immersion blender or in a food processor until smooth.
4. Serve topped with the salsa and cilantro.
5. Store cooled leftover soup in a sealed container in the refrigerator for up to 4 days, or in the freezer for up to 1 month.

PER SERVING

Sodium: 381mg; Calories: 127; Total Fat: 7g; Saturated Fat: 1g; Total Carbohydrates: 32g; Net Carbs: 26g; Fiber: 6g; Protein: 5g; Potassium: 473mg; Cholesterol: 0mg

Spiced Pumpkin Soup

Prep time: 15 minutes | Cook time: 35 minutes | Serves 4

- 1 tablespoon olive oil
- 1 sweet onion, chopped
- 1 tablespoon grated peeled fresh ginger
- 2 teaspoons minced garlic
- 6 cups low-sodium vegetable broth
- 5 cups diced fresh or frozen pumpkin
- 2 tablespoons honey
- ½ teaspoon ground nutmeg
- ½ teaspoon ground cinnamon
- ⅛ teaspoon ground cloves
- ½ cup coconut milk

1. Heat the oil in a large saucepan over medium-high heat. Sauté the onion, ginger, and garlic until softened, about 4 minutes.
2. Add the broth, pumpkin, honey, nutmeg, cinnamon, and cloves.
3. Bring the soup to a boil, reduce the heat to low, and simmer until the pumpkin is tender, about 30 minutes.
4. Remove the soup from the heat and puree with an immersion blender or in a food processor until very smooth.
5. Return to the saucepan and whisk in the coconut milk.
6. Serve.
7. Store any cooled leftover soup in a sealed container in the refrigerator for up to 4 days, or in the freezer for up to 1 month.

PER SERVING

Sodium: 247mg; Calories: 187; Total Fat: 10g; Saturated Fat: 6g; Total Carbohydrates: 26g; Net Carbs: 23g; Fiber: 3g; Protein: 3g; Potassium: 650mg; Cholesterol: 0mg

Turkey Rice Soup

Prep time: 15 minutes | Cook time: 25 minutes | Serves 6

- 1 tablespoon olive oil
- 1 sweet onion, diced
- 3 celery stalks with leaves, sliced
- 2 teaspoons minced garlic
- 2 carrots, sliced
- 6 cups no-salt-added chicken broth
- 2 cups chopped cooked turkey
- 1 cup medium-grain white rice
- 2 cups green beans, cut into 1-inch pieces
- Freshly ground black pepper
- 2 tablespoons chopped fresh parsley, for garnish

1. Heat the oil in a large saucepan over medium-high heat. Sauté the onion, celery, and garlic until softened, about 4 minutes.
2. Add the carrots and sauté for 3 minutes more.
3. Stir in the chicken broth, turkey, and rice and bring to a boil.
4. Reduce the heat to low and simmer until the rice is just tender, about 15 minutes.

5. Stir in the green beans and simmer for 2 minutes.
6. Season with black pepper and serve topped with parsley.
7. Store any cooled leftover soup in a sealed container in the refrigerator for up to 4 days, or in the freezer for up to 1 month.

PER SERVING

Sodium: 197mg; Calories: 279; Total Fat: 20g; Saturated Fat: 2g; Total Carbohydrates: 32g; Net Carbs: 27g; Fiber: 5g; Protein: 22g; Potassium: 298mg; Cholesterol: 60mg

Tuscan Chicken & Kale Soup

Prep Time: 10 minutes | Cook Time: 15 minutes | Serves 6

- 2 tablespoons olive oil
- 1 yellow onion, peeled and diced
- 2 carrots, peeled and diced
- 2 celery stalks, diced
- 1 pound boneless skinless chicken breast, cubed
- 4 cups chopped kale
- 2 to 3 garlic cloves, peeled and minced
- 2 tablespoons dried Italian seasoning
- ½ teaspoon kosher or sea salt
- ½ teaspoon ground black pepper
- 1 (15-ounce) can cannellini beans, rinsed and drained
- 1 (15-ounce) can no-salt-added petite diced tomatoes with juice
- 4 cups unsalted chicken stock
- ½ cup freshly grated Parmesan cheese

1. In a Dutch oven or stockpot, heat the oil over medium heat. Add the onion, carrots, and celery and cook for 3 to 4 minutes, until they start to soften. Stir in the cubed chicken breast and cook for 3 to 4 minutes, until slightly browned on the edges. Stir in the kale, garlic, Italian seasoning, salt, and black pepper until the kale is slightly wilted.
2. Add the cannellini beans, diced tomatoes, and stock and bring to a simmer for about 10 minutes, stirring occasionally. Taste and adjust the seasoning, if necessary.
3. Divide the soup evenly into bowls and top with the grated Parmesan.
4. Divide leftovers evenly into microwaveable airtight containers and store in the refrigerator for up to 5 days. Reheat in the microwave on high for 2 to 3 minutes, until heated through, stirring as needed.

PER SERVING

Calories: 267; Total Fat: 9g; Saturated Fat: 3g; Cholesterol: 53mg; Sodium: 543mg; Potassium: 195mg; Total Carbohydrate: 23g; Fiber: 6g; Sugars: 5g; Protein: 24g

Tomato Peach Soup

Prep Time: 10 minutes| Cook time: 12 minutes|Serves: 4

- ½ tablespoon olive oil
- 1 large ripe peach, halved, pitted, peeled and diced
- 1 cup carrots, shredded
- 2 garlic cloves, minced
- 1 can no-salt diced tomatoes in juice
- ½ teaspoon chili pepper, freshly ground
- 1 cup chicken broth, low-sodium
- 1 cup water
- 1 cup yogurt

1. Heat the olive oil in a large pot over medium heat.
2. Add the shredded carrots and cook, often stirring, about 5 minutes, or until carrots are tender. Sprinkle with garlic, and cook for 1 minute.
3. Remove the carrot mixture to a food processor.
4. Add the tomatoes and their juice, broth, chili pepper and water, and purée until smooth.
5. Return the purée to the pot, reduce heat to medium-low, cook the soup mixture for 5 minutes, or cook until cooked through.
6. Smear with the yogurt.
7. Enjoy.

PER SERVING

Calories 155 ;Fat 9g | Sodium 116mg;Carbs 17g ;Fiber 5g ;Sugar 4g ;Protein 5g

Asparagus Soup

Prep Time: 10 minutes|Cook time: 40 minutes|Serves: 2

- ½ tablespoon olive oil
- ¾ pound asparagus, trimmed and chopped
- 1½ scallions, chopped
- 2 cups low-sodium vegetable broth
- 1 tablespoon fresh lemon juice
- ½ Serrano pepper, seeded and chopped finely

1. Take a large frying-pan and heat the oil over medium heat and fry the scallion for about four to five minutes.
2. Stir in the asparagus and broth and bring it to a boil.
3. Reduce the heat to low and let it cook for about 25-30 minutes while covered.
4. Remove the pan from the heat and set aside to let it cool.
5. Now, transfer the soup into a food processor in two batches and pulse until we have a smooth mixture.
6. Transfer the soup into the same pan over medium-heat and cook for about four to five minutes.
7. Stir in the lemon juice, salt and black pepper and remove from the heat.
8. Serve hot.

PER SERVING

Calories: 85 ;Fat: 3.8g;Sat Fat: 0.6g ;Carbohydrates: 8.7g ;Fiber: 4g ;Sugar: 3.7g ;Protein: 6g

Slow-Cooked Mediterranean Chicken and Chickpea Soup

Prep Time: 4 hours 20 minutes | Cook Time: 20 minutes | Serves: 6

- 1½ cups dried chickpeas, soaked overnight
- 4 cups water
- 1 large yellow onion, finely chopped
- 1 (15 oz.) can no-salt-added diced tomatoes, preferably fire-roasted
- 2 tbsp. tomato paste
- 4 cloves garlic, finely chopped
- 1 bay leaf
- 4 tsp. ground cumin
- 4 tsp. paprika
- ¼ tsp. cayenne pepper
- ¼ tsp. ground pepper
- 2 lbs. bone-in chicken thighs, skin removed, trimmed
- 1 (14 oz.) can artichoke hearts, drained and quartered
- ¼ cup halved pitted oil-cured olives
- ½ tsp. salt
- ¼ cup chopped fresh parsley or cilantro

1. Drain the chickpeas and place them in a 6-quart (or larger) slow cooker. Add 4 cups water, onion, tomatoes and their juice, tomato paste, garlic, bay leaf, cumin, paprika, cayenne, and ground pepper. Stir to combine.
2. Add the chicken.
3. Cover and cook on low for 8 hours or on high for 4 hours.
4. Transfer the chicken to a clean cutting board and let it cool slightly. Discard the bay leaf.
5. Add the artichokes, olives, and salt to the slow cooker and stir to combine.
6. Shred the chicken, discarding the bones. Stir the chicken back into the soup.

PER SERVING

Calories 447 ;Protein 33.6g ; Carbohydrates 43g ;Dietary fiber 11.6g; Sugars 8.5g ;Fat 15.3g ;Sodium 761.8mg

Salmon & Veggie Soup

Prep Time: 10 minutes|Cook time: 30 minutes|Serves: 2

- ½ shallot, chopped
- ½ Jalapeno pepper, chopped
- 1 small bell peppers, seeded and chopped
- 1 boneless salmon fillets, cubed
- 1 tablespoon fresh lemon juice
- 1 tablespoon olive oil
- 1 garlic clove, minced
- 2½ cups low-sodium vegetable broth
- ½ head Chinese cabbage, chopped
- 2 tablespoons fresh cilantro, minced
- Fresh ground black pepper to taste

1. Take a large soup pan, heat oil over medium heat and fry shallot and garlic for about two to three minutes.
2. Add cabbage and bell peppers and fry them for about three to four minutes.
3. Add broth and bring to a boil over high heat.
4. Reduce the heat to medium-low and gently cook for about ten minutes.
5. Add salmon and cook for about five to six minutes.
6. Stir in the cilantro, lemon juice and black pepper and cook for about one to two minutes.
7. Serve hot and enjoy!

PER SERVING

Calories: 250 ;Fat: 13.2g ; Sat Fat: 1.9g ;Carbohydrates: 11.7g ;Fiber: 3.1g ;Sugar: 5.8g ;Protein: 23.8g

Jalapeño Chicken Soup

Prep time: 15 minutes | Cook time: 30 minutes | Serves 4

- 1 tablespoon olive oil
- 1 sweet onion, diced
- 2 celery stalks, chopped
- 1 jalapeño pepper, seeded and finely chopped
- 2 teaspoons minced garlic
- 6 cups low-sodium chicken broth
- 1½ cups chopped cooked chicken breast
- 1 cup canned low-sodium black beans, drained and rinsed
- 1 cup shredded spinach
- Juice of 1 lime
- Freshly ground black pepper
- 2 tablespoons chopped fresh cilantro, for garnish

1. Heat the oil in a large saucepan over medium-high heat. Sauté the onion, celery, pepper, and garlic until softened, about 4 minutes.
2. Stir in the chicken broth, chicken, and black beans and bring the soup to a boil.
3. Reduce the heat to low and simmer until the vegetables are tender, about 15 minutes.
4. Add the spinach and lime juice and simmer until the greens are wilted, about 2 minutes.
5. Season with black pepper and serve topped with cilantro.
6. Store any cooled leftover soup in a sealed container in the refrigerator for up to 3 days, or in the freezer for up to 1 month.

PER SERVING

Sodium: 564mg; Calories: 157; Total Fat: 18g; Saturated Fat: 1g; Total Carbohydrates: 9g; Net Carbs: 5g; Fiber: 4g; Protein: 18g; Potassium: 247mg; Cholesterol: 52mg

Tuscan Croutons Bean Stew

Prep Time: 15 minutes|Cook Time: 1 hour and 30 minutes|Serves: 6

CROUTONS:

- 1 tablespoon olive oil
- 2 garlic cloves, quartered
- 1 slice whole-grain bread, cut into ½-inch cubes
- Soup:
- 2 cups white beans, soaked and drained
- 6 cups water
- 1 bay leaf
- 2 tablespoons olive oil
- 1 cup yellow onion, chopped
- 3 carrots, peeled and chopped
- 6 garlic cloves, chopped
- ¼ teaspoon black pepper
- 1 tablespoon fresh rosemary chopped
- 1½ cups low-sodium vegetable stock

1. Add the oil to a large skillet and heat it.
2. Stir in the garlic and sauté for 1 minute.
3. Let it sit for 10 minutes, then remove the garlic from the oil.
4. Return the skillet with the oil to the heat and add the bread cubes.
5. Sauté for 5 minutes until golden brown, then set them aside.
6. Mix the white beans, water, and bay leaf in a pot.
7. Boil the beans on high heat, then reduce the heat to a simmer.
8. Partially cover the beans, then cook for 60 to 70 minutes until al dente.
9. Drain the beans and keep a ½ cup of the cooking liquid.
10. Discard the bay leaf and transfer the beans to a bowl.
11. Mix the reserved liquid with ½ cup of the beans in a bowl.
12. Mash this mixture to form a paste and return this mash to the remaining beans.
13. Place the cooking pot on the stove and heat olive oil in it.
14. Add the carrots and onion. Sauté for 7 minutes, then add the garlic.
15. Cook for 1 minute, then add the rosemary, pepper, bean mixture, and stock.
16. Allow the mixture to cool, then boil it and reduce the heat to a simmer.
17. Let it simmer for 5 more minutes.
18. Serve the soup with the croutons on top.
19. Garnish with a rosemary sprig and enjoy.

PER SERVING

Calories 301 ;Fat 6g ;Sodium 62mg;Carbs 24g ;Fiber 0.2g ;Sugar 1g ;Protein 16g

Chapter 11
Salads

Pork Salad with Orange Slices

Prep time: 5 minutes | Cook time: 5 minutes| Serves 4

- 1 tsp. crushed garlic
- ½ medium red bell pepper, chopped
- 4 medium spring onions, chopped
- 1 tin no-salt-added black beans, rinsed and drained
- 2 cups cooked pork tenderloin, no salt added, fat removed
- ½ tsp. French mustard
- ½ tsp. crushed dry oregano
- 2 tsp. extra-virgin olive oil
- 1½ tsp. brown sugar
- 2 tbsp. canola oil
- ¼ cup apple cider vinegar
- ¼ cup fresh parsley, chopped
- ¼ cup kalamata olives
- 1 cup baby tomatoes, halved
- 3 cups salad greens
- 1 medium orange, thinly sliced
- ½ cup green grapes (optional)

1. Using a large mixing bowl, combine the garlic, pepper, spring onions, black beans, and pork.
2. In a separate bowl, whisk together the mustard, oregano, olive oil, brown sugar, canola oil, vinegar, and fresh parsley until all of the sugar granules have disappeared.
3. Pour the dressing over the salad and toss to coat before covering and chilling for 30 minutes.
4. Once the salad is properly chilled, add the olives and tomatoes to the bowl and carefully mix until everything is just combined.
5. Serve the salad on a bed of salad greens, topped with orange slices and grapes (if included).

PER SERVING

Calories: 202; Sodium 71mg; Total Fat: 8½g; Saturated Fat: 1g; Cholesterol: 3mg; Total Carbohydrates: 15g; Fiber: 4g; Protein: 16g

Cheesy Brussels Sprout & Herb Salad

Prep time: 5 minutes | Cook time: 45 minutes| Serves 6

- 1 cup pearl barley
- 2 whole garlic cloves, peeled
- Himalayan salt
- 1 lb. Brussels sprouts, trimmed and halved
- Extra-virgin olive oil
- Freshly ground black pepper
- 1 can cranberry beans, rinsed and drained
- ¼ cup fresh chives, finely chopped
- 2 tbsp. balsamic vinegar
- ¼ cup chopped onions
- 1 tbsp. fresh lemon juice
- 1 tsp. lemon rind, finely shredded
- 1 cup ricotta cheese
- ¼ cup fresh parsley, chopped

1. Over high heat, in a large pot, combine the barley,

garlic cloves, and 1 pinch of salt with 6 cups of water. Once the water reaches a rolling boil, reduce the heat and allow the barley to simmer for 30-35 minutes, or until properly cooked. Strain and remove the garlic cloves before allowing the barley to rest for 10 minutes.

2. Cover a rimmed baking pan with tin foil and set the oven to preheat at 400°F.
3. In a large bowl, toss the halved sprouts with 1 tbsp. oil and a generous sprinkling of pepper until evenly coated. Fan the coated sprouts out over the prepared baking pan and place in the oven for 20-25 minutes, or until the sprouts are evenly browned and the edges are nice and crispy.
4. Meanwhile, heat the cranberry beans in the microwave with ¼ cup of water until heated through. Drain the beans and set aside on the counter in a large bowl.
5. Toss the roasted sprouts with the beans and chives. Add 1 tsp. oil and a small pinch of salt.
6. In a separate bowl, whisk together the vinegar, onions, lemon juice, lemon rind, 3 tbsp. oil, and a pinch of black pepper.
7. Gently fold the barley into the bowl with the beans and sprouts. Sprinkle the dressing over the dish and toss to combine.
8. Spoon the salad onto four plates in equal amounts. Garnish with ricotta and parsley before serving.

PER SERVING

Calories: 532; Sodium: 131mg; Total Fat: 19g; Saturated Fat: 4g; Cholesterol: 15mg; Total Carbohydrates: 74g; Fiber: 19g; Protein: 19g

Shrimp & Corn Chowder

Prep Time: 20 minutes|Cook Time: 30 minutes| Serves 6

- 3 tablespoons canola oil
- 1 yellow onion, peeled and diced
- 2 carrots, peeled and sliced
- 2 celery stalks, diced
- 4 baby Yukon Gold or red potatoes, diced
- 3 to 4 garlic cloves, peeled and minced
- ¼ cup all-purpose flour
- 3 cups unsalted vegetable or chicken stock
- ½ cup milk
- ¾ teaspoon kosher or sea salt
- ¼ teaspoon ground black pepper
- ¼ teaspoon ground cayenne pepper
- 4 cups fresh or frozen corn kernels
- 1 pound raw shrimp, peeled, deveined, and tails removed, chopped
- 2 scallions, thinly sliced

1. In a Dutch oven or stockpot, heat the oil over medium heat. Add the onion, carrots, celery, and potatoes to the pot. Cook for 5 to 7 minutes, until the vegetables are softened. Stir in the garlic and soften for one minute. Then stir in the flour to make a roux. Increase the heat to medium-high and slowly whisk in the stock and bring to a simmer, taking care to whisk out any lumps of roux so the stock is smooth. After the roux starts to turn brown, whisk in the milk, salt, black pepper, and cayenne pepper. Let simmer, stirring regularly, until thickened, 7 to 8 minutes.
2. Add the corn and shrimp and simmer for an additional 4 to 5 minutes, until the shrimp is fully cooked. Taste and adjust the seasoning, if necessary.
3. Divide the soup evenly into bowls and top with sliced scallions.
4. For leftovers, divide the chowder evenly into microwaveable airtight containers and store in the refrigerator for up to 5 days. Reheat in the microwave on high for 2 to 3 minutes, until heated through, stirring as needed.

PER SERVING

Calories: 340; Total Fat: 9g; Saturated Fat: 1g; Cholesterol: 115mg; Sodium: 473mg; Potassium: 613mg; Total Carbohydrate: 45g; Fiber: 5g; Sugars: 8g; Protein: 23g

Chicken & Mandarin Orange Salad with Sesame Ginger Dressing

Prep Time: 20 minutes|Cook Time: 12 minutes | Serves 4

FOR THE DRESSING:

- ¼ cup sodium-free rice wine vinegar
- 1 tablespoon sesame oil
- 1 tablespoon honey
- 2 garlic cloves, peeled and minced
- 1-inch piece fresh ginger, peeled and minced
- ¼ teaspoon kosher or sea salt

FOR THE SALAD:

- 1 tablespoon canola oil
- 1 pound boneless skinless chicken breasts
- ¼ teaspoon kosher or sea salt
- ¼ teaspoon ground black pepper
- 1 large head Napa cabbage, shredded
- 1 cup shredded red cabbage
- ½ cup shredded carrots
- ½ cup shelled edamame
- ½ cup sliced almonds
- 2 scallions, thinly sliced
- 8-ounce can mandarin oranges, drained
- TO MAKE THE DRESSING:
- Combine all the dressing ingredients in a jar or bowl and shake or whisk to combine. Refrigerate until ready to use.

TO MAKE THE SALAD:

1. Heat the canola oil in a skillet over medium heat. Season the chicken breasts with the salt and black pepper and place in the skillet. Cook for 5 to 6 minutes per side, until the internal temperature reaches 165°F. Place on a cutting board for 5 to 10 minutes to cool and then thinly slice against the grain.
2. In a large bowl, toss the Napa cabbage, red cabbage, carrots, and edamame together with the dressing. Divide into 4 bowls and top with the sliced chicken, almonds, scallions, and mandarin oranges.

PER SERVING

Calories: 394; Total Fat: 19g; Saturated Fat: 2g; Cholesterol: 70mg; Sodium: 544mg; Potassium: 494mg; Total Carbohydrate: 29g; Fiber: 5g; Sugars: 16g; Protein: 32g

Salmon & Avocado Cobb Salad with Buttermilk Ranch Dressing
Prep Time: 20 minutes | Cook Time: 12 minutes | Serves 4

FOR THE SALAD:
- 1 pound salmon fillets, skin removed
- 1 tablespoon olive oil
- ¼ teaspoon kosher or sea salt
- ¼ teaspoon ground black pepper
- 6 cups romaine lettuce, chopped
- 1 pint cherry tomatoes, halved
- 2 large hard-boiled eggs, peeled and quartered
- 1 avocado, peeled and diced
- 2 scallions, thinly sliced

FOR THE DRESSING:
- ⅓ cup low-fat buttermilk
- 2 tablespoons plain nonfat Greek yogurt
- 2 tablespoons mayonnaise
- Zest and juice of ½ lemon
- 1 tablespoon chopped fresh herbs of your choice like dill, parsley, or chives
- 1 to 2 garlic cloves, peeled and minced
- ½ teaspoon hot sauce
- ½ teaspoon ground black pepper
- ¼ teaspoon kosher or sea salt

TO MAKE THE SALAD:
1. Preheat the oven to 400°F. Place the salmon fillets in a greased baking dish. Drizzle with olive oil and season with salt and black pepper. Roast for 8 to 12 minutes, until the salmon flakes easily with a fork. Let slightly cool.
2. Assemble four salads by evenly distributing the romaine, cherry tomatoes, hard-boiled eggs, avocados, and scallions onto 4 large plates or in 4 large containers.
3. Whisk the dressing ingredients until combined.
4. Add the dressing to the salad and toss if serving immediately. Top with the salmon fillet. If storing, keep the salmon fillets and salad in airtight containers for up to 3 days. Store the dressing separately in small airtight containers.

PER SERVING
Calories: 365; Total Fat: 23g; Saturated Fat: 4g; Cholesterol: 158mg; Sodium: 486mg; Potassium: 548mg; Total Carbohydrate: 11g; Fiber: 6g; Sugars: 4g; Protein: 30g

Rustic Tomato Panzanella Salad
Prep Time: 15 minutes | Cook Time: 8 minutes | Serves 4

- 1 small baguette, cubed (about 5 ounces total)
- 3 tablespoons olive oil, divided
- 2 to 3 large ripe tomatoes, cubed
- 1 tablespoon red wine vinegar
- ¼ teaspoon kosher or sea salt
- ¼ teaspoon ground black pepper
- ¼ cup fresh basil leaves, torn

1. Preheat the oven to 400°F.
2. Place the cubed baguette on a baking sheet and drizzle with half of the olive oil. Roast in the oven for 8 minutes, until crisp. Transfer the croutons to a mixing bowl.
3. To the bowl, add the tomatoes, red wine vinegar, salt, black pepper, and remaining olive oil. Toss to combine, and top with the fresh basil. Serve immediately.

PER SERVING
Calories: 200; Total Fat: 11g; Saturated Fat: 1g; Cholesterol: 0mg; Sodium: 339mg; Potassium: 217mg; Total Carbohydrate: 18g; Fiber: 2g; Sugars: 0g; Protein: 3g

Baked Beetroot & Halloumi Salad
Prep time: 5 minutes | Cook time: 25 minutes | Serves 4

- 4 large beetroots, scrubbed
- 8 oz. salad greens
- ¼ cup balsamic vinegar
- ¼ cup halloumi cheese, shredded
- ¼ cup lightly toasted almond slivers

1. Set the oven to preheat at 350°F with the wire rack in the center of the oven.
2. Tightly wrap each beetroot in tin foil before placing them on a baking sheet.
3. Bake the beets in the oven for 25-35 minutes, or until a knife can easily slide in and out of each beet. Remove the sheet from the oven and allow the beets to cool.
4. When the beets are cool enough to work with, remove the foil and discard the skins. The skins should slide off the beets when properly cooked.
5. Slice the beets into semi-thick wedges before placing them in a bowl.
6. Add the salad greens to the bowl and toss in the vinegar until the beets and salad greens are evenly coated.
7. Garnish the salad with halloumi and almond slivers before serving.

PER SERVING
Calories: 197; Sodium: 171mg; Total Fat: 14g; Saturated Fat: 2g; Total Carbohydrates: 16g; Fiber: 4g; Protein: 6g

Spinach & Artichoke Grilled Cheese
Prep Time: 15 minutes|Cook Time: 15 minutes| Serves 4

- 2 cups baby spinach leaves, chopped
- 1 cup jarred marinated artichoke hearts, chopped
- ¼ cup nonfat plain Greek yogurt
- 2 to 3 garlic cloves, peeled and minced
- ¼ teaspoon ground black pepper
- ⅛ teaspoon kosher or sea salt
- 8 slices whole-wheat bread
- 4 slices mozzarella cheese
- 1 tablespoon olive oil

1. In a bowl, mix together the spinach, artichoke hearts, Greek yogurt, garlic, black pepper, and salt until combined.
2. Heat a skillet to medium. Prepare the sandwiches by placing 4 slices bread on a cutting board. Evenly distribute the spinach artichoke mixture onto each slice and top with a slice of mozzarella cheese. Top with another slice of bread. Brush top slices of bread with the olive oil. Place the sandwiches olive oil-side down in the hot skillet. Cook for 2 to 3 minutes, until browned. Brush the other slices of bread with the olive oil, then flip and cook for another 2 to 3 minutes, until the bottom is browned and the cheese is melted. Place a lid over the skillet, if necessary, to assist with melting the cheese.
3. Slice each sandwich in half and serve.

PER SERVING

Calories: 355; Total Fat: 13g; Saturated Fat: 4g; Cholesterol: 11mg; Sodium: 511mg; Potassium: 53mg; Total Carbohydrate: 44g; Fiber: 9g; Sugars: 7g; Protein: 16g

Strawberry, Chicken & Mozzarella Bow Tie Pasta Salad
Prep Time: 10 minutes|Cook Time: 20 minutes

FOR THE DRESSING:

- 2 tablespoons balsamic vinegar
- 1 tablespoon Dijon mustard
- 1 tablespoon honey
- ¼ cup olive oil
- ¼ teaspoon kosher or sea salt
- ¼ teaspoon ground black pepper

FOR THE SALAD:

- 8 ounces whole-grain bow tie pasta
- 1 tablespoon canola oil
- ½ pound boneless skinless chicken breasts
- ¼ teaspoon kosher or sea salt
- ¼ teaspoon ground black pepper
- 1 quart strawberries, hulled and sliced
- 1 cup fresh baby spinach
- ½ cup mini fresh mozzarella balls
- ¼ cup sliced almonds

FOR THE DRESSING:

- In a large bowl, whisk together the dressing ingredients until combined. Taste and adjust seasoning, if necessary.

FOR THE SALAD:

1. Bring a large pot of water to a boil. Cook the pasta according to the package directions.
2. In that same pot, heat the canola oil over medium heat. Season the chicken breasts with the salt and black pepper. Sauté the chicken for 6 to 7 minutes per side, until the internal temperature reaches 165°F. Place on a plate or cutting board to cool. Chop into bite-size pieces.
3. Place the strawberries, spinach, mozzarella, cooled pasta, and diced chicken into the bowl with the dressing and toss to combine. Refrigerate until chilled, and sprinkle the almonds on top before serving.

PER SERVING

Calories: 384; Total Fat: 18g; Saturated Fat: 3g; Cholesterol: 33mg; Sodium: 406mg; Potassium: 207mg; Total Carbohydrate: 40g; Fiber: 6g; Sugars: 8g; Protein: 17g

Mediterranean Chickpea Tuna Salad
Prep Time: 20 minutes |Cook Time: 10 minutes | Serves 4

FOR THE DRESSING:

- 2 tablespoons red wine vinegar
- Zest and juice of ½ lemon
- 1 tablespoon honey
- 1 teaspoon dried oregano leaves
- ¼ teaspoon kosher or sea salt
- ¼ teaspoon ground black pepper
- ¼ cup olive oil

FOR THE SALAD:

- 1 (15-ounce) can no-salt-added chickpeas, rinsed and drained
- 1 6.4-ounce pouch albacore tuna
- ½ English cucumber, diced
- 1 pint cherry tomatoes, quartered
- ¼ cup pitted kalamata olives
- 2 tablespoons crumbled feta cheese
- TO MAKE THE DRESSING:
- In a bowl, whisk together red wine vinegar, lemon zest and juice, honey, dried oregano, salt, and black pepper. Slowly whisk in the olive oil until combined.

TO MAKE THE SALAD:

1. In a separate bowl, add the chickpeas, tuna, cucumber, tomatoes, olives, and feta cheese.
2. If eating immediately, combine the salad and dressing in a large bowl. If eating later, store the salad and dressing separately in airtight containers. It will stay fresh in the refrigerator for up to 3 days.

PER SERVING

Calories: 347; Total Fat: 20g; Saturated Fat: 2g; Cholesterol: 22mg; Sodium: 574mg; Potassium: 367mg; Total Carbohydrate: 28g; Fiber: 6g; Sugars: 8g; Protein: 17g

Waldorf Chicken Salad

Prep Time: 20 minutes|Cook Time: 12 minutes

- ¼ cup plain nonfat Greek yogurt
- 2 tablespoons mayonnaise
- 2 tablespoons Dijon mustard
- 1 tablespoon honey
- ¼ teaspoon kosher or sea salt
- ¼ teaspoon ground black pepper
- 3 cups chopped cooked chicken breast
- 1 apple, diced
- 2 celery stalks, diced
- 1 cup green or red seedless grapes, halved
- ¼ cup chopped walnuts

1. In a bowl, whisk together the yogurt, mayonnaise, Dijon mustard, honey, salt, and black pepper. Fold in the cooked chicken, apple, celery, grapes, and walnuts.
2. Store in airtight containers in the refrigerator for up to 3 days.

PER SERVING

Calories: 353; Total Fat: 14g; Saturated Fat: 2g; Cholesterol: 92mg; Sodium: 475mg; Potassium: 283mg; Total Carbohydrate: 20g; Fiber: 2g; Sugars: 17g; Protein: 36g

Avocado Egg Salad

Prep Time: 10 minutes|Cook Time: 20 minutes| Serves 4

- 8 large eggs
- 2 avocados, peeled
- Zest and juice of ½ lemon
- ¼ cup flat-leaf Italian parsley, chopped
- ¼ teaspoon kosher or sea salt
- ¼ teaspoon ground black pepper

1. Place the eggs in a saucepan and cover with cold water. Bring to a boil, shut the heat off, and place a fitted lid on the top.
2. Set a timer for 17 to 18 minutes. Drain the hot water, and pour cold water over the eggs until cooled. Remove the shells and discard. Cut the eggs into smaller pieces.
3. In a bowl, mash the avocados. Add the eggs to the bowl, along with the lemon zest and juice, Italian parsley, salt, and ground black pepper. Stir to combine and serve.

PER SERVING

Calories: 289; Total Fat: 23g; Saturated Fat: 6g; Cholesterol: 422mg; Sodium: 292mg; Potassium: 453mg; Total Carbohydrate: 8g; Fiber: 6g; Sugars: 0g; Protein: 14g

Spicy Asian Chicken Salad

Prep time: 5 minutes | Cook time: 5 minutes| Serves 8

- ¾ cups raw basmati rice
- 2 tbsp. green bell peppers, diced
- 1 celery stalk, diced
- 4 spring onions, diced
- 10 oz. frozen green peas, defrosted
- 1½ lbs. diced chicken breast, cooked (no salt, fat discarded)
- ⅛ tsp. ground ginger
- ¼ tsp. hot chili oil
- 1 tbsp. low sodium French mustard
- 1 tbsp. low sodium soy sauce
- 2 tbsp. dry sherry
- 2 tbsp. extra-virgin olive oil
- ¼ cup plain rice vinegar
- Fresh coriander leaves, chopped for garnish

1. Prepare the rice by following the instructions on the package. (Note: Leave out any salt or oils, such as butter.) Drain and allow to cool to room temperature in a large bowl.
2. Once the rice is cool, gently fold in the bell peppers, celery, spring onions, peas, and cooked chicken.
3. In a separate bowl, whisk together the ginger, chili sauce, mustard, soy sauce, sherry, olive oil, and rice vinegar.
4. Sprinkle the vinaigrette over the salad and toss to coat. Cover the bowl with cling wrap and chill for a minimum of 30 minutes. (Note: You may also place the salad in a mold coated with cooking spray to allow for easy removal.)
5. Once the salad is properly chilled, transfer to a serving platter and garnish with coriander leaves before serving.

PER SERVING

Calories: 232; Sodium: 232mg; Total Fat: 6½g; Saturated Fat: 1g; Cholesterol: 54mg; Total Carbohydrates: 20g; Fiber: 3g; Protein: 22g

Old-Fashioned Saucy Bean Salad

Prep time: 5 minutes | Cook time: 5 minutes| Serves 6

- ½ medium yellow bell pepper, chopped
- ½ cup shallots, chopped
- 7 Oz. canned green beans, no salt added, rinsed and drained
- 7 Oz. canned turtle beans, no salt added, rinsed and drained
- 7 oz. canned kidney beans, no salt added, rinsed and drained
- ¼ tsp. white pepper
- ⅜ tsp. Himalayan salt
- 1 tbsp. extra-virgin olive oil
- 1½ tbsp. brown sugar
- 3 tbsp. red wine vinegar

1. Gently combine the bell pepper, shallots, green beans, turtle beans, and kidney beans in a medium bowl.
2. In a separate bowl, whisk together the white pepper, salt, olive oil, brown sugar, and red wine vinegar until properly combined, or until there are no more visible sugar granules.
3. Drizzle the vinaigrette over the salad and toss until all of the beans are evenly coated. Serve immediately.

PER SERVING

Calories: 110; Sodium: 148mg; Total Fat: 2½g; Saturated Fat: 0g; Cholesterol: 0mg; Total Carbohydrates: 18g; Fiber: 4g; Protein: 5g

Vinaigrette Potato Salad

Prep time: 5 minutes | Cook time: 15 minutes| Serves 6

- 12 oz. red potatoes, skin on
- ½ medium celery stalk, finely chopped
- ½ cup shallots, chopped
- ⅛ tsp. cayenne pepper
- ¼ tsp. Himalayan salt
- 2 tsp. crushed garlic
- 1 tsp. dried dill, crushed
- 2 tbsp. extra-virgin olive oil
- 3 tbsp. apple cider vinegar

1. Bring 8 cups of water to a rolling boil over high heat. Once the water is boiling, add the potatoes and cook for 18-20 minutes, or until the potatoes begin to soften and a knife can be easily inserted. Strain the potatoes through a colander and allow to cool until easy to handle (approx. 1 hour).
2. When the potatoes are cool enough to handle, slice them into semi-thick slices and toss them in a large bowl with the shallots and celery.
3. In a separate bowl, whisk together the cayenne pepper, salt, garlic, dried dill, olive oil, and apple cider vinegar.
4. Drizzle the vinaigrette over the salad and gently toss to combine. Refrigerate or serve immediately.

PER SERVING

Calories: 93; Sodium: 105mg; Total Fat: 4½g; Saturated Fat: ½g; Cholesterol: 0mg; Total Carbohydrates: 12g; Fiber: 2g; Protein: 1g

Middle-Eastern Mint Tabbouleh

Prep time: 5 minutes | Cook time: 15 minutes| Serves 4

- ⅓ cup fresh mint, chopped
- 4 medium spring onions, finely chopped
- 1 small English cucumber, sliced
- 1 medium red bell pepper, diced
- 2 cups fresh parsley, chopped
- ½ cup fine-grain bulgur, cooked
- ½ tsp. white pepper
- ¼ tsp. Himalayan salt
- 2 tsp. crushed garlic
- 2 tbsp. extra-virgin olive oil
- 2 medium lemons, juiced
- 20 cherry tomatoes, halved

1. In a large bowl, toss together the mint, spring onions, cucumber, red bell pepper, parsley, and cooked bulgur. Season with the white pepper and Himalayan salt.
2. In a small glass bowl, whisk together the garlic, olive oil, and lemon juice.
3. Drizzle the dressing over the salad and gently toss until all of the ingredients are evenly coated. Cover the bowl with cling wrap and chill for 3-4 hours.
4. Once the salad is properly chilled, garnish with the halved cherry tomatoes and serve.

PER SERVING

Calories: 73; Sodium: 73mg; Total Fat: 3g; Saturated Fat: ½g; Cholesterol: 0mg; Total Carbohydrates: 10g; Fiber: 3g; Protein: 2g

Mixed Vegetable Salad with Lime Dressing
Prep Time: 30 minutes|Cook Time: 30 minutes|Serves: 6

- ¼ cup canola oil
- ¼ cup extra-virgin olive oil
- 3 tbsp. lime juice
- 1½ tbsp. finely chopped fresh cilantro
- ½ tsp. salt
- ½ tsp. ground pepper
- 2 cups mixed vegetables, steamed (sliced small red potatoes, carrots or beets, green beans, peas) and raw (sliced radishes, cucumbers, or tomatoes)
- 6 leaves romaine or leaf lettuce
- 1 small bunch watercress, large stems removed
- 1 large hard-boiled egg, sliced
- 1 thick slice of red onion, broken into rings
- Crumbled Mexican queso fresco, feta, or farmer cheese for garnish

1. Whisk the canola and olive oils, lime juice, cilantro, salt, and pepper in a medium bowl until thoroughly blended. Add the mixed vegetables and toss to coat.

PER SERVING

Calories 214 ;Protein 2.6g ; Carbohydrates 7.7g ;Dietary fiber 1.9g ;Sugars 1.8g ;Fat 19.8g ;Sodium 216.6mg

Nutty Turmeric Tuna Salad
Prep time: 5 minutes | Cook time: 5 minutes| Serves 6

- ½ tsp. ground cumin
- 2 tsp. curry powder
- 1 tsp. turmeric powder
- 2 tbsp. almond milk
- ⅓ cup light mayonnaise
- 2 tins no salt added, albacore tuna (4½ oz. each)
- ⅓ cup raisins
- ½ cup lightly toasted almond slivers
- 2 medium celery stalks, finely chopped

1. Using a large bowl, combine the cumin, curry powder, turmeric, almond milk, mayonnaise, and tuna.
2. Add the raisins, almond slivers, and celery stalk to the bowl and mix until all of the ingredients are properly combined.
3. Chill for about 1 hour, or serve straight away. (Note: Do not press the salad down or try to compact the ingredients.)

PER SERVING

Calories: 162; Sodium: 158mg; Total Fat: 8½g: Saturated Fat: ½g; Cholesterol: 23mg; Total Carbohydrates: 11g; Fiber: 2g; Protein: 14g

Brussels & Berry Balsamic Slaw
Prep time: 5 minutes | Cook time: 5 minutes| Serves 4

- 1 tsp. raw honey
- 2 tbsp. balsamic vinegar
- ¼ cup extra-virgin olive oil
- Freshly ground black pepper
- ½ cup unsalted lightly toasted hazelnuts
- 1 cup strawberries, halved
- 1 cup blueberries
- 1 parsnip, grated
- 1 large carrot, shredded
- 1 jicama, peeled and shredded
- 4 cups Brussels sprouts, shredded

1. Using a small glass bowl, whisk together the honey, balsamic vinegar, and olive oil. Season to taste with pepper before setting aside on the counter.
2. In a separate large bowl, combine the hazelnuts, strawberries, blueberries, parsnip, carrot, jicama, and Brussels sprouts.
3. Drizzle the vinaigrette over the salad and gently toss until all the ingredients are evenly coated.
4. Serve immediately.

PER SERVING

Calories: 365; Sodium: 27mg; Total Fat: 23g; Saturated Fat: 3g; Cholesterol: 0mg; Total Carbohydrates: 37g; Fiber: 14g; Protein: 5g

Zucchini Pasta Salad
Prep time: 5 minutes | Cook time: 5 minutes| Serves 4

- ¼ cup parmesan, shredded
- 2 tbsp. balsamic vinegar
- ¼ cup extra-virgin olive oil
- freshly ground black pepper
- 1 tbsp. fresh basil, chopped
- 1 whole spring onion, chopped
- 2 bell peppers, orange and yellow, chopped
- 1 zucchini, chopped
- 1 cup cherry tomatoes, chopped
- 4 cup whole-grain elbow pasta, cooked

1. In a small glass bowl, use a fork to whisk the parmesan, balsamic vinegar, olive oil, and a pinch of black pepper together until properly combined.
2. In a separate large bowl, toss together the basil, spring onion, peppers, zucchini, cherry tomatoes, and elbow pasta.
3. Drizzle the balsamic vinaigrette over the pasta and gently stir until all of the ingredients are properly combined. Serve immediately.

PER SERVING

Calories: 307; Sodium: 159mg; Total Fat: 18g; Saturated Fat: 5g; Cholesterol: 12mg; Total Carbohydrates: 30g; Fiber: 6g; Protein: 10g

Spiralized Zucchini Pasta Salad

Prep time: 5 minutes | Cook time: 5 minutes| Serves 6

- 2 large zucchinis
- Extra-virgin olive oil
- 1 large red bell pepper, finely chopped
- 2 tsp. crushed garlic
- 2 tsp. dried basil, crushed
- 2 whole garlic cloves, peeled
- 2 tsp. fresh lemon juice
- ¼ cup plain, non-fat, unsweetened Greek yogurt
- 1 large Hass avocado
- Himalayan salt
- Freshly ground black pepper
- 2 cups frozen shelled edamame beans
- 3 tbsp. chives, finely chopped
- 15 oz. turtle beans, rinsed and drained
- 1 cup baby tomatoes, halved

1. Prepare the zucchinis by trimming the ends and carefully slicing them into spirals, either by hand or by machine. Transfer the spiralized zucchinis to a paper towel-lined bowl and set aside.
2. Heat a large skillet over medium-high heat before adding 1 tbsp. olive oil to the pan. Once the oil is nice and hot, gently toss the spiraled zucchini, red bell pepper, and garlic for about 6-8 minutes, or until the vegetables are tender. (Note: You don't want to overcook the zucchini spirals to the point where they fall apart.) Transfer the cooked vegetables to a plate once cooked.
3. While the vegetables are frying, pulse the basil, whole garlic cloves, lemon juice, yogurt, avocado, and 1 tbsp. olive until you have a lump-free dressing. Season to taste with a small pinch of salt and pepper. Set aside.
4. Microwave the frozen edamame beans on high for 3-5 minutes, or until properly cooked. Strain and transfer to a large bowl. The water from the frozen beans should be sufficient to cook the beans, but you may add 1-2 tbsp. water if you feel like the beans are drying out.
5. In the bowl with the cooked beans, gently toss in the chives, turtle beans, tomatoes, and cooked vegetables.
6. Drizzle the dressing over the salad and gently toss until all of the ingredients are properly combined.
7. Serve immediate.

PER SERVING

Calories: 259; Sodium: 27mg; Total Fat: 13g; Saturated Fat: 2g; Cholesterol: < 1mg; Total Carbohydrates: 26g; Fiber: 10g; Protein: 16g

Turkey & Baby Greens Salad

Prep time: 5 minutes | Cook time: 15 minutes| Serves 4

- 1 tbsp. sunflower oil
- 1 lb. turkey breast, cut into 1-inch cubes
- 2 tsp. extra-virgin olive oil
- 2 firm, but ripe avocados
- ¼ cup coriander leaves, chopped
- ¼ cup sunflower seeds
- 1 large heirloom tomato, chopped
- 1 small shallot, diced
- 8 cups mixed baby greens
- Himalayan salt
- Freshly ground black pepper

1. Heat the oil in a large skillet over medium-high heat. When the oil is nice and hot toss the turkey in the skillet for about 10 minutes, or until properly cooked. Transfer the cooked turkey to a covered dish and set aside on the counter while you prepare the rest of the dish.
2. Peel the avocados and remove the pips before slicing into semi-thick slices. Return the skillet to the heat with 1 tsp. olive oil and fry the avocado slices for 1-2 minutes, or until golden around the edges.
3. In a large bowl, toss together the coriander leaves, sunflower seeds, tomato, shallot, and baby greens. Season to taste with a small pinch of salt and pepper before drizzling with the remaining teaspoon of olive oil.
4. Serve the turkey cubes on a bed of the tossed baby greens salad.

PER SERVING

Calories: 370; Sodium: 137mg; Total Fat: 21g; Saturated Fat: 3g; Cholesterol: 70mg; Total Carbohydrates: 17g; Fiber: 10g; Protein: 33g

Sweet & Tangy Apple Slaw

Prep time: 5 minutes | Cook time: 5 minutes| Serves 2

- 2 tsp. raw honey
- 1 tbsp. extra-virgin olive oil
- 1 tbsp. balsamic vinegar
- 1 small green apple, thinly sliced
- 4 cups cabbage, shredded
- Freshly ground black pepper

1. In a large bowl, whisk together the honey, olive oil, and balsamic vinegar.
2. Toss in the apple and cabbage until all of the ingredients are properly combined. Season to taste with pepper.
3. Serve straight away.

PER SERVING

Calories: 176; Sodium: 34mg; Total Fat: 7g; Saturated Fat: 1g; Cholesterol: 0mg; Total Carbohydrates: 28g; Fiber: 6g; Protein: 3g

Shrimp Salad with Ginger Vinaigrette

Prep time: 5 minutes | Cook time: 5 minutes| Serves 2

- 1 cup frozen green peas
- 8 oz. shrimp, peeled, deveined, and cooked
- 2 tbsp. spring onions, chopped
- ¼ cup cashews, chopped
- 1 cup carrots, grated
- ⅓ tsp. cayenne pepper
- 1 tsp. low-sodium soy sauce
- ½ tbsp. sesame oil
- 1 tbsp. extra-virgin olive oil
- 2 tbsp. unseasoned rice vinegar
- 6 cups mixed baby greens

1. Bring a medium pot of water to a rolling boil over high heat. Once the water is boiling, add the peas and cook for about 3 minutes until the peas brighten in color. (Note: You don't want to overcook the peas.) Strain the peas using a colander before running them under cold water. Allow the peas to drain while you prepare the rest of the dish.
2. Chop the cooked shrimp into bite-sized portions before adding them to a large bowl. Toss in the cooked and drained peas along with the spring onions, cashews, red bell pepper, and carrots.
3. In a small glass bowl, whisk together the cayenne pepper, soy sauce, ginger, sesame oil, olive oil, and rice vinegar.
4. Drizzle the vinaigrette over the shrimp and toss until all the ingredients are evenly coated.
5. Serve the shrimp salad on a bed of mixed baby greens.

PER SERVING

Calories: 403; Sodium: 568mg; Total Fat: 18g; Saturated Fat: 3g; Cholesterol: 221mg; Total Carbohydrates: 23g; Fiber: 9g; Protein: 32g

Tomato & Feta Salad

Prep Time: 15 minutes|Serves: 2

- 1 large fresh tomato, sliced
- ½ tablespoon olive oil
- 1 scallions, chopped
- 1½ tablespoon Feta cheese, crumbled
- 3 cups fresh baby greens
- ½ red onion, sliced
- 1 tablespoon unsalted almonds, chopped
- 1 tablespoon fresh lemon juice

1. Take a bowl and add all the given ingredients except for almonds and cheese and toss to coat well.
2. Cover and refrigerate to let it sit and marinate for about six to eight hours.
3. Remove from the refrigerator and stir in the almonds.
4. Serve with the topping of Feta cheese.

PER SERVING

Calories: 150 ;Fat: 6.8g ;Sat Fat: 1.8g ;Carbohydrates: 18.3g ;Fiber: 6.8g ;Sugar: 4.3g ;Protein: 7.4g

Fresh Salmon & Lentil Salad

Prep time: 5 minutes | Cook time: 5 minutes| Serves 4

- 2 tbsp. fresh parsley, chopped
- 2 tbsp. balsamic vinegar
- 1 whole spring onion, chopped
- 6 radishes, thinly sliced
- 1 green bell pepper, chopped
- 1 small cucumber, chopped
- 2 cups baby kale, shredded
- 7 oz. no-salt-added, water-packed salmon (drained)
- 15 0z. no-salt-added lentils (drained)
- Freshly ground black pepper

1. In a large mixing bowl, toss together the parsley, balsamic vinegar, spring onion, radishes, bell pepper, cucumber, baby kale, salmon, and lentils.
2. Season to taste with freshly ground black pepper.
3. Cover the bowl with cling wrap and chill until ready to serve.

PER SERVING

Calories: 162; Sodium: 38mg; Total Fat: 1g; Saturated Fat: 0g; Cholesterol: 30mg; Total Carbohydrates: 24g; Fiber: 7g; Protein: 15g

Fig and Goat's Cheese Salad

Prep Time: 10 minutes|Cook Time: 10 minutes|Serves: 1

- 2 cups mixed salad greens
- 4 dried figs, stemmed and sliced
- 1 oz. fresh goat's cheese, crumbled
- 1½ tbsp. slivered almonds, preferably toasted
- 2 tsp. extra-virgin olive oil
- 2 tsp. balsamic vinegar
- ½ tsp. honey
- Pinch of salt
- Freshly ground pepper to taste

1. Combine the greens, figs, goat's cheese, and almonds in a medium bowl.
2. Stir together the oil, vinegar, honey, salt, and pepper.

PER SERVING

Calories 340 ;Protein 10.4g ; Carbohydrates 31.8g ; Dietary fiber 7g ;Sugars 21.8g ;Fat 21g; Sodium 309.5mg

Summer Squash Ribbons with Lemon and Ricotta

Prep time: 5 minutes | Cook time: 20 minutes| Serves 4

- 2 medium zucchini or yellow squash
- ½ cup ricotta cheese
- 2 tablespoons fresh mint, chopped, plus additional mint leaves for garnish
- 2 tablespoons fresh parsley, chopped
- Zest of ½ lemon
- 2 teaspoons lemon juice
- ½ teaspoon kosher salt
- ¼ teaspoon freshly ground black pepper
- 1 tablespoon extra-virgin olive oil

1. Using a vegetable peeler, make ribbons by peeling the summer squash lengthwise. The squash ribbons will resemble the wide pasta, pappardelle.
2. In a medium bowl, combine the ricotta cheese, mint, parsley, lemon zest, lemon juice, salt, and black pepper.
3. Place mounds of the squash ribbons evenly on 4 plates then dollop the ricotta mixture on top. Drizzle with the olive oil and garnish with the mint leaves.

PER SERVING

Calories: 90; Total fat: 6g; Saturated fat: 2g; Cholesterol: 10mg; Sodium: 180mg; Potassium: 315mg; Total Carbohydrates: 5g; Fiber: 1g; Sugars: 3g; Protein: 5g; Magnesium: 25mg; Calcium: 105mg

Sautéed Kale with Tomato and Garlic

Prep time: 5 minutes | Cook time: 10 minutes| Serves 4

- 1 tablespoon extra-virgin olive oil
- 4 garlic cloves, sliced
- ¼ teaspoon red pepper flakes
- 2 bunches kale, stemmed and chopped or torn into pieces
- 1 (14.5-ounce) can no-salt-added diced tomatoes
- ½ teaspoon kosher salt

1. Heat the olive oil in a wok or large skillet over medium-high heat. Add the garlic and red pepper flakes, and sauté until fragrant, about 30 seconds. Add the kale and sauté, about 3 to 5 minutes, until the kale shrinks down a bit.
2. Add the tomatoes and the salt, stir together, and cook for 3 to 5 minutes, or until the liquid reduces and the kale cooks down further and becomes tender.

PER SERVING

Calories: 110; Total fat: 5g; Saturated fat: 1g; Cholesterol: 0mg; Sodium: 222mg; Potassium: 535mg; Total Carbohydrates: 15g; Fiber: 6g; Sugars: 6g; Protein: 6g; Magnesium: 50mg; Calcium: 182mg

Roasted Broccoli with Tahini Yogurt Sauce

Prep time: 5 minutes | Cook time: 30 minutes| Serves 4

FOR THE BROCCOLI

- 1½ to 2 pounds broccoli, stalk trimmed and cut into slices, head cut into florets
- 1 lemon, sliced into ¼-inch-thick rounds
- 3 tablespoons extra-virgin olive oil
- ½ teaspoon kosher salt
- ¼ teaspoon freshly ground black pepper

FOR THE TAHINI YOGURT SAUCE

- ½ cup plain Greek yogurt
- 2 tablespoons tahini
- 1 tablespoon lemon juice
- ¼ teaspoon kosher salt
- 1 teaspoon sesame seeds, for garnish (optional)

TO MAKE THE BROCCOLI

1. Preheat the oven to 425°F. Line a baking sheet with parchment paper or foil.
2. In a large bowl, gently toss the broccoli, lemon slices, olive oil, salt, and black pepper to combine. Arrange the broccoli in a single layer on the prepared baking sheet. Roast 15 minutes, stir, and roast another 15 minutes, until golden brown.

TO MAKE THE TAHINI YOGURT SAUCE

1. In a medium bowl, combine the yogurt, tahini, lemon juice, and salt; mix well.
2. Spread the tahini yogurt sauce on a platter or large plate and top with the broccoli and lemon slices. Garnish with the sesame seeds (if desired).

PER SERVING

Calories: 245; Total fat: 16g; Saturated fat: 2g; Cholesterol: 2mg; Sodium: 305mg; Potassium: 835mg; Total Carbohydrates: 20g; Fiber: 7g; Sugars: 6g; Protein: 12g; Magnesium: 65mg; Calcium: 185mg

Green Beans with Pine Nuts and Garlic
Prep time: 5 minutes | Cook time: 20 minutes| Serves 4

- 1 pound green beans, trimmed
- 1 head garlic (10 to 12 cloves), smashed
- 2 tablespoons extra-virgin olive oil
- ½ teaspoon kosher salt
- ¼ teaspoon red pepper flakes
- 1 tablespoon white wine vinegar
- ¼ cup pine nuts, toasted

1. Preheat the oven to 425°F. Line a baking sheet with parchment paper or foil.
2. In a large bowl, combine the green beans, garlic, olive oil, salt, and red pepper flakes and mix together. Arrange in a single layer on the baking sheet. Roast for 10 minutes, stir, and roast for another 10 minutes, or until golden brown.
3. Mix the cooked green beans with the vinegar and top with the pine nuts.

PER SERVING

Calories: 165; Total fat: 13g; Saturated fat: 1g; Cholesterol: 0mg; Sodium: 150mg; Potassium: 325mg; Total Carbohydrates: 12g; Fiber: 4g; Sugars: 4g; Protein: 4g; Magnesium: 52mg; Calcium: 60mg

Roasted Harissa Carrots
Prep time: 5 minutes | Cook time: 20 minutes| Serves 4

- 1 pound carrots, peeled and sliced into 1-inch-thick rounds
- 2 tablespoons extra-virgin olive oil
- 2 tablespoons harissa
- 1 teaspoon honey
- 1 teaspoon ground cumin
- ½ teaspoon kosher salt
- ½ cup fresh parsley, chopped

1. Preheat the oven to 450°F. Line a baking sheet with parchment paper or foil.
2. In a large bowl, combine the carrots, olive oil, harissa, honey, cumin, and salt.
3. Arrange in a single layer on the baking sheet. Roast for 15 minutes. Remove from the oven, add the parsley, and toss together.

PER SERVING

Calories: 120; Total fat: 8g; Saturated fat: 1g; Cholesterol: 0mg; Sodium: 255mg; Potassium: 415mg; Total Carbohydrates: 13g; Fiber: 4g; Sugars: 7g; Protein: 1g; Magnesium: 18mg; Calcium: 53mg

Cucumbers with Feta, Mint, and Sumac
Prep time: 15 minutes | Cook time: 10 minutes| Serves 4

- 1 tablespoon extra-virgin olive oil
- 1 tablespoon lemon juice
- 2 teaspoons ground sumac
- ½ teaspoon kosher salt
- 2 hothouse or English cucumbers, diced
- ¼ cup crumbled feta cheese
- 1 tablespoon fresh mint, chopped
- 1 tablespoon fresh parsley, chopped
- ⅛ teaspoon red pepper flakes

1. In a large bowl, whisk together the olive oil, lemon juice, sumac, and salt. Add the cucumber and feta cheese and toss well.
2. Transfer to a serving dish and sprinkle with the mint, parsley, and red pepper flakes.

PER SERVING

Calories: 85; Total fat: 6g; Saturated fat: 2g; Cholesterol: 8mg; Sodium: 230mg; Potassium: 295mg; Total Carbohydrates: 8g; Fiber: 1g; Sugars: 4g; Protein: 3g; Magnesium: 27mg; Calcium: 80mg

Cherry Tomato Bruschetta
Prep time: 15 minutes | Cook time: 10 minutes| Serves 4

- 8 ounces assorted cherry tomatoes, halved
- ⅓ cup fresh herbs, chopped (such as basil, parsley, tarragon, dill)
- 1 tablespoon extra-virgin olive oil
- ¼ teaspoon kosher salt
- ⅛ teaspoon freshly ground black pepper
- ¼ cup ricotta cheese
- 4 slices whole-wheat bread, toasted

1. Combine the tomatoes, herbs, olive oil, salt, and black pepper in a medium bowl and mix gently.
2. Spread 1 tablespoon of ricotta cheese onto each slice of toast. Spoon one-quarter of the tomato mixture onto each bruschetta. If desired, garnish with more herbs.

PER SERVING

Calories: 100; Total fat: 6g; Saturated fat: 1g; Cholesterol: 5mg; Sodium: 135mg; Potassium: 210mg; Total Carbohydrates: 10g; Fiber: 2g; Sugars: 2g; Protein: 4g; Magnesium: 22mg; Calcium: 60mg

Roasted Red Pepper Hummus

Prep time: 15 minutes | Cook time: 10 minutes | Makes about 2 cups

- 1 (15-ounce) can low-sodium chickpeas, drained and rinsed
- 3 ounces jarred roasted red bell peppers, drained
- 3 tablespoons tahini
- 3 tablespoons lemon juice
- 1 garlic clove, peeled
- ¾ teaspoon kosher salt
- ¼ teaspoon freshly ground black pepper
- 3 tablespoons extra-virgin olive oil
- ¼ teaspoon cayenne pepper (optional)
- Fresh herbs, chopped, for garnish (optional)

1. In a food processor, add the chickpeas, red bell peppers, tahini, lemon juice, garlic, salt, and black pepper. Pulse 5 to 7 times.
2. Add the olive oil and process until smooth. Add the cayenne pepper and garnish with chopped herbs, if desired.

PER SERVING(¼ CUP)

Calories: 130; Total fat: 8g; Saturated fat: 1g; Cholesterol: 0mg; Sodium: 150mg; Potassium: 125mg; Total Carbohydrates: 11g; Fiber: 2g; Sugars: 1g; Protein: 4g; Magnesium: 20mg; Calcium: 48mg

Baked Eggplant Baba Ganoush

Prep time: 15 minutes | Cook time: 60 minutes | Makes about 4 cups

- 2 pounds (about 2 medium to large) eggplant
- 3 tablespoons tahini
- Zest of 1 lemon
- 2 tablespoons lemon juice
- ¾ teaspoon kosher salt
- ½ teaspoon ground sumac, plus more for sprinkling (optional)
- ⅓ cup fresh parsley, chopped
- 1 tablespoon extra-virgin olive oil

1. Preheat the oven to 350°F. Place the eggplants directly on the rack and bake for 60 minutes, or until the skin is wrinkly.
2. In a food processor add the tahini, lemon zest, lemon juice, salt, and sumac. Carefully cut open the baked eggplant and scoop the flesh into the food processor. Process until the ingredients are well blended.
3. Place in a serving dish and mix in the parsley. Drizzle with the olive oil and sprinkle with sumac, if desired.

PER SERVING(½ CUP)

Calories: 50; Total fat: 4g; Saturated fat: 1g; Cholesterol: 0mg; Sodium: 110mg; Potassium: 42mg; Total Carbohydrates: 2g; Fiber: 1g; Sugars: 0g; Protein: 1g; Magnesium: 7mg; Calcium: 28mg

White Bean Romesco Dip

Prep time: 15 minutes | Cook time: 10 minutes | Makes about 4 cups

- 2 red bell peppers, or 1 (12-ounce) jar roasted sweet red peppers in water, drained
- 2 garlic cloves, peeled
- ½ cup roasted unsalted almonds
- 1 6-inch multigrain pita, torn into small pieces
- 1 teaspoon red pepper flakes
- 1 (14.5-ounce) can no-salt-added diced tomatoes
- 1 (14.5-ounce) can low-sodium cannellini beans, drained and rinsed
- 1 tablespoon fresh parsley, chopped
- 1 teaspoon sweet or smoked paprika
- 1 teaspoon kosher salt
- ¼ teaspoon black pepper
- ¼ cup extra-virgin olive oil
- 2 tablespoons red wine vinegar
- 2 teaspoons lemon juice (optional)

1. If you are using raw peppers, roast them following the steps, then roughly chop. If using jarred roasted peppers, proceed to step 2.
2. In a food processor, add the garlic and pulse until finely minced. Scrape down the sides of the bowl and add the almonds, pita, and red pepper flakes, and process until minced. Scrape down the sides of the bowl and add the bell peppers, tomatoes, beans, parsley, paprika, salt, and black pepper. Process until smooth.
3. with the food processor running, add the olive oil and vinegar, and process until smooth. Taste, and add the lemon juice to brighten, if desired.

PER SERVING(½ CUP)

Calories: 180; Total fat: 10g; Saturated fat: 1g; Cholesterol: 0mg; Sodium: 285mg; Potassium: 270mg; Total Carbohydrates: 20g; Fiber: 4g; Sugars: 3g; Protein: 6g; Magnesium: 40mg; Calcium: 65mg

Kidney Beans Curry

Prep Time: 10 minutes|Cook time: 25 minutes|Serves: 2

- 1 cup water
- 1 large plum tomato, chopped finely
- ⅛ teaspoon Cayenne pepper
- ½ teaspoon ground cumin
- ½ cup low-sodium tomato sauce
- ½ garlic cloves, minced
- ⅛ cup olive oil
- ¼ teaspoon ground turmeric
- ½ teaspoon ground coriander
- 1 tablespoon fresh ginger, minced
- ½ medium onion, chopped finely
- Fresh ground black pepper to taste

1. Grab a large frying pan and heat oil over medium heat and fry onion, garlic and ginger for about four to five minutes.
2. Stir in tomato sauce and spices and cook for about five minutes.
3. Stir in tomatoes, kidney beans and water and bring it to a boil over high heat.
4. Lessen the heat to medium and gently cook for about ten to 15 minutes or until we have the desired thickness.
5. Serve hot and enjoy!

PER SERVING

Calories: 628 ;Fat: 14.6g ;Sat Fat: 2.1g;Carbohydrates: 96.1g ;Fiber: 23.8g ;Sugar: 8.4g ;Protein: 33.4g

Roasted Cherry Tomato Caprese

Prep time: 15 minutes | Cook time: 10 minutes| Serves 4

- 2 pints (about 20 ounces) cherry tomatoes
- 6 thyme sprigs
- 6 garlic cloves, smashed
- ½ teaspoon kosher salt
- 8 ounces fresh, unsalted mozzarella, cut into bite-size slices
- ¼ cup basil, chopped or cut into ribbons
- Loaf of crusty whole-wheat bread for serving

1. Preheat the oven to 350°F. Line a baking sheet with parchment paper or foil.
2. Put the tomatoes, thyme, garlic, olive oil, and salt into a large bowl and mix together. Place on the prepared baking sheet in a single layer. Roast for 30 minutes, or until the tomatoes are bursting and juicy.
3. Place the mozzarella on a platter or in a bowl. Pour all the tomato mixture, including the juices, over the mozzarella. Garnish with the basil.
4. Serve with crusty bread.

PER SERVING(EXCLUDING BREAD)

Calories: 250; Total fat: 17g; Saturated fat: 7g; Cholesterol: 31mg; Sodium: 157mg; Potassium: 425mg; Total Carbohydrates: 9g; Fiber: 2g; Sugars: 4g; Protein: 17g; Magnesium: 35mg; Calcium: 445mg

Italian Crepe with Herbs and Onion

Prep time: 15 minutes | Cook time: 20 minutes| Serves 6

- 2 cups cold water
- 1 cup chickpea flour
- ½ teaspoon kosher salt
- ¼ teaspoon freshly ground black pepper
- 3½ tablespoons extra-virgin olive oil, divided
- ½ onion, julienned
- ½ cup fresh herbs, chopped (thyme, sage, and rosemary are all nice on their own or as a mix)

1. In a large bowl, whisk together the water, flour, salt, and black pepper. Add 2 tablespoons of the olive oil and whisk. Let the batter sit at room temperature for at least 30 minutes.
2. Preheat the oven to 450°F. Place a 12-inch cast-iron pan or oven-safe skillet in the oven to warm as the oven comes to temperature.
3. Remove the hot pan from the oven carefully, add ½ tablespoon of the olive oil and one-third of the onion, stir, and place the pan back in the oven. Cook, stirring occasionally, until the onions are golden brown, 5 to 8 minutes.
4. Remove the pan from the oven and pour in one-third of the batter (about 1 cup), sprinkle with one-third of the herbs, and put it back in the oven. Bake for 10 minutes, or until firm and the edges are set.
5. Increase the oven setting to broil and cook 3 to 5 minutes, or until golden brown. Slide the crepe onto the cutting board and repeat twice more. Halve the crepes and cut into wedges. Serve warm or at room temperature.

PER SERVING

Calories: 135; Total fat: 9g; Saturated fat: 1g; Cholesterol: 0mg; Sodium: 105mg; Potassium: 165mg; Total Carbohydrates: 11g; Fiber: 2g; Sugars: 2g; Protein: 4g; Magnesium: 30mg; Calcium: 20mg

Pita Pizza with Olives, Feta, and Red Onion

Prep time: 15 minutes | Cook time: 10 minutes| Serves 4

- 4 (6-inch) whole-wheat pitas
- 1 tablespoon extra-virgin olive oil
- ½ cup hummus
- ½ bell pepper, julienned
- ½ red onion, julienned
- ¼ cup olives, pitted and chopped
- ¼ cup crumbled feta cheese
- ¼ teaspoon red pepper flakes
- ¼ cup fresh herbs, chopped (mint, parsley, oregano, or a mix)

1. Preheat the broiler to low. Line a baking sheet with parchment paper or foil.
2. Place the pitas on the prepared baking sheet and brush both sides with the olive oil. Broil 1 to 2 minutes per side until starting to turn golden brown.
3. Spread 2 tablespoons hummus on each pita. Top the pitas with bell pepper, onion, olives, feta cheese, and red pepper flakes. Broil again until the cheese softens and starts to get golden brown, 4 to 6 minutes, being careful not to burn the pitas.
4. Remove from broiler and top with the herbs.

PER SERVING

Calories: 185; Total fat: 11g; Saturated fat: 2g; Cholesterol: 8mg; Sodium: 285mg; Potassium: 13mg; Total Carbohydrates: 17g; Fiber: 3g; Sugars: 3g; Protein: 5g; Magnesium: 18mg; Calcium: 91mg

Cajun Baked Trout

Prep Time: 10 minutes| Cook time: 15 minutes|Serves: 4

- ¼ teaspoon chili powder
- 1 teaspoon Treacle sugar
- 1 teaspoon brown onion powder
- 1 teaspoon paprika powder
- 2 teaspoon dried parsley
- 1 teaspoon dried oregano
- 1 teaspoon garlic powder
- 1 teaspoon ground cumin
- Black pepper to taste
- 17 ounces broccoli florets
- 4, 6 ounces Rainbow trout fillets
- 1 teaspoon olive oil
- 1 lemon, cut into four pieces

1. Make the crust for the fish by mixing all the dried spices and herbs in a bowl.
2. Lightly oil the fish fillets and then pat the spice crust onto them evenly. Place them on a well-oiled baking tray.
3. Preheat the oven to 425° F and lightly oil a baking tray.
4. Dress the broccoli with a little olive oil and pepper and place on the second oiled baking tray.
5. Bake both trays in the oven simultaneously, for about 12-15 minutes, or until the fish and broccoli

are superbly cooked.
6. The trout should pull apart effortlessly and have a crisp, dark crust.

PER SERVING

Calories 280 ;Fat 11g ; Sodium 227mg;Carbs 10g ;Fiber 4g ;Sugar 7g ;Protein 38g

Sweet and Sour Cabbage with Pork Chops

Prep Time: 10 minutes| Cook time: 1 hour 10 minutes|Serves: 4

- Sweet and Sour Cabbage:
- 1 tablespoon olive oil
- 1 medium red onion, sliced
- 2 rashers low sodium back bacon, cut into cubes
- ½ medium-sized white cabbage, sliced
- ¼ cup white grape vinegar
- 3 tablespoon golden syrup
- ¼ cup water
- 2 crisp green apples, peeled and diced
- Black pepper to taste
- Pork Chops:
- Olive oil cooking spray
- 4 ounces pork chops, fat removed
- Black pepper to taste

1. Heat the oil in a pan, add the onion and fry for 1 minute. Then add the bacon pieces and cook until crispy and browned.
2. Add ⅓ of the cabbage, and sprinkle over ⅓ of the vinegar.
3. Repeat this process until the cabbage and vinegar are all incorporated. Then add the syrup, water, apples, and black pepper and reduce the heat. Leave to simmer on low for about 1 hour.
4. Ten minutes before the cabbage is ready, heat and oil a nonstick pan.
5. Place the pork chops in the pan and fry until golden brown on each side, about 3 minutes aside.
6. While cooking, add black pepper to taste. Set aside covered to keep warm.
7. Transfer the cabbage mixture to the hot chops pan and stir well on high for 3 minutes.
8. Enjoy.

PER SERVING

Calories 356 ;Fat 10g ; Sodium 377mg;Carbs 39g ;Fiber 6g ;Sugar 8g ;Protein 29g

Roasted Za'atar Chickpeas

Prep time: 5 minutes | Cook time: 60 minutes| Serves 8

- 3 tablespoons za'atar
- 2 tablespoons extra-virgin olive oil
- ½ teaspoon kosher salt
- ¼ teaspoon freshly ground black pepper
- 4 cups cooked chickpeas, or 2 (15-ounce) cans, drained and rinsed

1. Preheat the oven to 400°F. Line a baking sheet with foil or parchment paper.
2. In a large bowl, combine the za'atar, olive oil, salt, and black pepper. Add the chickpeas and mix thoroughly.
3. Spread the chickpeas in a single layer on the prepared baking sheet. Bake for 45 to 60 minutes, or until golden brown and crispy. Cool and store in an airtight container at room temperature for up to 1 week.

PER SERVING

Calories: 150; Total fat: 6g; Saturated fat: 1g; Cholesterol: 0mg; Sodium: 230mg; Potassium: 182mg; Total Carbohydrates: 17g; Fiber 6g; Sugars: 3g; Protein: 6g; Magnesium: 32mg; Calcium: 52mg

Roasted Rosemary Olives

Prep time: 5 minutes | Cook time: 30 minutes| Serves 4

- 1 cup mixed variety olives, pitted and rinsed
- 2 tablespoons lemon juice
- 1 tablespoon extra-virgin olive oil
- 6 garlic cloves, peeled
- 4 rosemary sprigs

1. Preheat the oven to 400°F. Line the baking sheet with parchment paper or foil.
2. Combine the olives, lemon juice, olive oil, and garlic in a medium bowl and mix together. Spread in a single layer on the prepared baking sheet. Sprinkle on the rosemary. Roast for 25 minutes, tossing halfway through.
3. Remove the rosemary leaves from the stem and place in a serving bowl. Add the olives and mix before serving.

PER SERVING

Calories: 100; Total fat: 9g; Saturated fat: 1g; Cholesterol: 0mg; Sodium: 260mg; Potassium: 31mg; Total Carbohydrates: 4g; Fiber: 0g; Sugars: 0g; Protein: 0g; Magnesium: 3mg; Calcium: 11mg

Cauliflower & Peas Curry

Prep Time: 20 minutes|Cook time: 15 minutes|Serves: 6

- ½ cup water
- 4 medium tomatoes, chopped
- 4 cup cauliflower, chopped
- 4 tablespoons olive oil
- 6 garlic cloves, minced
- 2 teaspoons Cayenne pepper
- 2 teaspoons ground cumin
- 2 teaspoons ground coriander
- 1 tablespoon fresh ginger, minced
- ½ teaspoon ground turmeric
- 2 cup fresh green peas, shelled
- Fresh ground black pepper to taste
- Pinch of salt
- 1 cup warm water

1. Take a food processor, add tomatoes and half cup of water and pulse until you have a smooth puree.
2. Set aside the formed mixture.
3. In a large saucepan, heat the oil over medium heat and fry the garlic, green chilies and spices for about a minute.
4. Add the cauliflower, peas and tomato puree to the pan and cook for about three to four minutes.
5. Now, pour warm water and bring it to a boil.
6. Reduce the heat to medium-low and let it cook for about eight to ten minutes while covered.

PER SERVING

Calories: 163 ;Fat: 10.1g ;Sat Fat: 1.5g;Carbohydrates: 16.1g ;Fiber: 5.6g ;Sugar: 6.7g ;Protein: 5.1g

Spiced Maple Nuts

Prep time: 5 minutes | Cook time: 10 minutes| Makes about 2 cups

- 2 cups raw walnuts or pecans (or a mix of nuts)
- 1 teaspoon ground sumac
- ½ teaspoon pure maple syrup
- ¼ teaspoon kosher salt
- ¼ teaspoon ground ginger
- 2 to 4 rosemary sprigs

1. Preheat the oven to 350°F. Line a baking sheet with parchment paper or foil.
2. In a large bowl, combine the nuts, olive oil, sumac, maple syrup, salt, and ginger; mix together. Spread in a single layer on the prepared baking sheet. Add the rosemary. Roast for 8 to 10 minutes, or until golden and fragrant.
3. Remove the rosemary leaves from the stems and place in a serving bowl. Add the nuts and toss to combine before serving.

PER SERVING(¼ CUP)

Calories: 175; Total fat: 18g; Saturated fat: 2g; Cholesterol: 0mg; Sodium: 35mg; Potassium: 110mg; Total Carbohydrates: 4g; Fiber: 2g; Sugars: 1g; Protein: 3g; Magnesium: 35mg; Calcium: 23mg

Chapter 13
Desserts

Baked Apples with Cherries and Walnuts

Prep time: 10 minutes | Cook time: 35 to 40 minutes | Serves 6

- ⅓ cup dried cherries, coarsely chopped
- 3 tablespoons chopped walnuts
- 1 tablespoon ground flaxseed meal
- 1 tablespoon firmly packed brown sugar
- 1 teaspoon ground cinnamon
- ⅛ teaspoon nutmeg
- 6 Golden Delicious apples, about 2 pounds total weight, washed and unpeeled
- ½ cup 100 percent apple juice
- ¼ cup water
- 2 tablespoons dark honey
- 2 teaspoons extra-virgin olive oil

1. Preheat the oven to 350°F.
2. In a small bowl, toss together the cherries, walnuts, flaxseed meal, brown sugar, cinnamon, and nutmeg until all the ingredients are evenly distributed. Set aside.
3. Working from the stem end, core each apple, stopping ¾ of an inch from the bottom.
4. Gently press the cherries into each apple cavity. Arrange the apples upright in a heavy ovenproof skillet or baking dish just large enough to hold them.
5. Pour the apple juice and water into the pan.
6. Drizzle the honey and oil evenly over the apples, and cover the pan snugly with aluminum foil. Bake until the apples are tender when pierced with a knife, 35 to 40 minutes.
7. Transfer the apples to individual plates and drizzle with the pan juices. Serve warm.

PER SERVING

Calories: 162; Total Fat 5g; Saturated Fat: 1g; Cholesterol: 0mg; Sodium: 4mg; Potassium: 148mg; Total Carbohydrate: 30g; Fiber: 4g; Protein: 1g

Easy Peach Crumble

Prep time: 10 minutes | Cook time: 30 minutes | Serves 8

- 8 ripe peaches, peeled, pitted and sliced
- 3 tablespoons freshly squeezed lemon juice
- ½ teaspoon ground cinnamon
- ¼ teaspoon ground nutmeg
- ½ cup oat flour
- ¼ cup packed dark brown sugar
- 2 tablespoons margarine, cut into thin slices
- ¼ cup quick-cooking oats

1. Preheat the oven to 375°F. Lightly coat a 9-inch pie pan with cooking spray. Arrange peach slices in the prepared pie plate and sprinkle with the lemon juice, cinnamon, and nutmeg.
2. In a small bowl, whisk together the flour and brown sugar. with your fingers, crumble the margarine into the flour-sugar mixture. Add the uncooked oats and stir to mix. Sprinkle the flour mixture over the peaches.
3. Bake until the peaches are soft and the topping is browned, about 30 minutes.
4. Cut into 8 even slices and serve warm.

PER SERVING

Calories: 130; Total Fat 4g; Saturated Fat: 0g; Cholesterol: 0mg; Sodium: 42mg; Potassium: 255mg; Total Carbohydrate: 28g; Fiber: 3g; Protein: 2g

Cinnamon Oranges

Prep time: 10 minutes| Serves 4

- 4 navel oranges
- 2 tablespoons orange juice
- 2 tablespoons lemon juice
- 1 tablespoon sugar
- ½ teaspoon ground cinnamon
- ½ cup fresh raspberries
- 4 sprigs fresh mint

1. Using a sharp knife, remove the rind and white pith from the oranges. Cut each orange into 5 or 6 segments and arrange on 4 plates.
2. Whisk together the orange and lemon juices, sugar, and cinnamon, and spoon the mixture over the orange slices.
3. Top each serving with several raspberries and a sprig of fresh mint. Serve immediately.

PER SERVING

Calories: 90; Total Fat 0g; Saturated Fat: 0g; Cholesterol: 0mg; Sodium: 2mg; Potassium: 0mg; Total Carbohydrate: 20g; Fiber: 4g; Protein: 1g

Banana Ice Cream

Prep time: 3 to 5 minutes| Serves 2

- 2 ripe bananas, sliced and frozen
- OPTIONAL ADD-INS
- soy milk (or other milk)
- nuts
- nut butters
- fresh or dried fruit
- spices (cinnamon, mint, cardamom, ginger)
- cocoa

1. Add the frozen bananas and any desired additions to the bowl of a food processor and blend.
2. Occasionally scrape down the sides and continue to blend until smooth, approximately 3 to 5 minutes.
3. Scoop into 2 serving bowls and enjoy immediately as a soft serve. For firmer ice cream, place in an airtight, freezer-safe container and freeze for at least 1 hour.

PER SERVING

Calories: 122; Total Fat 0g; Saturated Fat: 0g; Cholesterol: 0mg; Sodium: 2mg; Potassium: 487mg; Total Carbohydrate: 31g; Fiber: 4g; Protein: 2g

Lemon Thins

Prep time: 15 minutes | Cook time: 8 to 10 minutes | Makes 30 cookies

- Cooking spray
- 1¼ cups whole wheat pastry flour
- ⅓ cup corn starch
- 1½ teaspoons baking powder
- ¾ cup sugar, divided
- 2 tablespoons butter, softened
- 2 tablespoons extra-virgin olive oil
- 1 large egg white
- 3 teaspoons freshly grated lemon zest
- 1½ teaspoons vanilla extract
- 4 tablespoons freshly squeezed lemon juice

1. Preheat the oven to 350°F. Coat two baking sheets with cooking spray.
2. In a mixing bowl, whisk together the flour, cornstarch, and baking powder.
3. In another mixing bowl beat ½ cup of the sugar, the butter, and olive oil with an electric mixer on medium speed until fluffy.
4. Add the egg white, lemon zest, and vanilla and beat until smooth. Beat in the lemon juice.
5. Add the dry ingredients to the wet ingredients and fold in with a rubber spatula just until combined.
6. Drop the dough by the teaspoonful, 2 inches apart, onto the prepared baking sheets.
7. Place the remaining ¼ cup sugar in a saucer. Coat the bottom of a wide-bottomed glass with cooking spray and dip it in the sugar. Flatten the dough with the glass bottom into 2½-inch circles, dipping the glass in the sugar each time.
8. Bake the cookies until they are just starting to brown around the edges, 8 to 10 minutes. Transfer to a flat surface (not a rack) to crisp.

PER SERVING (1 COOKIE)

Calories: 40; Total Fat 2g; Saturated Fat: 1g; Cholesterol: 2mg; Sodium: 26mg; Potassium: 3mg; Total Carbohydrate: 5g; Fiber: 1g; Protein: 1g

Banana Cream Pie

Prep time: 10 minutes | Bake time: 5 minutes, plus 6 hours to overnight cooling time | Serves 8

- 3 cups whole milk
- ¾ cup white sugar
- ⅓ cup all-purpose flour
- 3 egg yolks, slightly beaten, or Egg Beaters
- 2 tablespoons unsalted butter
- 1 teaspoon vanilla
- 3 bananas
- 1 (9-inch) prebaked pie crust

1. In a large saucepan, scald the milk.
2. In another large saucepan, combine the sugar and flour. Over medium heat, gradually stir in the scalded milk, stirring constantly, and cook until thickened.
3. Cover and cook for 2 minutes more, stirring occasionally.
4. Stir ¼ cup of the hot sugar-milk mixture into the beaten egg yolks. When thoroughly combined, stir the yolk mixture into the remaining sugar-milk mixture. Cook for 1 minute more, stirring constantly.
5. Remove from the heat and blend in the butter and vanilla. Let the pie sit until it's cool.
6. When cool, slice the bananas and scatter on the pie crust. Pour the lukewarm sugar-milk mixture over the bananas. Wait until the pie is cool before serving, or refrigerate overnight for at least 6 hours.

PER SERVING

Calories: 333; Total Fat 13g; Saturated Fat: 6g; Cholesterol: 88mg; Sodium: 151mg; Potassium: 342mg; Total Carbohydrate: 49g; Fiber: 2g; Protein: 6g

Snickerdoodle Chickpea Blondies

Prep time: 10 minutes | Cook time: 30 to 35 minutes| Serves 15

- 1 (15-ounce) can chickpeas, drained and rinsed
- 3 tablespoons nut butter of choice
- ¾ teaspoon baking powder
- 2 teaspoons vanilla extract
- ⅛ teaspoon baking soda
- ¾ cup brown sugar
- 1 tablespoon unsweetened applesauce
- ¼ cup ground flaxseed meal
- 2¼ teaspoons cinnamon

1. Preheat the oven to 350°F. Grease an 8-by-8-inch baking pan.
2. Blend all ingredients in a food processor until very smooth. Scoop into the prepared baking pan.
3. Bake until the tops are medium golden brown, 30 to 35 minutes. Allow the brownies to cool completely before cutting.

PER SERVING

Calories: 85; Total Fat 2g; Saturated Fat: 0g; Cholesterol: 0mg; Sodium: 7mg; Potassium: 62mg; Total Carbohydrate: 16g; Fiber: 2g; Protein: 3g

Chocolate Chia Seed Pudding

Prep time: 15 minutes, plus 3 to 5 hours or overnight to rest| Serves 4

- 1½ cups unsweetened vanilla almond milk
- ¼ cup unsweetened cocoa powder
- ¼ cup maple syrup (or substitute any sweetener)
- ½ teaspoon vanilla extract
- ⅓ cup chia seeds
- ½ cup strawberries
- ¼ cup blueberries
- ¼ cup raspberries
- 2 tablespoons unsweetened coconut flakes
- ¼ to ½ teaspoon ground cinnamon (optional)

1. Add the almond milk, cocoa powder, maple syrup, and vanilla extract to a blender and blend until smooth. Whisk in chia seeds.
2. In a small bowl, gently mash the strawberries with a fork. Distribute the strawberry mash evenly to the bottom of 4 glass jars.
3. Pour equal portions of the blended milk-cocoa mixture into each of the jars and let the pudding rest in the refrigerator until it achieves a pudding like consistency, at least 3 to 5 hours and up to overnight.
4. Portion into serving bowls and top with blueberries, raspberries, coconut flakes, and cinnamon (if using).

PER SERVING

Calories: 189; Total Fat 7g; Saturated Fat: 2g; Cholesterol: 0mg; Sodium: 60mg; Potassium: 232mg; Total Carbohydrate: 28g; Fiber: 10g; Protein: 6g

Chocolate-Mint Truffles

Prep time: 45 minutes | Bake time: 5 hours| | Makes 60 small truffles

- 14 ounces semisweet chocolate, coarsely chopped
- ¾ cup half-and-half
- ½ teaspoon pure vanilla extract
- 1½ teaspoon peppermint extract
- 2 tablespoons unsalted butter, softened
- ¾ cup naturally unsweetened or Dutch-process cocoa powder

1. Place semisweet chocolate in a large heatproof bowl.
2. Microwave in four 15-second increments, stirring after each, for a total of 60 seconds. Stir until almost completely melted. Set aside.
3. In a small saucepan over medium heat, heat the half-and-half, whisking occasionally, until it just begins to boil. Remove from the heat, then whisk in the vanilla and peppermint extracts.
4. Pour the mixture over the chocolate and, using a wooden spoon, gently stir in one direction.
5. Once the chocolate and cream are smooth, stir in the butter until it is combined and melted.
6. Cover with plastic wrap pressed on the top of the mixture, then let it sit at room temperature for 30 minutes.
7. After 30 minutes, place the mixture in the refrigerator until it is thick and can hold a ball shape, about 5 hours.
8. Line a large baking sheet with parchment paper or a use a silicone baking mat. Set aside.
9. Remove the mixture from the refrigerator. Place the cocoa powder in a bowl.
10. Scoop 1 teaspoon of the ganache and, using your hands, roll into a ball. Roll the ball in the cocoa powder, the place on the prepared baking sheet. (You can coat your palms with a little cocoa powder to prevent sticking).
11. Serve immediately or cover and store at room temperature for up to 1 week.

PER SERVING

Calories: 21; Total Fat 2g; Saturated Fat: 1g; Cholesterol: 2mg; Sodium: 2mg; Potassium: 21mg; Total Carbohydrate: 2g; Fiber: 1g; Protein: 0g

Personal Mango Pies

Prep time: 15 minutes | Cook time: 14 to 16 minutes| Serves 12

- Cooking spray
- 12 small wonton wrappers
- 1 tablespoon corn starch
- ½ cup water
- 3 cups finely chopped mango (fresh, or thawed from frozen, no sugar added)
- 2 tablespoons brown sugar (not packed)
- ½ teaspoon cinnamon
- 1 tablespoon light whipped butter or buttery spread
- Unsweetened coconut flakes (optional)

1. Preheat the oven to 350°F.
2. Spray a 12-cup muffin pan with nonstick cooking spray.
3. Place a wonton wrapper into each cup of the muffin pan, pressing it into the bottom and up along the sides.
4. Lightly spray the wrappers with nonstick spray. Bake until lightly browned, about 8 minutes.
5. Meanwhile, in a medium nonstick saucepan, combine the cornstarch with the water and stir to dissolve. Add the mango, brown sugar, and cinnamon and turn heat to medium.
6. Stirring frequently, cook until the mangoes have slightly softened and the mixture is thick and gooey, 6 to 8 minutes.
7. Remove the mango mixture from heat and stir in the butter.
8. Spoon the mango mixture into wonton cups, about 3 tablespoons each. Top with coconut flakes (if using) and serve warm.

PER SERVING

Calories: 61; Total Fat 1g; Saturated Fat: 0g; Cholesterol: 2mg; Sodium: 52mg; Potassium: 77mg; Total Carbohydrate: 14g; Fiber: 1g; Protein: 1g

Lightened Whipped Cream

Prep time: 25 minutes | Cook time: 40 minutes| Serves 16

- ⅓ cup evaporated nonfat milk, chilled
- 2 tablespoons granulated sugar
- 2 tablespoons plain low-fat yogurt

1. Pour milk into a deep mixing bowl, and place in the freezer for 30 minutes.
2. Remove bowl from freezer and whip with an electric mixer at high speed until the milk is the consistency of fluffy whipped cream, 1 to 2 minutes.
3. Add sugar and yogurt, and whip until thickened, 3 minutes. Serve immediately.

PER SERVING

Calories: 20 ;Fat: 0 Grams; Cholesterol: 0 Milligrams;-Sodium: 7 Milligrams ;Carbohydrates: 4 Grams;Fiber: 0 Grams ;Protein: 0 Grams

Fruit Kebabs

Prep time: 15 minutes | Cook time: 20 minutes| Serves 8

- 3 tablespoons lime juice
- 3 tablespoons orange juice
- 1 tablespoon jarred minced ginger
- ¾ cup cantaloupe chunks
- ¾ cup star fruit, cut into ½-inch slices
- ¾ cup strawberries
- ¾ cup peach chunks
- One 6-ounce container nonfat vanilla yogurt
- ⅛ teaspoon cayenne pepper

1. In a shallow lasagna pan, combine lime juice, orange juice, and ginger.
2. Thread cantaloupe, star fruit, strawberries, and peaches onto eight skewers. Arrange on top of juice mixture and turn to coat.
3. In a small bowl, combine yogurt and cayenne.
4. Remove skewers from marinade, and serve with spiced yogurt.

PER SERVING

Calories: 91; Fat: 1 Gram ;Cholesterol: 2 Milligrams;Sodium: 20 Milligrams Carbohydrates: 21 Grams;Fiber: 1 Gram ;Protein: 2 Grams

Pumpkin Seed Brittle

Prep time: 5 minutes | Cook time: 25 minutes| Serves 10

- ½ teaspoon cayenne pepper
- ¼ teaspoon grated nutmeg
- 1 cup roasted, unsalted pumpkin seeds
- 1 cup granulated stevia
- ½ cup granulated sugar
- ¼ cup water

1. Line a jelly roll pan with parchment paper or a baking mat. Combine cayenne, nutmeg, and pumpkin seeds in a small bowl and set aside.
2. In a large sauté pan, combine the stevia, sugar, and water, and cook over high heat, stirring constantly with a silicone spatula, until the mixture begins to boil, about 6 minutes. Using a pastry brush, swab down sides of pan so all sugar cooks evenly. Cook 3 more minutes without stirring.
3. Reduce heat to medium. Cook for another 15 to 20 minutes, checking frequently, until the mixture turns a golden, light brown color. Remove from heat.
4. Using a silicone spatula, quickly stir the pumpkin seed mixture into the sugar mixture. Pour into the prepared baking pan, and press firmly with the spatula to make a single, even layer.
5. Cool completely, then break into pieces and serve.

PER SERVING

Calories: 20; Fat: 0 Grams ;Cholesterol: 0 Milligrams;-Sodium: 7 Milligrams Carbohydrates: 4 Grams;Fiber: 0 Grams ;Protein: 0 Grams

Chocolate Pudding

Prep time: 5 minutes | Cook time: 20 minutes| Serves 4

- 2 tablespoons unsweetened cocoa powder
- ½ tablespoon arrowroot powder
- 1 cup evaporated skim milk
- 2 tablespoons agave nectar or brown rice syrup
- 1 teaspoon vanilla extract
- 4 tablespoons roasted slivered almonds

1. In a medium nonstick pan, whisk together the cocoa powder and arrowroot powder.
2. Over medium heat, add evaporated skim milk and agave nectar to cocoa powder mixture, and whisk to combine. Bring just to a simmer, whisking constantly to make sure it does not boil.
3. Cook 3 to 5 minutes, or until pudding is thick. Remove from heat. Stir in vanilla.
4. Allow to rest 30 minutes before serving or chill overnight. Spoon into four bowls. Top each bowl with 1 tablespoon of the almonds, and serve.

PER SERVING

Calories: 89 ;Fat: 3.7 Grams ;Cholesterol: 0 Milligrams;-Sodium: 60.3 Milligrams Carbohydrates: 11.5 Grams;Fiber: 1.4 Grams; Protein: 5.8 Grams

Fudgy Sauce

Prep time: 5 minutes | Cook time: 10 minutes| Serves 8

- 2 tablespoons unsweetened cocoa powder
- 1 teaspoon instant coffee
- 1 teaspoon arrowroot powder
- ½ cup evaporated skim milk
- ¼ cup blackstrap molassas

1. In a small nonstick sauté pan, stir together the cocoa, instant coffee, and arrowroot powder. Whisk in the milk; then the molasses.
2. Place the pan over medium heat. Cook, stirring constantly, until the sauce is smooth and thickened, 5 to 10 minutes. Remove from heat, and allow sauce to cool 4 minutes before serving.

PER SERVING

Calories: 39 ;Fat: 0.3 Gram ;Cholesterol: 0 Milligrams;-Sodium: 20.9 Milligrams Carbohydrates: 9.4 Grams;Fiber: 0.7 Gram ;Protein: 1.4 Grams

Figs with Chocolate Sauce

Prep time: 5 minutes | Cook time: 10 minutes| Serves 4

- 8 fresh or dried figs
- ¼ cup honey
- 2 tablespoons unsweetened cocoa powder
- ½ cup plain low-fat Greek-style yogurt

1. If using dried figs, place the figs in a small heat-proof bowl. Add boiling water to cover. Let rest in the hot water for 5 to 15 minutes; then drain before continuing.
2. Combine the honey and cocoa powder in a small bowl, and mix well to form a syrup.
3. Cut the figs in half and place cut side up. Drizzle with the syrup, top with a dollop of yogurt, and serve.

PER SERVING

Calories: 142.6; Fat: 0.6 Gram Cholesterol: 0 Milligrams;Sodium: 12.2 Milligrams Carbohydrates: 35.1 Grams;Fiber: 3.3 Grams; Protein: 3.7 Grams

Berries with Balsamic Vinegar and Black Pepper

Prep time: 15 minutes | Cook time: 10 minutes| Serves 4

- ¼ cup balsamic vinegar
- 1 tablespoon brown sugar
- ¼ teaspoon freshly ground pepper
- ½ cup sliced strawberries
- ½ cup blueberries
- ½ cup raspberries
- 4 tablespoons plain, unsweetened low-fat whipped cream or yogurt

1. In a small bowl, whisk together balsamic vinegar, brown sugar, and pepper until combined.
2. Add berries, stir to combine, and let rest for 10 minutes.
3. Serve in dessert bowls, topped with whipped cream or yogurt.

PER SERVING

Calories: 44 ;Fat: 0.2 Gram ;Cholesterol: 0 Milligrams;Sodium: 7.2 Milligrams Carbohydrates: 10.7 Grams;Fiber: 2 Grams ;Protein: 0.4 Gram

Spiced Peaches with Ricotta
Prep time: 15 minutes | Cook time: 10 minutes| Serves 4

- 6 ripe peaches, pitted and thinly sliced
- ¼ cup water
- 2 tablespoons Sucanat, or other raw or brown sugar
- 1½ tablespoons lemon juice
- 1 cup low-fat ricotta
- 2 teaspoons lemon zest

1. In a heavy, medium-sized skillet, combine peaches, water, Sucanat, and lemon juice. Bring just to a simmer, stirring frequently. Remove from heat.
2. In a small bowl, combine ricotta and lemon zest. Mix well.
3. Divide peaches between four bowls. Top with ricotta and serve.

PER SERVING

Calories: 165 ;Fat: 5.2 Grams Cholesterol: 19.1 Milligrams;Sodium: 59 Milligrams Carbohydrates: 25.6 Grams;Fiber: 2.9 Grams ;Protein: 8 Grams

Black Bean Cheese Wrap
Prep time: 5 minutes | Cook time: 3 minutes| Serves 6

- 1½ cups black beans, drained
- 3 tablespoons cilantro, chopped
- 1½ cups corn kernels
- 2 tablespoons green chili peppers, chopped
- 4 green onions, diced
- 1 tomato, diced
- 1 tablespoon chopped garlic
- 6 fat-free whole-grain tortilla wraps
- ¾ cup shredded cheddar cheese
- ¾ cup salsa

1. Toss the black beans with the corn, chili peppers, onions, garlic, tomato, and cilantro in a bowl.
2. Heat the mixture in a microwave for 1 minute, stirring halfway through.
3. Spread 2 tortillas between paper towels and heat them in the microwave for 20 secs.
4. Warm the remaining tortillas in the same way.
5. Add ½ cup of the bean mixture, 2 tablespoons of salsa, and 2 tablespoons of cheese to each tortilla.
6. Roll them and serve instantly.

PER SERVING

Calories 280 ;Fat 8g ;Sodium 39mg;Carbs 26g ;Fiber 1g ;Sugar 2g ;Protein 12g

Fruited Oatmeal Cookies
Prep time: 15 minutes | Cook time: 20 minutes| Makes 40 Cookies

- 1⅓ cups uncooked old-fashioned oats or quick-cooking rolled oats
- 1 cup whole-wheat flour
- 1 teaspoon baking powder
- 1 teaspoon ground cinnamon
- ½ cup loosely packed brown sugar
- ⅓ cup plain low-fat yogurt
- 2 tablespoons canola oil
- 1 egg
- 1 teaspoon vanilla extract
- ½ cup mixed dried fruit
- ½ cup dark chocolate chips

1. Preheat oven to 350°F. Line two baking sheets with baking mats or parchment paper.
2. In a medium bowl, stir together oats, flour, baking powder, cinnamon, mace, and sugar.
3. In a large bowl, stir together yogurt, oil, egg, and vanilla. Add flour mixture to yogurt mixture. Using a spatula, mix until just combined. Stir in dried fruit and chocolate chips.
4. Using a tablespoon, drop cookie dough onto baking sheet about 2 inches apart.
5. Bake 10 to 12 minutes, until lightly browned. Remove from oven and cool on a wire rack.

PER SERVING

Calories: 78 ;Fat: 3 Grams Cholesterol: 0 Milligrams;-Sodium: 4 Milligrams Carbohydrates: 12 Grams;Fiber: 2 Grams; Protein: 2 Grams

Mango Tortillas
Prep Time: 15 minutes|Serves: 2

- 2 whole-wheat tortillas, warmed
- ½ cup purple cabbage, shredded
- ½ tablespoon Dijon mustard
- 1 tablespoon fresh lime juice
- ½ cup mango, peeled, pitted and cubed
- ⅛ cup fresh cilantro, chopped
- 1 tablespoon olive oil
- Fresh ground black pepper to taste

1. Take a large bowl, add mustard, lime juice, oil and black pepper and beat until well combined.
2. Add mango, cabbage and cilantro and toss them all to coat well.
3. Arrange the tortillas onto a smooth surface.
4. Place mixture over each tortilla, leaving about one inch border all around.
5. Carefully fold the edges of each tortilla over the filling to roll up.
6. Cut each roll in half cross-wise.
7. Serve and enjoy!

PER SERVING

Calories: 229 ;Fat: 10.7g ; Sat Fat: 2.2g ; Carbohydrates: 20g;Fiber: 2.9g ;Sugar: 6.8g ;Protein: 15.1

Ginger Molasses Cookies

Prep time: 15 minutes | Cook time: 20 minutes | Makes 40 Cookies

- 3 tablespoons unsalted butter, softened
- 1 egg white
- 1 teaspoon vanilla extract
- 2 teaspoons blackstrap molasses
- ¾ cup whole-wheat flour
- ½ cup all-purpose flour
- ⅓ cup granulated sugar
- 1 teaspoon baking soda
- ½ teaspoon ground ginger
- ½ teaspoon ground cinnamon
- ¼ teaspoon ground nutmeg
- 1 teaspoon chopped crystallized ginger
- Cooking spray

1. Preheat oven to 350°F.
2. In a large bowl, combine the butter, egg white, vanilla, and molasses. Mix until well blended.
3. In a medium bowl, whisk together the whole-wheat flour, all-purpose flour, sugar, baking soda, ground ginger, cinnamon, nutmeg, and crystallized ginger.
4. Add dry ingredients to wet ingredients, stirring until well mixed.
5. Using a tablespoon, drop dough 2 inches apart onto two baking sheets lightly coated with cooking spray. Bake for 15 minutes, or just until the cookies begin to brown on top and the edges.
6. Remove the baking sheets from the oven, and allow the cookies to sit on the sheets for 2 minutes before transferring them to a wire rack to cool.

PER SERVING

Calories: 61 ;Fat: 2 Grams Cholesterol: 6 Milligrams;Sodium: 44 Milligrams Carbohydrates: 10 Grams;Fiber: 0 Grams ;Protein: 1 Gram

Lemony Angel Food Mini Cakes

Prep time: 15 minutes | Cook time: 20 minutes | Makes 8 Mini Cakes

- 2 tablespoons powdered sugar
- ½ cup all-purpose white flour
- 6 egg whites
- ¾ teaspoon cream of tartar
- 1 teaspoon lemon flavor or lemon extract
- ½ cup granulated sugar

1. Preheat oven to 350°F. Spray mini cake pans or 8 cups of a cupcake pan with cooking spray.
2. In a medium bowl, sift together the powdered sugar and the flour until it is very fine. Sift two or three times to ensure even consistency.
3. Using a stand mixer or hand held mixer on high speed, whip the egg whites, cream of tartar, and lemon flavor or extract until just combined, 1 to 2 minutes. Add the granulated sugar, 1 tablespoon at a time, until the egg whites form stiff peaks. Do not overwhip the eggs.
4. Using a spatula, slowly fold the flour mixture into the egg whites until just combined. Pour batter into prepared pans, stopping ½ inch before the rim.
5. Place cake pans on a baking sheet. Bake for 15 minutes. To check for doneness, gently push on the top of the cakes. If they spring back, they're ready. If not, bake for 2 to 5 more minutes until done.
6. Cool on a wire rack.

PER SERVING

Calories: 120 ;Fat: 2 Grams Cholesterol: 0 Milligrams;Sodium: 1 Milligram Carbohydrates: 22.6 Grams;Fiber: 0.5 Gram ;Protein: 5 Grams

Cinnamon Apple Cake

Prep time: 15 minutes | Cook time: 20 minutes | Serves 16

- Cooking spray
- 1¾ cups granulated sugar
- 3 teaspoons ground cinnamon
- 1½ cups all-purpose flour
- 1½ teaspoons baking powder
- ½ teaspoon ground ginger
- ¼ teaspoon ground nutmeg
- ¼ teaspoon ground mace
- ½ cup (4 ounces) low-fat cream cheese
- ⅓ cup unsweetened applesauce
- 2 tablespoons canola oil
- 1 teaspoon vanilla extract
- 2 egg whites
- 3 Fuji apples, peeled and chopped into 1-inch pieces

1. Preheat oven to 350°F. Spray an 8-inch springform pan or four mini springform pans with cooking spray.
2. In a small bowl, mix ¼ cup of the sugar with 2 teaspoons of the cinnamon. Set aside.
3. In a medium bowl, combine flour, baking powder, ginger, nutmeg, mace, and remaining teaspoon cinnamon. Set aside.
4. In the bowl of a stand mixer fitted with the paddle attachment, beat 1½ cups sugar, cream cheese, applesauce, canola oil, and vanilla extract until well blended, about 4 minutes. Add egg whites to batter and continue beating until incorporated. Add flour mixture to batter, ¼ cup at a time, mixing until well incorporated.
5. In another small bowl, mix the apples with 3 tablespoons of the cinnamon sugar mixture. Gently stir the apple-cinnamon mixture into the batter.
6. Pour the batter into the pan or pans, and sprinkle with the remaining cinnamon sugar.
7. Bake for 20 minutes, or until a toothpick inserted in the center comes out clean. Individual pans will cook more quickly; check after 12 minutes.

PER SERVING

Calories: 341; Fat: 12 Grams Cholesterol: 62 Milligrams;-Sodium: 137 Milligrams Carbohydrates: 57 Grams;Fiber: 3 Grams ;Protein: 4 Grams

Appendix 1 Measurement Conversion Chart

Volume Equivalents (Dry)

US STANDARD	METRIC (APPROXIMATE)
1/8 teaspoon	0.5 mL
1/4 teaspoon	1 mL
1/2 teaspoon	2 mL
3/4 teaspoon	4 mL
1 teaspoon	5 mL
1 tablespoon	15 mL
1/4 cup	59 mL
1/2 cup	118 mL
3/4 cup	177 mL
1 cup	235 mL
2 cups	475 mL
3 cups	700 mL
4 cups	1 L

Volume Equivalents (Liquid)

US STANDARD	US STANDARD (OUNCES)	METRIC (APPROXIMATE)
2 tablespoons	1 fl.oz.	30 mL
1/4 cup	2 fl.oz.	60 mL
1/2 cup	4 fl.oz.	120 mL
1 cup	8 fl.oz.	240 mL
1 1/2 cup	12 fl.oz.	355 mL
2 cups or 1 pint	16 fl.oz.	475 mL
4 cups or 1 quart	32 fl.oz.	1 L
1 gallon	128 fl.oz.	4 L

Temperatures Equivalents

FAHRENHEIT(F)	CELSIUS(C) APPROXIMATE)
225 °F	107 °C
250 °F	120 ° °C
275 °F	135 °C
300 °F	150 °C
325 °F	160 °C
350 °F	180 °C
375 °F	190 °C
400 °F	205 °C
425 °F	220 °C
450 °F	235 °C
475 °F	245 °C
500 °F	260 °C

Weight Equivalents

US STANDARD	METRIC (APPROXIMATE)
1 ounce	28 g
2 ounces	57 g
5 ounces	142 g
10 ounces	284 g
15 ounces	425 g
16 ounces (1 pound)	455 g
1.5 pounds	680 g
2 pounds	907 g

Appendix 2 The Dirty Dozen and Clean Fifteen

The Environmental Working Group (EWG) is a nonprofit, nonpartisan organization dedicated to protecting human health and the environment Its mission is to empower people to live healthier lives in a healthier environment. This organization publishes an annual list of the twelve kinds of produce, in sequence, that have the highest amount of pesticide residue-the Dirty Dozen-as well as a list of the fifteen kinds ofproduce that have the least amount of pesticide residue-the Clean Fifteen.

THE DIRTY DOZEN	
The 2016 Dirty Dozen includes the following produce. These are considered among the year's most important produce to buy organic:	
Strawberries	Spinach
Apples	Tomatoes
Nectarines	Bell peppers
Peaches	Cherry tomatoes
Celery	Cucumbers
Grapes	Kale/collard greens
Cherries	Hot peppers

The Dirty Dozen list contains two additional itemskale/collard greens and hot peppers-because they tend to contain trace levels of highly hazardous pesticides.

THE CLEAN FIFTEEN	
The least critical to buy organically are the Clean Fifteen list. The following are on the 2016 list:	
Avocados	Papayas
Corn	Kiw
Pineapples	Eggplant
Cabbage	Honeydew
Sweet peas	Grapefruit
Onions	Cantaloupe
Asparagus	Cauliflower
Mangos	

Some of the sweet corn sold in the United States are made from genetically engineered (GE) seedstock. Buy organic varieties of these crops to avoid GE produce.

Appendix 3 Index

MICHELE D. BUTLER

CPSIA information can be obtained
at www.ICGtesting.com
Printed in the USA
LVHW022017300523
748293LV00007B/271